CHANGED *into* HIS IMAGE

Few books made such an early impact on our church as did Jim Berg's *Changed into His Image*. We have profited from its use in small groups, in one-on-one discipleship, and in our counseling ministry. Jim's organization, style, illustrations, and thoroughness combine to make this book a classic for personal sanctification. I anticipate God using this new edition in your life as well.

—**Kevin Carson**, Pastor, Sonrise Baptist Church, Ozark, Missouri; Department Chair of Biblical Counseling, Baptist Bible College and Theological Seminary

Our dad intentionally discipled us, and we're thankful that he wrote down how he did it. What began as a series of "Letters from Dad" was eventually developed into a timeless and profound treatise on biblical growth! Dad is a gifted, passionate, and compassionate communicator, illustrating truth in a way that is easily understandable to any Christian who desires to grow in Christlikeness. We are proud to say that Dad still faithfully lives according to the biblical truths contained in this book.

—**Kirsten Berg Daulton**, **Angela Berg McMorris**, **Michelle Berg Radford**

Dr. Jim Berg is one of the best communicators of God's truths in the church today. *Changed into His Image* is an indispensable discipleship resource that teaches Christians how to understand and kill sin, renew their minds, and behold Jesus. As they learn this, it will allow them to image Christ and magnify his name. Jim has been an invaluable teacher in my life, and this book is one that I love and use with those I counsel and mentor, as well as myself. It is a treasure to God's children.

—**Kelli Dionne**, Biblical Counselor, Faith Biblical Counseling Ministries, Spokane, Washington; Author, *James and His Weird Mad*

For many years, I have been using *Changed into His Image* as a foundational study within my congregation and with my students at the Bible college. It is theologically sound and practically effective in leading individuals into the understanding and process of developing in progressive sanctification.

—**Nicolas Ellen**, Senior Pastor, Community of Faith Bible Church, Houston, Texas; Senior Professor of Biblical Counseling, College of Biblical Studies

Changed into His Image feels like a modern book of Proverbs. As a reader, you feel like a kind, wise, life-tested father is sitting down with you to share what he's learned about the heart of the Christian life and living it out earnestly. Filled with memorable analogies and thoughtful applications, this book points you constantly toward maturity in Christ.

—**Alasdair Groves**, Executive Director, Christian Counseling & Educational Foundation

For those who desire a resource that is theologically driven with resources on how to practically apply God's Word in real-life situations, I strongly recommend this book to you. This book is one of those books that will literally change your life!

—**Kevin E. Hurt**, Founding Pastor, Grace Bible Church, Clayton, Georgia

A friend once asked me to list the five best books I had ever read. *Changed into His Image* was, and still is, one of them. Jim Berg is an excellent communicator who has written an organized, thoughtful, resolute, and compassionate volume for any reader who seeks genuine heart change for any type of issue. I recommend it without hesitation to anyone who believes in the sufficiency of the Scriptures to bring about biblical heart change.

—**Mark E. Shaw**, Founder, Truth in Love Ministries; Author, *The Heart of Addiction*

CHANGED *into* HIS IMAGE

God's Plan for Transforming Your Life

JIM BERG

P&R PUBLISHING
P.O. BOX 817 • PHILLIPSBURG • NEW JERSEY 08865-0817

First edition © 1999 BJU Press
Second edition © 2018 BJU Press
Third edition 2023 from P&R Publishing

Italics within Scripture quotations indicate emphasis added.

The letter on pages 116–19 is used by permission of Carol L. Wilkinson.

Cover design by Jelena Mirkovic

ISBN: 978-1-62995-978-8 (pbk)
ISBN: 978-1-62995-979-5 (ePub)

Printed in the United States of America

Library of Congress Cataloging-in-Publication Data has been applied for.

To Kirsten, Angie, and Michelle, my beloved daughters,
in whom I am well pleased

CONTENTS

Part 3: Reflecting Your Lord

PREFACE

In August of 1996, I presented the original draft of this book to my three daughters with a personal letter that outlined my intent for its writing. I had occasionally written "letters from Dad" to them about biblical truths I wanted to be sure they understood. I soon realized there were many truths I wanted them to not soon forget—truths they had heard repeatedly at home and during their formative years growing up on the campus of Bob Jones University. In order for you, the reader, to get a better grasp of the passion I felt for this project from its beginning, I have, with the permission of my daughters, reproduced here a portion of the letter that accompanied their original draft of this book.

> Dear Kirsten, Angie, and Michelle,
>
> These chapters are the lengthiest "letter from Dad" you have received yet, and perhaps the most important one. In December of 1993 we forged a family mission statement together that God has used to mold our direction as a family. I want to restate it here so that you can see where these chapters fit into the picture.

The Mission of Our Family

To passionately know our God,
and to love and please him by
living together in harmony,
serving each other in humility,
growing together in godliness,
helping others with cheerfulness,
and thereby, as a family,
to provide a "living advertisement"
of Christlikeness
for others in this generation

and for our children
in the generations to come.

Ever since we together crafted this statement, I have been burdened to make sure you have in your hands the information you need about the Christian life to ensure that our family can indeed be a "living advertisement" of Christlikeness. This book is one means to that end. It is written in such a way that others outside our family might benefit from it, but I want you to know that it was written for you. If no one else ever reads it, I have accomplished my primary goal by placing it in your hands.

I have told you before that your mother and I will probably not be able to pass on to you any kind of earthly inheritance. If we can pass on to you a passion for God, however, we will have given you something more valuable than silver, gold, or rubies and more satisfying than anything a mortal can experience (see Prov. 3:13–15). Your mother and I can honestly say that "[we] have no greater joy than to hear that [our] children are walking in the truth" (3 John 4). Our prayer is that "our daughters may be as corner stones, polished [as for] a palace" (Ps. 144:12 KJV).

May God use all of this book to draw you to a greater love and devotion to our matchless Savior, Jesus Christ. You truly are our beloved daughters in whom we are well pleased.

Love, Dad

The two years I devoted to writing this book were two of the most spiritually refreshing of my entire life. Writing this book forced me to clear away the chaff in my thinking about the Christian life and drove me to consider only the fundamental issues of life with God. As I culled through sermon notes of messages I preached or classroom lectures I delivered, I was compelled to continually ask myself, "Do I consider the material I am examining essential for my daughters' pursuit of God and godliness, or is it merely peripheral? Is this idea or that thought indispensable for their walk in the Spirit, or is it only incidental? And most important, will it stir within them a thirst for God, a hunger for his Word, and a desire to represent him well as salt in the earth?"

I intended this book to be a sort of travel brochure for my daughters, enticing them to fellowship with God and to behold for themselves the breathtaking vistas of the glories of God in Christ Jesus. It was also to be a basic road map of Christian growth, showing them the way to that kind of relationship with God. It was an attempt to present to them in writing a biblical overview of the Christian life. Decades later, every goal I had in the beginning remains the same—for them and for you.

Please keep in mind that the illustrations you will encounter as you read this text have been greatly changed "to protect the guilty." Names and details have been altered so that no situation, as it is printed, represents any actual individual in my acquaintance. While I do not wish for anyone's personal identity to be exposed, I would hope that all of us would see ourselves often in the various scenarios so that biblical truth can be more readily understood and applied.

Although the primary target audience for this book was my daughters, it is also my prayer that you too will have a greater passion for our God and will be enabled by God's Spirit to have a godly impact in this darkening age that precedes the imminent return of our blessed Lord. We shall stand before him soon! There is much to be done in us and through us before then.

ACKNOWLEDGMENTS

I WOULD BE remiss if I did not give "honor to whom honor is owed" (Rom. 13:7). This has not been a solo project. I am indebted to Gail Yost and Dr. Guenter Salter who read my first, very rough draft and who provided needed insight in the beginning stages of the project. I owe special thanks as well to those who read the final manuscript and offered valuable critiques: Dr. Michael Barrett, Dr. Steve Hankins, Dr. Randy Leedy, Dr. Greg Mazak, and Ted Harris, MD. Many other friends in the pastorate—too numerous to mention—have read the manuscript in its various stages and have offered valuable suggestions and enthusiastic encouragement.

Rebecca Moore, who edited the initial manuscript so that it could be field-tested in small-group studies and individual counseling situations, and Elizabeth Berg, my sister-in-law and member of the editorial staff at BJU Press, worked grammatical miracles on the various drafts of the book. Nancy Lohr provided skillful assistance as well. They have my deepest admiration and sincerest thanks for their craftsmanship and heart for this project.

Many thanks go to the seminary faculty of Bob Jones University, who were used of God to instill within me an unshakable confidence in God's Word. My professors provoked me to love God for myself as I observed their passion for him when they stood before me in the classroom. Although that was decades ago, the fire the Holy Spirit kindled in my heart through their example and instruction still remains, and I "esteem them very highly in love because of their work" (1 Thess. 5:13).

I have been humbled that God has chosen to bless this book with translations into multiple foreign languages and with over one hundred thousand English copies in print. I pray that he would be pleased to continue to use this book to encourage others of his children to grow in likeness to his Son, Jesus.

Finally, I am deeply grateful to and for my wife, Patty. I have watched her pursue God for the past fifty-plus years of our marriage. Her daughters have followed her example and have made the truths of this book their own and are passing on to their children the same spiritual fervor and instruction that they received from their mother. Patty's love for her Savior, her confidence in her God, and her thirst for his Word have been a constant delight to behold. She has contributed her life to this book. Her daughters "rise up and call her blessed; her husband also, and he praises her" (Prov. 31:28).

1

UNDERSTANDING BIBLICAL CHANGE AND DISCIPLESHIP

Do not be conformed to this world, but be transformed by the renewal of your mind, that by testing you may discern what is the will of God, what is good and acceptable and perfect. (Rom. 12:2)

HAVE YOU EVER set out to help someone, not really knowing what you were doing or how you were going to do it? Have you ever tried to tackle some gnawing problem in your own life but didn't have a clue about how to get started? Christopher Columbus experienced this problem when he set out to find a westward passage to Asia.

Because the explorer had little idea about what he was doing, someone proposed that the Christopher Columbus Award be given to those who emulate him: "This award goes to those who, like good old Chris, when they set out to do something, don't know where they are going; neither do they know how to get there. When they arrive, they don't know where they are, and when they return, they don't know where they've been."

Tragically, many Christians set out in life with little more understanding of what they are doing than Mr. Columbus. While he possessed no accurate charts to lead him to Asia, the journey that we take as believers has been very carefully mapped out for us by the captain of our salvation (see Heb. 2:10).

This book is about sanctification. *Sanctification* is the word used to describe the Bible's teaching about how we are made holy ("sanctified"). The Bible teaches that people become Christians by accepting

Jesus Christ as their personal substitute for the penalty of sin. Once they become children of God, God begins a process in them that changes them to become more like Christ in their attitudes, ambitions, and actions. God uses many things to accomplish this change, including temptations and trials, the local church and Christian friends, his Word and his Spirit.

Sanctification, in the sense we are discussing in this book, is progressive. A person's likeness to Christ is not something that happens all at once. It is a process of change that the Bible calls growth. As we look at various aspects of the Christian life in this book, remember that whenever you see the phrases change and grow, becoming like Christ, or biblical change, we are talking about the Bible doctrine of progressive sanctification.

The discussion of growth toward Christlikeness in this book will help you to more skillfully navigate the sometimes treacherous waters of daily living. A sea captain who understands the basics of navigation and sailing knows how to make progress no matter what the direction of the winds or currents. In much the same way, if you understand these basics for biblical change, you can experience growth in your life no matter what challenges confront you at any given moment. Furthermore, you can effectively help others to change and grow as well.

Not Just Any Change Will Do

The title of this book announces that the subject under discussion is change—but for the Christian not just any change will do. Consider the following scenarios:

- A spoiled teen may stop his sulking (a desirable change), but only because his parents have acquiesced and have given him the car he wanted.
- A depressed wife may become her old cheerful self again (a desirable change), but only because her alcoholic husband has granted her a divorce.
- A college student may be getting better grades (a desirable change), but only because she has found a boyfriend whose affection has lifted her spirits so that she feels like studying again.
- An embittered dockworker may stop his complaining about the foreman's decisions (a desirable change), but only because the foreman was transferred to another terminal.

As you can see, we have to be specific about what kind of change we are talking about and how it is to be accomplished. Mere relief from symptoms of despair, anger, fear, and so forth does not necessarily mean the real problem has been solved.

The real problem in the scenarios above is not that these people lack a car, have an alcoholic husband, lack a boyfriend, or have a foreman with poor judgment. The real problem goes much deeper. Dr. Bob Wood, a colleague of mine who is now with the Lord, used to remind us of an important Bible principle we need to understand about change. He would often say, "Our greatest problems are never *around us; they are in us.*"

Jesus said it this way in Mark 7:21–23:

> For from within, out of the heart of man, come evil thoughts, sexual immorality, theft, murder, adultery, coveting, wickedness, deceit, sensuality, envy, slander, pride [arrogance], foolishness. All these evil things come from within, and they defile a person.

The apostle James tells us the same thing in James 4:1: "What causes quarrels and what causes fights [the outward, visible problems] among you? Is it not this, that your passions [the inward desires of the heart] are at war within you?"

Since the fall of man in the garden of Eden, we have attempted to blame someone or something for our trouble. Adam attempted to shift responsibility to God and Eve. Eve pointed an accusing finger at the serpent (see Gen. 3:12–13). God's Word is clear, however, that our real problems are not the result of pressures from someone or something outside ourselves. We do not sin because of financial, social, medical, or circumstantial pressures. We sin because each of us has a sinful heart.

We can illustrate this biblical truth this way. When we take a tea bag, place it in a teacup, and fill the cup with hot water, the water activates the tea in the bag, unleashing its taste into the water around it. The hot water didn't create the taste; it merely drew out what was already in the bag.[1]

This depicts what happens in the human heart. The pressures around us (the unfavorable circumstances, the temptations, and the

1. Tea bag illustration adapted from J. Allan Petersen, *Your Reactions Are Showing* (Lincoln: Back to the Bible, 1967), 14–15.

commands of God to love him and our neighbor) merely draw out of our hearts what is already in them. We cannot blame the hot water for the taste in the cup. The contents of the tea bag determine the flavor of the tea. If we don't like that particular taste, we need to seep a bag that contains a different kind of tea. Similarly, we cannot shift the blame for any bitterness, anger, despair, deception, cruelty, or other emotional response that we display when we are under pressure. The pressures merely expose how unlike Christ we really are.

Acts 16:22–24 tells us of a hot-water experience Silas and the apostle Paul had while in Philippi. Because of their preaching,

> the crowd joined in attacking them, and the magistrates tore the garments off [Paul and Silas] and gave orders to beat them with rods. And when they had inflicted many blows upon them, they threw them into prison, ordering the jailer to keep them safely. Having received this order, he put them into the inner prison and fastened their feet in the stocks.

The hot water of suffering revealed the nature of the hearts of these two men. We see their response in the next verse: "About midnight Paul and Silas were praying and singing hymns to God, and the prisoners were listening to them" (16:25). Although other believers might react to such mistreatment with bitterness and anger or with despair and discouragement, Paul and Silas responded with praise and thanksgiving. Why the difference? Their hearts had been changed to be like the heart of Christ, who responded in a similar fashion to his suffering (see 1 Peter 2:21–23).

This book is about change—change that involves warring against this sinful disposition within. As we shall see, this is not a change we can make on our own. Furthermore, we must have God's goal in mind as we seek to change. Remember, not just any change will do.

The Goal of Change

While living on this earth, Jesus Christ exemplified the characteristics of a man controlled by the Holy Spirit and abiding in perfect fellowship with God. As the result of the sanctification process, believers look increasingly like him—they become "grown-up Christians" as they are brought "to the measure of the stature of the fullness of Christ" (Eph. 4:13). When the nature of God is reflected fully through a human nature, as it was in Christ, the blend produces a person who is the Father's humble servant. Spiritually mature humanity is in essence Christlike humility, which is the humility of a servant.

Please note that this biblical goal of Christlike humility is a far cry from many popular, but unworthy, goals for helping others. Our Lord did not come to this planet, live a perfect life, and become a worthy atonement for the sins of the world so that those who become his children can merely be well-adjusted, live morally upright lives, and enjoy personal happiness and success. He died to redeem us from the penalty and power of a sinful heart that keeps us from being useful servants of the living God. A truly humble servant of God will be well-adjusted, will have a morally sensitive conscience, and will enjoy the blessedness of life with God—but these are byproducts of godliness, not primary goals for the Christian life.

The leading passage of Scripture that describes the servanthood of Christ is Philippians 2:1–11. Theologian B. B. Warfield said about this passage:

> A life of self-sacrificing unselfishness is the most divinely beautiful life that man can lead. He whom as our Master we have engaged to obey, whom as our example we are pledged to imitate, is presented to us here as the great model of self-sacrificing unselfishness. "Let this mind be in you, which was also in Christ Jesus," is the apostle's pleading. We need to note carefully, however, that it is not self-depreciation, but self-abnegation, that is thus commended to us. If we would follow Christ, we must, every one of us, not in pride but in humility, yet not in lowness but in lowliness, not degrade ourselves but forget ourselves, and seek every man not his own things but those of others.[2]

Only when a believer looks like a humble servant of the Father does he look like Jesus Christ, of whom the Father said, "Behold, my servant whom I have chosen, my beloved with whom my soul is well pleased" (Matt. 12:18).

2. B. B. Warfield, "Imitating the Incarnation," in *The Person and Work of Christ,* ed. John J. Hughes (Phillipsburg, NJ: P&R Publishing, 2023), 610–11.

This change from the self-centered ways of our sinful heart to the self-sacrificing ways of our Lord will require divine assistance. This kind of change is not a do-it-yourself project. We must understand, therefore, the source of our power to change.

Let me illustrate that power.

I grew up on my grandfather's cattle farm in South Dakota. My father was the mechanic for the many pieces of machinery that were required to farm three thousand acres. Even though my grandfather owned several tractors, two combines, and many other farm implements, my favorite piece of machinery was a yellow bulldozer, a D6 Caterpillar. My grandfather used the Cat for such things as moving small buildings, digging a water reservoir on the property, compacting silage in one of several large silage pits, or pulling an eight bottom-disc plow with thirty-two-inch discs that would turn up new sod a foot deep, eight rows at one time. If he had a hard job that required much power, the Cat was the solution.

Suppose my grandfather wanted to plow an eighty-acre field and went out to the machinery yard to pull the several-thousand-pound disc plow by hand. What would happen? About all he would be able to do in his own power would be to lift the hitch. He could never move the plow even one inch in his own strength. If he were first to start the Cat's powerful diesel engine and then hitch the plow to it, however, he could get out into the field. When quitting time came, he could say, "I plowed the field." To make his statement more accurate, he could add, "Yet not I, but the bulldozer did it for me." Without the bulldozer, he would be helpless to get any serious plowing done.

As believers, we can no more please and serve God effectively in our own strength than my grandfather could pull a plow in his own strength. The bulldozer enabled him to carry out his work in the field. In the same fashion, the Holy Spirit is the divine power behind everything believers do that counts for God. We need, therefore, to understand as much as we can about the Holy Spirit because of the crucial role he plays in biblical change.

The Person of Change

The Holy Spirit is not some mystical, impersonal influence or force. He is one of the three persons of the Godhead—God the Father, God the Son, and God the Holy Spirit. He is the agent who shows us our need of Christ and imparts Christ's life to us at salvation. He then begins the work of changing our lives to become like Christ's through sanctification, and he empowers us for service to Christ.

We are changed by him as we cooperate with his leading. Paul testified that the Holy Spirit's leadership in believers' lives is one of the chief evidences of their salvation: "All who are led by the Spirit of God are sons of God" (Rom. 8:14).

The apostle is not teaching in Romans 8:14 that we should expect the Spirit of God to give us mystical leadings and nudgings and thereby direct our lives. Rather he writes in the context of Romans 6–8, which speaks of the sanctification that God is working out in our lives—a process initiated and orchestrated by the Spirit of God. He is the divine leader whose convicting voice calls our attention to the times when we are intent on going our own way. He leads us into an understanding of the Scriptures and leads us into "paths of righteousness" (Ps. 23:3) by which we reflect Christ's life. Those who experience this kind of leadership—away from sin and toward Christ's likeness—"are sons of God" (Rom. 8:14).

The leadership of the Spirit toward Christlikeness takes place as we obey Paul's admonition in Ephesians 5:18 to "be filled with [controlled by] the Spirit." Note three things about the Greek verb for *filled* that Paul uses in this passage.

- *It is in the imperative.* That means it is a command. God must command us to yield to the Holy Spirit's control because we are not automatically so inclined. We naturally wish to control ourselves.
- *It is in the present tense.* That means it is something that should be continually happening in the here and now. Being filled with the Spirit should be an ongoing action; we should keep on being filled with (controlled by) the Spirit.
- *It is in the passive voice.* This means that the empowering is done to us. We do not do it to ourselves. The Holy Spirit is the one who empowers us when we choose to cooperate with him.

The filling of the Spirit refers to the supernatural work of the Spirit within a believer whereby that believer is enabled or empowered to become *like Christ* (sanctification) and become useful *to Christ* (service). Many believers are virtually powerless to overcome the lusts of their flesh and of their mind because of failure in this very area. They continue for years manifesting the same anger, driven by the same pride, motivated by the same fears, crippled by the same sense of hopelessness, or consumed with the same lusts that they have had for years. How tragic that so many years of blessing and usefulness have been forfeited because these powerless believers never learned how to be or did not practice being controlled by the Holy Spirit. There is no doubt that he is the person of change.

Let's look for a few minutes at how he works in the process of change—sanctification.

The Process of Change

I heard it said years ago that sanctification is the "Christianizing of the Christian." Preachers through the years have described it as the process by which the Spirit of God takes the Word of God and changes us to become like the Son of God.

The Bible teaches that believers have three main spiritual responsibilities in the sanctification process. God, the Holy Spirit, is the primary initiator in all these activities, but believers must cooperate with what the Holy Spirit is doing in their lives. Those three responsibilities are listed in the first column of the following chart. Take a minute to look

Our Personal Responsibility	Paul's Instruction (Eph. 4:22–24)	James's Instructions (James 1:21–25)	The Holy Spirit's Result
1. Mortification of the flesh	"put off [the ways of] your old [unregenerate] self" (v. 22)	"put away all filthiness" (v. 21)	The flesh is restrained through the Spirit's enablement.
2. Meditation on the Word	"be renewed in the spirit of your minds" (v. 23)	"receive . . . the implanted word" (v. 21)	The mind is renewed through the Spirit's illumination.
3. Manifestation of Christlikeness	"put on [the ways of] the new self [in Christ]" (v. 24)	"be doers of the word, and not hearers only" (v. 22)	Christ is revealed through the Spirit's fruit.

over them and notice the passages written by Paul and James that refer to each activity. Notice also in the last column that the Holy Spirit, when he enables believers in those activities, produces a certain kind of fruit: their flesh is restrained, their minds are renewed, and Christ is revealed through their example and ministry to others.

Although every believer has a personal responsibility to carry out these commands, the Bible clearly teaches that these activities can be performed *only* in the power of the Holy Spirit. Keep in mind that sanctification has been designed by God to be a cooperative venture between God and us. Notice the joint responsibility in the following verses:

> For if you live according to the flesh you will die, but if by the Spirit you put to death the deeds of the body, you will live. (Rom. 8:13)

> I have been crucified with Christ. It is no longer I who live, but Christ who lives in me. And the life I now live in the flesh I live by faith in the Son of God, who loved me and gave himself for me. (Gal. 2:20)

In each case, we are commanded to do something: "put to death the deeds of the body" and "live [in our bodies] by faith in the Son of God." At the same time, God says he is doing something: the Spirit allows us to put the deeds of the body to death, and Christ lives in us.

This book is divided into three parts that correspond to the three personal responsibilities illustrated in the chart above. Understanding and practicing these three personal responsibilities are not incidental in the sanctification process. They are necessary. Every failure in Christian living is due to a failure to cooperate with God in these responsibilities by the power of the Spirit.

So essential are these truths to the biblical process of change and growth that they are the touchstone for evaluating any theory or advice offered today in the fields of Christian education, parenting, biblical counseling, and pastoral ministry. Truly biblical counsel emphasizes to believers, not merely mentions in passing, that to change they must "put off [the ways of] the old [unregenerate] self," "be renewed in the spirit of [their] minds," and "put on [the ways of] the new self [in Christ]."

For this reason, these three components of sanctification form the structure of this book on change. We will look at each one in great depth and will especially note the Holy Spirit's role in the sanctification process as believers yield themselves to the Spirit's control. This is God's plan! Therefore, it is our only answer and our wonderful hope. It is the continued work of the gospel in us.

Spiritual Parenting

Although this book is about *sanctification,* it is also about *discipleship.* Through the years, the term *discipleship* has come to mean different things to different groups. To some, discipleship is a tightly regimented curriculum complete with discussion groups and study guides. Attendees who have filled in all the blanks and attended all the sessions have been discipled. To others, discipleship is something akin to taking monastic vows and moving into a religious commune removed from the rest of civilization. To yet another group, it is merely their denomination's yearly four-week emphasis on daily Bible reading and prayer.

Biblical discipleship is not primarily a program. It is a certain kind of relationship between two believers with a very specific spiritual goal in mind. Discipleship is helping other believers to make biblical change toward Christlikeness—helping others in the sanctification process. It is the spiritual parenting Paul spoke of in Galatians 4:19, when he addressed the members of the church as "my little children, for whom I am again in the anguish of childbirth until Christ is formed in you!"

This book on sanctification and discipleship therefore can serve as a beginning study for assisting new Christians in their growth in Christ. Perhaps, however, it can best function as a training manual for pastors, Christian educators, biblical counselors, and parents since these leaders are involved in helping others to change. Specific sections at the end of each chapter provide disciple makers with additional information that will aid them in their ministry to others.

The Centrality of Discipleship

I want us to look briefly at several common relationships in life that involve biblical change. Perhaps having an idea of how fundamental these principles of change and growth are to every significant area of your life will increase your motivation to master them and practice them at every level of your God-given responsibilities.

When relationships in the following areas are crumbling, you can be sure that biblical responsibilities for discipleship and basic issues of sanctification and life with God are being ignored or defied. You can neither effectively build the following relationships nor troubleshoot them without a biblical understanding of your discipleship responsibilities in each. You must also master God's methods for bringing about change and growth in the lives of his people. To do so, you must understand what constitutes discipleship.

Parenting Is Discipleship

Parenting, when understood biblically, is basically a discipling relationship. When God gives children to Christian couples, they must realize that their little bundles of joy are essentially lost souls. Their biblical mission is to evangelize them and then to equip them for usefulness to Christ. This mission is, in essence, discipleship. This is what Paul teaches in Ephesians 6:4 when he tells fathers to "bring [their children] up in the discipline and instruction of the Lord."

Sadly, the goal of many Christian parents is merely "to raise a good kid." Through moral training and consistent discipline, they might even rear children of whom they are proud. These children may never cause them any real heartache but still not be useful to Christ due to materialism, impatience, impulsiveness, anxiety, stubbornness, or any other fleshly attitudes and actions. In that case, the biblical parenting goal has not been reached, even though these children never got into serious trouble or seriously embarrassed their parents. The biblical goal was not reached because their parenting efforts did not produce disciples of Jesus Christ—people like the Master and therefore useful to the Master.[3]

Parents who do not understand the role that discipleship and sanctification play in Christian parenting often find themselves off course when their children reach the teen years. In the early years, these parents chart the wrong courses on the sea of early child-rearing and, consequently,

3. This is not to say that every failure of a child to follow God's way is entirely the fault of the parents. God himself said, "Children have I reared and brought up, but they have rebelled against me" (Isa. 1:2). He certainly didn't make any mistakes in his parenting goals or methods. Every child has the inclination to turn "every one—to his own way" (Isa. 53:6). God does, however, place a heavy responsibility on parents to exemplify godliness and to saturate their child-rearing environment with the ways and the words of the living God lest their children forget the Lord (see Deut. 6:5–13).

encounter unnecessary dangers in the teen years. Tragically, they may never reach their anticipated port.

Many parenting failures also reflect a lack of biblical discipleship between husband and wife and a failure to understand and practice the principles of biblical change and growth within the marriage itself. Husbands and wives who are not actively helping each other to grow in Christlikeness within their marriages will not see the importance of doing so with their children either. Neither will they know how to apply the issues of sanctification to the lives of their children, since they have not practiced doing so in their own lives.

Edification in the Local Church Is Discipleship

The mission of the church is laid out in Ephesians 4:12–16. It is to be a place where God-called and Spirit-gifted leaders help the saints to mature "for the work of ministry" (v. 12) as they grow "to mature manhood, to the measure of the stature of the fullness of Christ" (v. 13). This is clearly a call to disciple the flock.

The New Testament pastoral role is much like that of an Israelite shepherd in Bible times who led the whole flock to pasture and water but often had to give individual attention to sheep that had become ill, injured, or lost. Likewise, the shepherd of the local assembly, through his Bible-preaching ministry, is to "shepherd the flock of God" en masse (1 Peter 5:2), but he must also meet with individual members who need personal explanation, encouragement, and exhortation. Whether by public preaching or by private counseling, the pastor's role is that of a disciple maker.

Of course, his ministry to the flock becomes a pacesetter for every other ministry of the local assembly. Those leading Sunday school classes, special ministries to children and youth, vacation Bible school, and various outreach ministries must also have a passion not only to bring in sheep but also to help them grow. Christ called his disciples to bring forth fruit that would reproduce itself and would abide (see John 15:1–16). Without a passion to disciple believers to Christlikeness through the ministries of the church, the church will focus merely on perpetuating its programs, and the sheep will grow sickly and unfruitful. The edification ministry of the local church is therefore a discipling effort—helping believers to make biblical change toward Christlikeness.

Christian Education Is Discipleship

Christian education, an extension of the Christian home and the church, is also essentially discipleship. The following statements about Christian education point this out.[4]

> In following God they [the students] imitate both His nature and His works. The imitation of God's nature results in holiness of character. . . . The fruit of the Spirit (Gal. 5:22–23) is the expression of the holiness of God in the believer's character. The imitation of God's works results in service.
>
> Academic subjects—whether in the humanities or in the natural sciences, whether general or strictly vocational—are studied not as ends in themselves but as means of improving the student as a servant of God.
>
> In endeavoring to fulfill the purpose of Christian education—the development of Christlikeness in redeemed man—the Christian school teaches, as a consequence of the knowledge of God, the imitation of God. Students learn of God so that they may imitate Him. They are to become "followers of God" (Eph. 5:1).

When principals, teachers, parents, school board members, and students forget this driving motive behind Christian education, the results are disappointing, even disastrous. Well-ordered classrooms, high academic achievement, cultural appreciation, and athletic accomplishment are not the measure of success in Christian education. If those overseeing the sports, fine arts, student discipline, and classroom instruction do not see their arena of responsibility as a means of developing Christlikeness and do not actively and consciously pursue it as such, Christian education will produce only highly trained rebels.

For example, student misbehavior and disinterest at school are not just interruptions in the educational process—they are revelations of the students' heart condition. Spiritual processes of Christian change and growth have been stymied in the students' lives and must be addressed biblically. Christian teachers must remember that while the goal of most

4. Ronald A. Horton, ed., *Handbook of Christian Education* (Greenville, SC: BJU Press, 2017), 12.

businesses is to *please* customers, making them consumers, the goal of Christian education is to *change* customers, making them contributors, servants. Discipleship must be the driving concern. For that reason, every Christian teacher must understand the principles of biblical change.

Biblical Counseling Is Discipleship

Discipleship must be the primary concern in the realm of biblical counseling as well. Too many who attempt to counsel do not have the biblical process of progressive sanctification in mind when they try to help someone. They do not see themselves involved primarily in a discipleship relationship of helping their counselee grow in Christlikeness.

Counselees may come to such counselors for relief from despair, anxiety, anger, guilt, or fear. They may want help in getting their spouses back or may desire direction in restoring wayward teens. They may be struggling with the effects of sexual abuse or the life-dominating clutches of drugs, alcohol, or homosexuality. They may be grieving after miscarriages or the discovery of malignant tumors. In each case, change and growth toward Christlikeness are the needs of the hour. When the counselor's mindset is not truly biblical, the counseling process will not intentionally move toward biblical goals.

For example, when a woman who was sexually abused as a child by her now-deceased uncle comes to such a counselor for help, he may think she needs to recover hidden memories or build her self-esteem. Or he may believe her "damaged emotions" need to be healed or her "inner child" needs to be re-parented. He may suppose that a "Christianized" twelve-step recovery program is the solution or assume that giving her "insight" into why her uncle was abusive in the first place can help her get some "closure."

In the process, the counselee may find some temporary relief from whatever was troubling her most. She may even learn some spiritual truths she had not known before. But unless the path of sanctification is clearly charted for her, she will spend months, and perhaps years, steering from one navigational heading to another looking for lasting help. What she needs is a counselor who understands that God's "recovery program" is sanctification. She can become godly and useful to Christ as an adult, no matter what her past, if the counselor helps her to learn and practice the basics of biblical change. To attempt to produce love, joy, peace, endurance, and contentment apart from the Spirit of God is to rely on strategies that compete with God.

Management in Christian Work Is Discipleship

Paul had an enormous management responsibility on his shoulders—the daily "care of all the churches" (2 Cor. 11:28 KJV). How did he do it? A look at Ephesians 4:11–13 shows that he expected the "saints" to do the "work of ministry" (v. 12) as they were brought to maturity by the leadership of the church. Christian leaders today must have the same focus. The work must be done, but the whole job isn't done unless the saints are developed in the process.

Some Christian organizations tolerate the anger, disobedience, harshness, or critical spirit of Christian workers or leaders just because they are productive workers or have important positions. Paul, however, demonstrated that individuals must be addressed and must be disciplined if there is no change—they cannot simply be moved to a less damaging position in the organization. He did not hesitate to personally address uncharitable and sinful behavior of the workers and leaders under his oversight (see 1 Cor. 5:1–7; 6:7–8; Gal. 2:11–16; Phil. 4:2; 2 Tim. 2:16–18), nor did he ignore the reports he received from others about selfish behavior within the ranks (see 1 Cor. 1:11; 5:1; 11:18; 2 Thess. 3:11). He was concerned that "a little leaven leavens the whole lump" (1 Cor. 5:6). Entire sections of his epistles were "staff development manuals" to specific groups, and sometimes he had to address the whole organization for its petty arguments and carnality. Concerned for the corporate testimony, he spent much time addressing individual and corporate problems.[5]

We may speak today within Christian organizations about our "personnel problems." There is nothing at all wrong with this terminology, but we must remember to look at these problems biblically. Paul called the believers with "envying, and strife, and divisions" he saw within the church "carnal" (1 Cor. 3:3 KJV). He did not pacify or arbitrate divisions. In Philippians 2:1–16, he called the conflicting parties to repentance and to a like-mindedness that reflected the mind that "was also in Christ Jesus" (v. 5 KJV).

5. For more examples of how individual and corporate problems are addressed to maintain God's blessing upon the group, see how Moses and Joshua dealt with the children of Israel.

Christian leaders must humbly address fleshly actions and attitudes within their organizations and help wrongdoers to make biblical change through the remedies offered in God's plan of progressive sanctification. This emphasis on developing Christlikeness within the Christian worker is called discipleship.

Your Role in Discipleship

As you can see, God's concern about godly living encompasses every area of life. Believers must share that concern and be committed to God's purposes and plans for themselves and for other believers.

Keep in mind as you study this book that you cannot effectively help others to change toward Christlikeness unless you adequately understand the basics of biblical change for yourself. You must have a working knowledge of the doctrine of progressive sanctification and must, by God's grace, be practicing it in your own life. Paul gave his disciple Timothy the following instructions:

> Practice these things, *immerse yourself in them*, so that all may see your progress. *Keep a close watch on yourself* and on the teaching. Persist in this, for by so doing you will save both yourself and your hearers. (1 Tim. 4:15–16)

If you have picked up this book to help someone else, resist the urge to skip over parts 1 and 2. Before you can become useful to Christ as a disciple maker, the fruit of your own walk with Christ must be apparent to others. Humbly study these opening truths, asking God to enable you to apply them to your life. Then move on to part 3 about helping others.

Understand that God has called all believers to disciple those around them. He said we are to be "teaching [others] to observe all that [he has] commanded [us]" (Matt. 28:20). Paul told his disciple Timothy, "What you have heard from me in the presence of many witnesses entrust to faithful men, who will be able to teach others also" (2 Tim. 2:2). God has placed others around you who need to grow in Christ—your spouse, your children, your friends, your students, your roommate, your congregation, and your coworkers. All believers are to take up the challenge to "instruct" (Rom. 15:14) and to "exhort" (Heb. 3:13) one another.

Some have the unbiblical mindset that religion is a personal matter and that they shouldn't "meddle" in other people's lives; they think, "It's their life—if they want to throw it away, that's their business." The writer to the Hebrews warns such people in Hebrews 5:11–14, where he addresses those who "ought to be teachers" but are not (v. 12). The apostle insists that those who have an attitude of noninterference in the lives of others need biblical change themselves: they are "dull of hearing" (v. 11), "unskilled in the word of righteousness" (v. 13), and need to place themselves under basic instruction again. Avoiding the responsibility to biblically challenge others is a sure way to remain a spiritual baby.

The church at Thessalonica was of an entirely different persuasion. They were so grateful for what God had done for them that they ministered to anyone who would listen.[6] May God use this book on biblical change to help you to become like the Thessalonian Christians, whom Paul commended for becoming "imitators of [the apostles] and of the Lord, for [they] received the word" (1 Thess. 1:6).

A Final Word

The goal of this book is to give you a thoroughly biblical overview of the Christian life, of man, and of our relationship with God. When we do not understand God's ways and are not properly related to God, chaos results. You will not be able to lead others out of that self-centered chaos unless you understand life from God's perspective, model the proper relationship to God yourself, and know how to lead others to the change that will bring them back to a right relationship with God. There is no true biblical change toward Christlikeness unless you handle life and its problems God's way.

Take Time to Reflect

1. Do you understand the biblical teaching of sanctification? Could you briefly outline its main points for people who want to know how to biblically change something in their lives? We will thoroughly unpack this concept throughout this book; for now, ascertain what you already know.

6. See 1 Thessalonians 1 and 2 for the remarkable ministry of both the apostle Paul and of his converts in this church.

2. Have you unwittingly accepted unbiblical solutions to solving life's problems? Are there concepts you need to rethink and perhaps abandon in light of God's Word? Keep a running list of them as they come to mind while you read this book. Don't let anyone's solution, including your own ideas, go unchecked against the Word of God. If you find that the idea you are espousing is not taught in the Word of God as part of the sanctification process, you must abandon it and learn God's ways to handle life's problems.
3. What is your attitude toward and involvement in your local church? The Christian home and the local church are God's primary means of providing the instruction, accountability, and practical experience necessary for Christian growth. God intends to use our meeting together as a means of "encouraging one another" (Heb. 10:25). Would your attendance and service record demonstrate a commitment to spiritual growth and mutual discipleship?
4. What is your attitude toward involving yourself in the lives of others? Do you stay out of their problems because you are unprepared to help them? If so, pay close attention to the following chapters. God intends to use every believer to help others.
5. If you are uninvolved, is it because you think the problems of others are none of your business? If so, are you willing to ask God to teach you his way of thinking about this? A position of neutrality may sound justified, but it is often a way for us to protect ourselves from the vulnerability that comes in ministry to others. Yet God uses this vulnerability to stimulate our own change and growth.
6. Perhaps you are the kind of person who is always involved in other people's lives (maybe even a busybody who has an opinion about everything), but you never see them experience lasting biblical change. Are you attempting to help by giving them your ideas and opinions? Are you "practicing medicine without a license"? Can you show biblical passages that back up your "prescriptions"? Would the apostle Paul have given the same advice you give?

A Word to Disciple Makers

How to Use This Book

THE TERM *DISCIPLE MAKERS*, as used in this book, refers to those who are helping other believers to make biblical change toward Christlikeness. This includes Christian leaders, who have official responsibilities for others, as well as Christian laypeople, who have no official authority over others but nonetheless have a biblical responsibility to help fellow believers. You can use this book in several ways when working with others.

Individual Discipleship

If you are working with individuals, have them read each chapter and then write out the answers to the questions for each chapter's "Take Time to Reflect" section. You might also ask them to find and write down *five* statements in the chapter that had the most significance to them. Having to search for the five—not four, not six—most significant statements will force them to concentrate on the material as they read it. Writing them down will mentally reinforce them one more time. Sharing them with you when you next meet will further cement them in their thinking. At the same time, the significant statements they chose and their answers to the "Take Time to Reflect" section will show you where God is currently working in their lives. If you are having the individuals read one chapter each week, encourage them to read the chapter early in the week so that they have time to reflect on what they have read and to see how their lives either measure up to or fall short of what they have learned.

Small Group Study

Small groups that could benefit from studying this book together include Sunday school classes, elder or deacon groups, members of the church and Christian school staff, men's or women's Bible studies, church or Christian school teen leadership councils, and Christian biblical counselor training programs. Organizations that serve the local church, such as Christian camps, can use the book for staff training as well.

If you are working with a small group of people reading through this book, you can ask them to follow the same process described above and then have them share with the group what statements were significant to them and why those statements had an impact on them. Sharing with others reinforces the truths they have seen while encouraging others who saw the same ideas. It also highlights that truth for others who missed it in their reading.

Family Bible Study

The small group process described above is a wonderful way for a father to go through this book with teenage children who can grasp the material—in fact, this was the initial intent of this book. If there is a wide range of ages and abilities in the family, he can study the book with his wife or individually with each child who is old enough to understand it.

Premarital and Early Marriage Growth

Engaged couples and newlyweds can study through the book following the process described for individual discipleship. Individually answering the questions in the "Take Time to Reflect" sections, writing out the five most significant statements for that chapter, and then discussing the results together will pay huge dividends in their relationship. They will find out a great deal about each other while at the same time learning of God's ways of handling life's problems. If there are areas that puzzle them or points of disagreement between them about something they studied, they can seek out the help of their pastor or a mature Christian friend to clarify the issue. Growing together spiritually in this way will help them to launch their marriage with the biblical like-mindedness that forms the bedrock of a solid Christian marriage.

Part One

RESTRAINING YOUR FLESH

You have heard about [Christ] and were taught in him, as the truth is in Jesus, to put off [the ways of] your old self, which belongs to your former manner of life and is corrupt through deceitful desires. (Eph. 4:21–22)

2

RECOGNIZING THE EVIL WITHIN

There is a way that seems right to a man, but its end is the way to death. (Prov. 14:12)

As we saw in the introduction, Paul starts his threefold discussion of biblical change with a command to "put off [the ways of] your old self" (Eph. 4:22). Although technically the old self—all that we were before salvation—has been "crucified with [Christ]" (Rom. 6:6) and sin's absolute rule over us has been broken (as we shall see in chapter 5 of this book), we still possess a residual effect of that old self even after salvation. We still have an indwelling principle of sin in us that corrupts every part of us. Paul sometimes calls it the *flesh*. It is in constant conflict with the Spirit of God and represents everything within us that attempts to make life work apart from God (see Rom. 7:15–25; 8:6; Gal. 5:17). The flesh is the source of our tendency to dethrone God and to view ourselves as the ruling entity for our lives.

Bible teacher A. W. Tozer captures the propensity of the human heart this way: "The witness of the saints has been in full harmony with prophet and apostle, that an inward principle of self lies at the source of human conduct, turning everything men do into evil. To save us completely Christ must reverse the bent of our nature."[1] No honest person can deny that something is desperately wrong with humanity.

In this chapter we want to take a spiritual MRI to find out what is going on inside us that causes all our problems. I'm sure by now you may have a feeling that what we will find is not a pretty sight. But don't

1. A. W. Tozer, *The Knowledge of the Holy* (New York: Harper & Row, 1961), 31.

put this book down in despair or throw it away in anger. The Bible's message not only reveals the extent of human wickedness but also offers us our only hope—redemption. God not only redeems believers from the penalty of sin but also continues renewing within them the image of God, a likeness distorted in the fall in Eden. It is to this end that we are moving. Do not grow faint of heart in the journey, though the portrait of us is not at all flattering.

Getting the View of Man Right

On page 2 of this book, we saw four scenarios. The people in the scenarios thought their lives wouldn't be complete unless something specific changed. One thought he had to have a new car, while another wanted a divorce. One yearned for a boyfriend, while another wanted a new boss. Something did need to change, but they didn't understand their real problem: major change was needed in their own hearts.

Unfortunately, we often do not understand the treachery that lies in our hearts. We sometimes think we are pretty good people who mess up once in a while. The biblical picture is just the opposite: we are all pretty bad people who do right only by the grace of God. The Puritan writer John Owen reminds us of the danger within our own being: "[Since] there is such a law [of indwelling sin] in Christians, then it is our duty to find it out, as if a fire were in our home. Our earnestness for grace, our watchfulness, and our diligent obedience depends upon this discovery. Upon this one hinge the whole course of our lives will turn."[2]

It is certainly instructive that Paul opens his great epistle to the Romans with three chapters on the sinful nature of man. He does this before he speaks of salvation in Romans 4 and 5 and before he reveals to us the wonderful truths of progressive sanctification in Romans 6 through 8. Most Christians who have had any training in personal evangelism are familiar with the idea of getting people lost before they can be saved. Unless we see ourselves as sinners, we will not reach for the only remedy to that condition—salvation by grace through faith.

Paul's sequence of topics in the book of Romans shows us that the same understanding of human nature is prerequisite for rightly

2. John Owen, *Sin and Temptation*, James M. Houston, ed. (Minneapolis: Bethany House Publishers, 1996), 9.

understanding the remedy of sanctification in believers. So essential is a right view of man that Professor Charles Williams writes,

> One cannot hold a Scriptural view of God and the plan of salvation without having a Scriptural idea of sin. One cannot proclaim a true theory of society unless he sees the heinousness of sin and its relation to all social ills and disorders. No man can be a successful New Testament evangelist publishing the Gospel as "the power of God unto salvation to every one that believeth," unless he has an adequate conception of the enormity of sin. Nor can a man hold a consistent theory of ethics or live up to the highest standard of morality, unless he is gripped with a keen sense of sin's seductive nature.[3]

Those are powerful and foundational statements! Much goes awry in Christian parenting, Christian education, and Christian counseling because of a faulty anthropology—a faulty understanding of human nature. If the nature of man's problem is misdiagnosed, a faulty prescription is sure to follow.

Misdiagnosis in Parenting

All kinds of faulty reasons for teenage rebellion are swallowed hook, line, and sinker by parents because they do not have a biblical picture of their teens' hearts. They believe they are fighting a hormonal battle or a natural struggle for independence from parental control. Others feel that peer pressure and its resulting worldliness are the main predators on family unity, or they feel their teens are suffering from low self-esteem or merely being immature.

The solution to these diagnoses is for parents to batten down the hatches while they ride out the storms of raging hormones or negotiate a peace accord with their teens by doling out more freedom in return for some cooperation and civility at home. Those who see peer pressure as the main culprit try various restrictions to keep their teens from bad company, while others, noticing what they call *low self-esteem*, will do everything they can to help their teens feel good about themselves.

3. Charles B. Williams, "Paul's Testimony to the Doctrine of Sin," in *The Fundamentals: A Testimony to the Truth*, eds. R. A. Torry and A. C. Dixon (Los Angeles: The Bible Institute of Los Angeles, 1917), 3:25.

Parents who see their teens as immature can hope only that somehow—and, they hope, sometime soon—they grow out of it.

Although some of these issues can certainly influence a teen's thoughts and choices and need to be addressed, not one of them strikes at the root of the problem—the teen's heart itself. Hormones, peer pressure, immaturity, and so on are not the cause of teenage rebellion. Rather, in most cases, they reveal what is going on in teenagers' hearts. That is good news for parents who understand God's view of the heart, because they can then begin to address the problem God's way.

Incidentally, parents who do not understand the nature of the human heart will not be aware of how their own hearts' corruption is a further stumbling block to their children's hearts. A parent's own inconsistency, anger, moodiness, materialism, sensuality, or deception can be a far more serious stumbling block to the teen's life than whatever problem the parent is trying to address.

Misdiagnosis in Counseling

The same confusion of causes and cures exists in the field of Christian counseling. Unbiblical theories of human problems focus on codependency, low self-esteem and insecurities, "damaged emotions," an unparented "inner child," a dysfunctional upbringing, unmet needs, longings for security and significance—the list goes on and on. Since none of these theories grow out of a biblical anthropology, none of the attendant solutions are God-honoring or truly effective.

In the same way, to label counselees' problems as one or more of countless psychological disorders is a deficient psychological solution that avoids dealing with the inner corruption and deception of the human heart. Without a full understanding of the deceptive and exceedingly wicked nature of the heart, there appears to be no satisfying explanation—and therefore no truly effective remedy—for psychotic breaks, deviant sexual behavior, eating disorders, the plethora of anxiety disorders, addictions, mood disorders . . . again, the list goes on and on. The view from heaven, however, is that "the heart is deceitful above all things, and desperately wicked" (Jer. 17:9 KJV).

Often popular Christian theories of change miss the mark as well. So-called deliverance ministries assert that demonic activity is behind the increase in addictions, disorders, conflicts, and struggles of the

Christian life. Extensive tests for the presence of demons, exorcisms, and "adversarial praying" are presented as means for breaking the "bondage" of the powers of darkness. Although the Scriptures are clear about the powerful presence of demonic forces, an obsession with demons is largely a result of a faulty view of the human heart—which can easily enslave and corrupt a person without any outside help—and a faulty exegesis of Scripture passages that deal with Satan and the spirit world.

Misdiagnosis in the Local Church

In some churches where the true nature of the human heart is not understood and biblical discipleship is not seen as a sanctification issue, wrong means may be employed to help church members who struggle with some area of their lives. For example, people who are fighting the lusts of their flesh may be told that they wouldn't have such battles if they were out evangelizing more or if they got busy helping in the jail ministry. Strugglers may indeed need to make better use of their time and influence, but local church involvement is not the primary means of heart sanctification. In addition to their involvement in profitable service, the heart issues of these members must be addressed biblically before the problem of lust can be conquered. The tree itself must be healthy if it is to produce fruit that tastes truly Christlike.

Misdiagnosis in Christian Education

Williams wrote that "one cannot proclaim a true theory of society unless he sees the heinousness of sin and its relation to all social ills and disorders."[4] Pastors and Christian educators need to take special note here because they are entrusted by God with the leadership and discipleship of a certain "society" of people. Biblical standards for Christian schools and church covenants cannot be forged upon an unbiblical view of man. Human nature is such that we *will* go astray.

Many Christians today believe the lie that whatever people decide for themselves is all right and that no one else should interfere with their decisions. But we need accountability. We must be made to look at our lives through someone else's eyes. Initially those eyes are those of our parents, teachers, and church leaders. Eventually, we need to see beyond

4. Williams, 3:25.

those authority figures to the God who deputized them to "watch" on his behalf (Heb. 13:17). Ultimately, we must realize that God is watching us all the time, that he knows not only our actions but also the "thoughts and intentions of the heart" (Heb. 4:12), and that our hearts are "naked and exposed to the eyes of him to whom we must give account" (v. 13).

Accountability is the constant watchfulness and enforcement behind every effective discipleship effort. School administrators who do not ensure the presence of responsible teachers and chaperones in student classrooms and at activities are only reinforcing the inclination of students' hearts to avoid restraining the sinful impulses of the flesh. The result is chaos and disorderly conduct at best and perversion at worst.

God uses accountability to stimulate change (see Ps. 10:13; Rom. 14:12; 2 Cor. 5:10) and makes it a primary part of the ministry of the leaders he has appointed—prophets, apostles, parents, and other spiritual leaders (see Ezek. 33; Rom. 13; Heb. 13:17). Please understand, however, that sanctification is not accomplished by keeping rules. The rules for which students are held accountable are merely the guardrails on the highway that keep them from destroying themselves and others while they learn how to drive—how to walk in the Spirit for themselves.

Man also needs continual reminding. God constantly repeated his standards and warnings to Israel because they continually "forgot the Lord" or "remembered not his commandments." God was not above repeating his expectations and penalties for the society he led. So too godly leaders must see the necessity of a "ministry of repetition."[5]

This does not mean that correction should be withheld when reminders are ignored; both reminders and correction are necessary. Teachers and leaders who feel their students are too mature to be reminded don't have an accurate picture of the human heart or a biblical picture of their responsibility. Sensitive believers are aware of this ministry of repetition in their own lives as well, since the Holy Spirit repeatedly convicts and instructs when believers are straying.

This section is not by any means a fully developed philosophy of discipline: it merely shows that a biblical view of man is crucial to the leadership of any "society" of believers. It is impossible to have right

5. See 2 Peter 1:12–13, 15: "I intend always to remind you of these qualities. . . . I think it right . . . to stir you up by way of reminder. . . . I will make every effort so that after my departure you may be able at any time to recall these things."

standards or right remedies for wrongdoing without a right view of human nature. Through the years, the Christian institutions that have felt that restraint and accountability are passé have spiraled downward spiritually and morally and have become the doors through which countless young people have gone to destruction.

More Misdiagnosis

I have seen in my own thoughts in years past a deficient view of the human heart as I have looked at my own heart. There have been times when I have willfully and foolishly ignored God's ways and have sinned grievously against him. When I stopped later to reflect on what I had done, I thought with a mixture of horror and grief, "I can't believe I did that!" But once I learned the truth about my flesh, I was truly surprised I hadn't failed a whole lot more!

The variations on the above theme are numerous. If we have a biblical view of the human heart, the actions of others will certainly grieve us, but never will they surprise us. Another flavor of this same idea is "I trust my kids; they would never do something like that!" It may be true that your children are demonstrating some wonderful spiritual growth in their lives that would make certain actions uncharacteristic at this moment, but it is never outside the realm of possibility. Bob Jones Sr. used to put it this way: "Any sin that any sinner ever committed, every sinner under proper provocation could commit."

Unbelievers often comment, with various degrees of contempt, "I can't believe God would damn anyone to hell." Those with a biblical view of man, however, exclaim in grateful humility, "I'm surprised God would save any of us!" When we begin to see the human heart as God has been seeing it all along, we are stunned that he would want to redeem the likes of us. We all are truly deserving of nothing but his wrath and judgment.

I also remember times when God had been dealing with my heart about something he wanted me to surrender to him—the kind of music I listened to as a teen, whether I would serve him in a full-time vocational ministry, whether I would forgive someone who had wronged me, and so forth. Once the issue was settled and I had committed myself to God's way of handling it, I would begin to have all sorts of trouble doing right. I remember thinking, "The devil is really fighting me now." Although

Satan certainly wants to see my downfall, it is doubtful that I was experiencing direct attacks from the Evil One; I was more likely experiencing the true strength of the tendencies of my flesh, whose power I did not fully know until I resisted it. This phenomenon is very much like the experience of rowing a boat. As long as you are going with the current, you have no idea how strong the current really is. Only when you decide to turn your boat around and start rowing against the current do you experience its true strength.

Believers who have been giving in to the pull of their flesh never learn the extent of its power over them. When they decide to "row upstream," however, they meet the "current" of indwelling sin full force. They quickly realize that life lived against their sinful bent is not only difficult—it is impossible. They must learn how desperately they need God.

The Nature of Our Nature

The apostle Paul testified in Romans 7:21, "I find it to be a law that when I want to do right, evil lies close at hand." Three verses earlier, he said, "For I know that nothing good dwells in me, that is, in my flesh. For I have the desire to do what is right, but not the ability to carry it out" (v. 18). Notice further the unflattering picture God paints of the unredeemed human heart in Romans 3:10–18.

> "None is righteous, no, not one;
> no one understands;
> no one seeks for God.
> All have turned aside; together they have become worthless;
> no one does good,
> not even one."
> "Their throat is an open grave;
> they use their tongues to deceive."
> "The venom of asps is under their lips."
> "Their mouth is full of curses and bitterness."
> "Their feet are swift to shed blood;
> in their paths are ruin and misery,
> and the way of peace they have not known."
> "There is no fear of God before their eyes."

This is what we are up against. Paul, in this passage, is describing the hearts of unbelievers, but this is also a portrait of every believer's sinful tendency—a tendency that is not exterminated at salvation. Its absolute power over us is broken when we are saved, as we shall see later, but it is still present with us and can still wield its influence on us.

Our natural response to all this ugliness is to cry out with the apostle Paul, "Wretched man that I am! Who will deliver me from this body of death?" (Rom. 7:24). Fortunately, Paul didn't stop on that note. This blessed apostle, who knew full well by experience and by revelation the treachery of his own heart, follows that cry of desperation with a glorious note of triumphant hope. He exclaims, "Thanks be to God through Jesus Christ our Lord!" (v. 25). There is a way out! There is deliverance! There is hope! And with that Paul launches into his instruction on how to "walk . . . according to the Spirit" (Rom. 8:4).

But before we get to a discussion of his teaching, we need to get a more detailed picture of the nature of our nature—a full picture, not just a passing glimpse. We don't want the biblical view of our hearts to be soon forgotten. We want it to be burned indelibly on our minds. With that purpose in mind, let's go back to the start of all this ugly mess. Let's go back to Eden.

Have It Your Way

Years ago a popular fast-food chain advertised its hamburgers by telling customers that they could have any number of options on their burgers. They wanted you to come in and "have it your way." Whether or not the slogan sold more hamburgers, it certainly appealed to the most basic desire of human nature. We all, left to ourselves, want life our way.

It started in the garden of Eden. "The Devil did not tempt Adam and Eve to steal, to lie, to kill, to commit adultery; he tempted them to live independent of God."[6] It is this passion for autonomy, for independence from God, that prompted C. S. Lewis to write, "Fallen man is not simply an imperfect creature who needs improvement: he is a rebel who must lay down his arms."[7] As we have seen already, Isaiah exposes the very essence of this rebellion when he declares, "All we like sheep have gone

6. *Chapel Sayings of Dr. Bob Jones Sr.* (Greenville, SC: Bob Jones University, n.d.), 13.
7. C. S. Lewis, *Mere Christianity* (repr., New York: HarperCollins, 2001), 56.

astray; we have turned—*every one—to his own way*" (Isa. 53:6). Our biggest problem then is not the environment in which we have been reared; it is not the evil that has been done to us by others; it is not the limitations we feel so acutely. Our biggest problem is a heart that wants its own way in opposition to God's way.

Let's take a few moments to reflect on what God has to say about our hearts. Thoughtfully read through the passages listed below—a small sampling of those available in Scripture—and consider how often God targets our *own way* as our most basic problem.

> Everyone did what was right in his *own eyes*. (Judg. 17:6)

> So I gave them up unto their *own hearts' lust*:
> and they walked in their *own counsels*. (Ps. 81:12 KJV)

> Trust in the LORD with all your heart,
> and do not lean on your *own understanding*. (Prov. 3:5)

> Be not wise in your *own eyes*;
> fear the LORD, and turn away from evil. (Prov. 3:7)

> The way of a fool is right in his *own eyes*. (Prov. 12:15)

> Cease from thine *own wisdom*. (Prov. 23:4 KJV)

> Whoever trusts in his *own mind* is a fool. (Prov. 28:26)

> Woe to those who are wise in their *own eyes*,
> and shrewd in their *own sight*! (Isa. 5:21)

> Never be wise in your *own sight*. (Rom. 12:16)

> [Love] does not insist on its *own way*; it is not irritable or resentful. (1 Cor. 13:5)

> For they all seek their *own interests*, not those of Jesus Christ. (Phil. 2:21)

> For men shall be lovers of their *own selves.* (2 Tim. 3:2 KJV)

> These are grumblers, malcontents, following their *own sinful desires.* (Jude 1:16)

This *own way* tendency of our flesh is the culprit. Let's look more closely at how dangerous it is and how thoroughly it has penetrated every part of our being.

The Flesh Defies God

Speaking through the prophet Isaiah, God is clear that our natural ways and his ways are mutually exclusive. The prophet appeals to God's people to turn back from their own way.

> Seek the Lord while he may be found;
> call upon him while he is near;
> let the wicked forsake his way,
> and the unrighteous man his thoughts;
> let him return to the Lord, that he may have compassion on him,
> and to our God, for he will abundantly pardon.
> For my thoughts are not your thoughts,
> neither are your ways my ways, declares the Lord.
> For as the heavens are higher than the earth,
> so are my ways higher than your ways
> and my thoughts than your thoughts. (Isa. 55:6–9)

There can be little doubt that God sees our independent spirit—the very thing the world considers a virtue—as the root problem of man. Our heart says, "I will make life work my own way!" It raises a clenched fist toward the heavens and asserts, "I will do it my way!" Williams says, "Its root principle is the assertion of a will that is not subject to the will of God."[8]

Here then is the defiance of our flesh. Paul says it is "hostile [it has deep-seated antagonism] to God, for it does not submit to God's law; indeed, it cannot" (Rom. 8:7). This fleshly nature is perpetually at war

8. Williams, "Paul's Testimony," 3:44.

with God. It *will not* be subject. It *will not* be ruled. It is no wonder then that when we begin to submit to the Spirit of God as he works in our lives, our flesh rises up and resists that work of God. We possess within us a reflection of Satan's own nature to live independently of God.

If you at the moment are not experiencing this warfare, do not be lulled into complacency. Either you are drifting with its current and therefore not feeling its strength as it carries you to ruin, or it is craftily deceiving you by its silence only to strike when you are not watching. Thus, Paul warns, "Let anyone who thinks that he stands take heed lest he fall" (1 Cor. 10:12). Peter admonishes us to "be sober-minded; be watchful" (1 Peter 5:8) and our Lord himself says, "Watch and pray that you may not enter into temptation. The spirit indeed is willing, but the flesh is weak" (Matt. 26:41).

Since the Enemy has a base of operation within your own soul, there is never a time when you can let down your guard. He has infiltrated your ranks and will continue both his guerrilla warfare and his outward frontal attacks. His goal is to break your fellowship with your God and render you useless for service to your Redeemer, Jesus Christ. Tozer says, "So subtle is self that scarcely anyone is conscious of its presence. Because man is born a rebel, he is unaware that he is one. His constant assertion of self, as far as he thinks of it at all, appears to him a perfectly normal thing."[9]

No wonder the wisest man, Solomon, said, "Whoever trusts in his own mind is a fool" (Prov. 28:26). A traitor lives within! It will betray us to the Enemy at every turn. It cannot be trusted. It cannot be appeased. And until we stand before God, it cannot be eradicated. Until then its presence must be acknowledged, its tactics studied, its attacks discovered and resisted, and its victories confessed. Williams says,

> It scarcely requires stating that modern ideas about sin receive no countenance from Scripture, which never speaks about sin as "good in the making," as "the shadow cast by man's immaturity," as "a necessity determined by heredity and environment," as "a stage of upward development of a finite being," as a "taint adhering to man's corporeal frame," as a "physical disease," "a mental infirmity," "a constitutional weakness," and least of all "as a figment of the imperfectly enlightened,

9. Tozer, *Knowledge of the Holy*, 29.

> or theologically perverted, imagination," but always as the free act of an intelligent, moral and responsible being asserting himself against the will of his Maker, the supreme Ruler of the universe.[10]

The Flesh Defiles Man

Some who acknowledge the presence of an essential wickedness within, however, fail to realize the pervasive scope of its influence. The Bible teaches that the sin principle has infected every part of a person's being. We call this truth *total depravity*. Man is depraved—fundamentally crooked, as we have just seen. Total depravity does not mean that people are as wicked as is possible but that their fundamental crookedness has penetrated their total being. No part of their bodies or of their immaterial being is left untouched.

The sin principle has darkened all peoples' understanding so that without supernatural intervention they cannot comprehend spiritual things (see Eph. 4:18; 1 Cor. 2:14). The will has been made stubborn by the influence of indwelling sin, and the mind and its affections have been perverted so that we need continual reminders to "set [our] minds on things that are above, not on things that are on earth." (Col. 3:2) and "seek the things that are above" (v. 1). Furthermore, "it dulls the conscience, that vice regent of God in the soul, [and] renders it less quick to detect the approach of evil, less prompt to sound a warning against it and sometimes so dead as to be past feeling about it (Eph. 4:19). In short there is not a faculty of the soul that is not injured by it."[11]

We must face it then; we are totally infiltrated by the Enemy. What cautiousness this should bring to our plans and deliberations. How frequently do we rush through our days making decision after decision, touching lives in this way or that, with no thought of what corruption has tainted those decisions? Are they decisions that cannot please God? How have we defiled those with whom we have companied? This is why God so forcefully asserts,

> If you live according to the flesh you will die, but if by the Spirit you put to death the deeds of the body, you will live. (Rom. 8:13)

10. Williams, "Paul's Testimony," 3:10.
11. Williams, 3:14.

> Abstain from the passions of the flesh, which wage war against your soul. (1 Peter 2:11)

> Walk by the Spirit, and you will not gratify the desires of the flesh. For the desires of the flesh are against the Spirit, and the desires of the Spirit are against the flesh, for these are opposed to each other, to keep you from doing the things you want to do. (Gal. 5:16–17)

> For the one who sows to his own flesh will from the flesh reap corruption. (Gal. 6:8)

There is hope for us, but it will not be found by looking within. Paul says, "I know that nothing good dwells in me, that is, in my flesh" (Rom. 7:18). Our destruction has been an inside job. Our only hope is for outside intervention. Let us put away then any thought of how we must become confident within ourselves or must trust in ourselves. While the absolute power of this sinful bent over us is broken at salvation, the intrinsic corruption still remains as long as we are in our mortal bodies. It is ever present and ever active. We dare not forget about it or fail to arm ourselves against it.

The Flesh Deceives Man

Perhaps you are saying right now, "Do we have to look at this picture in any more detail? Can't we just leave things here and go on?" We could if God had not wanted us to know anything further. But he has wisely chosen to show us two other aspects of our sinful tendency that we must consider before moving on to the remedy for sin's pull. The first is the deceptive nature of the human heart. We all know by experience the intrinsic pull to be dishonest. None of us had to be taught to lie. It was natural the first time and remains natural now.

We are warned in Hebrews 3:13 to "exhort one another every day . . . that none of you may be hardened by the *deceitfulness of sin*." Jeremiah 17:9 warns us that "the heart is *deceitful above all things, and desperately sick*." James 1:22 speaks of how easy it is for believers to *deceive themselves*. And our key text for this part of our discussion, Ephesians 4:22, says that the "old self . . . is corrupt through *deceitful desires.*"[12] The serpent "deceived" Eve (Gen. 3:13; 2 Cor. 11:3). Deception is one of the two fundamental characteristics of the devil (see John 8:44)—the other being the destructiveness of his nature.

We must ask ourselves, then, in what way the fleshly nature within us is deceitful. It is deceptive in that it conceals truth. A fundamental characteristic of God is that he is truth (see John 14:6). Satan wishes to keep the God of truth hidden from the eyes of men and women and wishes to conceal from us any of the realities of life that would make redeemed humanity useful to God. Several of those realities are that

- God exists, and he made me.
- My sin is against him, and he will hold me accountable for it unless I turn to him for salvation.
- The way of the transgressor is hard.
- There is only one way of salvation, not many.
- Without him I can do nothing.
- He loves me and skillfully orders my ways for my ultimate good and his ultimate glory.
- His Word is the only trustworthy account of reality.
- He has promised his grace for every trial and challenge of life.

The list could go on and on. I can no more ignore these truths and live a life pleasing and useful to God than I can ignore the reality of gravity and fly. Indwelling sin generates lies—fantasies about life that conceal reality. Once sin has deceived the mind, believers are sure to sin. John Owen effectively portrays the influence of deception on the mind.

> The basis for the efficacy of deceit is its effect on the mind. For sin deceives the mind. When sin attempts to enter into the soul by some other way (such as by the affections), the mind checks and controls it. But when deceit influences the mind, the chance of sinning multiplies.
>
> The mind is the leading faculty of the soul. When the mind fixes on an object or course of action, the will and the affections follow

12. Other passages cautioning us not to be deceived abound. See Luke 21:8; 1 Corinthians 6:9; 15:33; Galatians 6:7; and Ephesians 5:6.

> suit. They are incapable of any other consideration. Thus, while the entanglement of the affections in sin is often very troublesome, it is the deceit of the mind that is always the most dangerous situation because of its role in all other operations of the soul. The mind's office is to guide, to direct, to choose, and to lead. "If then the light in [us] is darkness, how great is the darkness!" (Matt. 6:23).[13]

James 1:14 tells us that the sin principle within us conceals the hook (i.e., the consequences of our sin) by deceiving the mind, thus making the bait look entirely good to the affections. It looks like something to be desired, and so the will chooses it. The will chooses what appears to be good to the affections because the mind has been deceived.

No wonder Paul frequently talked about the mind. He saw how sin "waging war against the law of [his] *mind*" could then bring him into captivity (Rom. 7:23). He said, "So then, I myself serve the law of God with my *mind*, but with my flesh I serve the law of sin" (v. 25). Part 2 of this book deals extensively with being "renewed in . . . [our] *minds*" (Eph. 4:23) so that we are not deceived. You should now be able to see why that renewal of the mind is so crucial—if the mind is deceived, the battle is lost.

The Flesh Destroys Man

The Bible's teaching is plain and simple: "Sin when it is fully grown brings forth *death*" (James 1:15); "if you live according to the flesh you will *die*" (Rom. 8:13). Death means separation from something. Of course, the death spoken of here cannot mean eternal separation from God, for these passages are written to believers. It means that the design of the Serpent is to separate believers from their Master's fellowship, rendering them useless in the Master's service. It also means that the Enemy seeks to ultimately separate believers' bodies from their souls in physical death so that they can no longer be useful to their Master on this earth.

The toxicity of the heart is so potent that when God wants to judge people, all he has to do is turn them over to their own hearts. Romans 1 describes the degradation of the human heart. You and I have enough evil residing in us that if God were to let us have our own way, we would destroy ourselves. Rather than demanding our own way, we ought to be

13. Owen, *Sin and Temptation*, 36–37.

begging God never to let us have what our flesh demands. We ought to pray, "Dear God, limit me, bind me, restrict me. Do whatever you have to, but please don't let me have my own way."

Can you see now why doing right is so hard? Can you also see why it is just not possible to live the Christian life on your own without divine assistance? You and I are no match for the enemy within. Do you see now why we don't have to look for any causes outside people themselves to explain or excuse their behavior? Their environment, circumstances, hormones, health, and genetics will never account for the level of wickedness that their hearts can generate on their own.

The picture is bleak. If there were no help from God, knowledge of this condition would lead only to despair. It ought to lead us rather to repentance and dependence. We will look more specifically in the next chapter at how that sinful heart manifests itself in so many different ways in all of us.

Anthropology and Authority

Before leaving this chapter, I want to present one last matter for your reflection. I hope by now you have a healthy fear of the destructive nature of your flesh. To trust in it and obey it is to guarantee disaster. When Adam and Eve defied God, their hearts were corrupted with a reflection of Satan's own heart to live independently of God. You and I have inherited that same sinful bent. A biblical anthropology demands that we understand that, if left to ourselves, we think and act just like the Evil One himself. The worst thing that can happen to us is for God to allow us to have the desires of our own hearts.

Once Adam and Eve fell, God immediately reinforced his structure of authority—not as a punishment but as a protection. Think carefully about this for a moment. Before the fall, Adam and Eve instinctively desired fellowship with their Creator and knew what their place was in his scheme of life. As long as they acted consistently with that reality, there was no conflict or chaos. Once they listened to the Serpent's lies and defied God's order, they no longer instinctively desired to be under God. The corrupted heart within them instinctively wanted to rule itself. They now embraced "the way of the Serpent"—do your own thing.

After the fall, God reiterated the human authority of the husband over the wife and later set up the institutions of civil government and the church because if this evil nature is not restrained, it will destroy itself and everything around it. In addition, he even placed *himself* within us, in the person of the Holy Spirit, to convict us every time we begin to go our own way.

Why all this accountability? Why all this emphasis on authority in the Word of God? Because an unrestrained sinful heart is destructive (see Rom. 3:10–18; 8:13). When we are presented with a restriction by some governing authority in our lives, we have the opportunity to face once again our corrupt hearts and submit once again to God's ways of handling life. Our tendency is to evaluate merely the *rightness of the rule* we are being told to obey. The real issue is more often our authority's *right to rule* in God's scheme of life. A refusal to acknowledge our authority's right to rule is a rejection of God's ways and an evidence that our corrupt nature is ruling our lives at the moment.

Most people today have the idea that they are not free unless they are making their own decisions. The fallacy of this line of thinking is seen by reflecting on the condition of our society. We have more people making more decisions about their own lives than at any other time in the history of civilization, yet this has led to great civil and personal turmoil, misery, and discontent. You see, the practice of making decisions is not necessarily helpful unless the decisions are *wise*—that is, they are in line with God's scheme of life. If they are not wise decisions, they add even more corruption to a decision-maker's life and to the society he touches. Remember this: the same pride in people that demands the right to make its own decisions will pollute every decision that they make. That is why we are told in Proverbs 4:23, "Keep [watch over; guard] your heart with all vigilance, for from it flow the springs of life."

When we have humbled ourselves before God and have acknowledged his right to superintend all our choices, we are ready to make the choices that make us truly useful to him. As long as our old, sinful heart still rules our lives, its choices can only be destructive.

Take Time to Reflect

1. How does what we have seen about the human heart fit with the common boasts we hear from those who are engaged in sinful habits (for example, "Don't worry about me. I can handle it")?
2. If people have been engaged in life-dominating sins such as

drinking, doing drugs, practicing disordered eating, gambling, engaging in sexual perversions, and behaving self-destructively, why won't ten or twelve simple steps restore them to usefulness and Christlikeness?

3. Why is it impossible to genuinely help people by encouraging them to feel good about themselves?
4. When in your life are you prone to raise a clenched fist to God and demand your own way?
5. How has your heart deceived you regarding sin in the past? What evidence do you see that it may be deceiving you in such a way again?
6. In what areas of your life is sin's destruction making headway?

A Word to Disciple Makers

The Sight of Blood

Though no one likes to see a loved one go through hard and humiliating times, Hebrews 12:6 is very clear that "the Lord disciplines the one he loves, and chastises every son whom he receives." In God's perfect love, he wisely chastens us "for our good" (v. 10). He must confront us with our own sinfulness because left on our own, we would destroy ourselves.

Just as a person who cannot stand the sight of blood will have a hard time being a nurse, a believer who cannot bear to see someone hurting from God's chastening will struggle to be an effective disciple maker. Instead of shielding our children or fellow believers from the consequences of their wrong choices, parents and other disciple makers must not put themselves at cross-purposes to what God is doing. The ones we are trying to help will not undergo biblical change unless they humble themselves when God exposes their sin.

Sometimes chastened believers say they could take the chastening more patiently if they knew God was the one doing the chastening. They may argue that they have a harder time being corrected by other people—especially if those other people have some problems of their own or if the correction is not given in a spirit the receivers respect. It is helpful to remind such people that one of God's ordained functions for authority is to bear the sword (see Rom. 13:1–5). Authorities are sent by God "to punish those who do evil" (1 Peter 2:14). God is fully aware of and has authorized every rebuke and every correction that comes into the lives of believers. It is truly God who "works in [us], both to will and to work for his good pleasure" (Phil. 2:13), and even when others mean "evil against [us]; . . . God mean[s] it for good" (Gen. 50:20).

God's admonition to chastened believers is "do not regard lightly the discipline" or "be weary when reproved" (Heb. 12:5). If we truly want to help to bring about biblical change, we will encourage those who are being disciplined to take the whole situation very seriously instead of regarding it lightly (literally, *looking down on* it) or minimizing it. We will encourage them to endure through the full effects of the situation instead of becoming weary. Cutting the corrective process short (for example, by attempting to deflect the consequences) violates the instruction of James 1:3–4, which says to let the trial produce the endurance that, in turn, matures the believer.

If you are a disciple maker who "can't stand the sight of blood," perhaps you need to examine your own heart for motives that are not centered on God. It may be that your own way of making life work is to be a rescuer with a soft spot in your heart. Perhaps you think that if you are firm with others, you will lose their approval or your reputation for being a compassionate helper. Or perhaps you feel such a great responsibility to turn other people around that you think anything negative will keep that from happening.

Remember, we are never anyone's messiah; we are not saviors! We are, like John the Baptist, just *voices* that herald the Lamb of God. Our primary responsibility is to be faithful stewards of the opportunity to teach other people God's ways. Furthermore, we have a responsibility to do so in a way that does not erect unnecessary stumbling blocks in their paths. The responsibility for their outcomes, however, is entirely theirs before the Lord. We may have further concern for them, but we have no responsibility for their outcome (see 1 Cor. 3:5–8). To assume more is to assume a crushing, frustrating burden that God never intended for us to bear.

Jesus himself said, "Those whom I love, I reprove and discipline, so be zealous and repent" (Rev. 3:19). We cannot be Christlike unless we, like our Lord, are willing to rebuke, chasten, and call to repentance those we minister to. Remember, God did not use David, Peter, or Paul (and countless other Bible characters) because they had great potential. He instead exposed their rebellion, and when they humbled themselves, he forgave them and gave grace to them as they humbly worked through any lasting consequences.

Now that you understand the danger of this fleshly nature within, perhaps you can more readily see why God is so insistent that we "shall reason frankly" with our sinning "neighbor, lest you incur sin because of him" (Lev. 19:17). He commands us to get any brother or sister who is "caught in any transgression" involved in the restoration process (Gal. 6:1) and to live such self-examined lives that we are ready at any time to help to remove a "speck out of [our] brother's eye" (Matt. 7:5). We need each other's help. We are too easily deceived and destroyed if sin is allowed to remain unchecked.

3

IDENTIFYING YOUR OWN WAY

But each person is tempted when he is lured and enticed by his own desire. (James 1:14)

As WE HAVE seen, all of us are born with sinful hearts that demand to have their own way. If you look around you, however, you will observe that not everyone seems to have the *same* own way. Some people seem obsessed with possessions; other people feel that they will die if they don't have certain friends; still others make achievement their ultimate goal in life.

The Nature of Our Nurture

Although all of us are born with certain natural bodily desires (for food, water, air, and sexual satisfaction when puberty is reached), most of the rest of the things we desire we learn from our surroundings. They are nurtured in us—taught to us from our earliest stages of life. For instance, babies are born hungry (a natural bodily desire) but not with an innate desire for designer clothes or for certain kinds of music. They learn from their families, cultures, and peers to want those things as they grow older. These desires are called "desires of . . . the mind" in Ephesians 2:3. They are created by the way we think.

The field of advertising depends on our human ability to learn to desire something. Companies spend much money teaching their audience that they will have happier, healthier, more successful, and more fulfilled lives if they buy their products. Those who begin thinking about the benefits of a product and begin imagining themselves possessing the product begin to desire it. They may think about it so much that they feel they cannot continue without having it. Of course, that is exactly how the product manufacturer wants them to feel. It is a small step from this strong desire to a decision to buy.

Fortunately, desires that are learned can be unlearned. Fashions that teens desired a decade ago are no longer desired by today's teens. Desires changed when thinking changed about the importance or desirability of the fashion.

Many nurtured or learned desires are not wrong in themselves. James makes it clear, however, that whenever we have a strong personal desire, we can easily be lured by our flesh to pursue that desire in a sinful fashion or for a sinful motive. Remember, the flesh is that part of us that tries to usurp God's control and replace it with our own way. Notice in James 1:13–15 how our desires become the target for temptation:

> Let no one say when he is tempted, "I am being tempted by God," for God cannot be tempted with evil, and he himself tempts no one. But each person is tempted when he is lured and enticed by his *own* desire. Then desire when it has conceived gives birth to sin, and sin when it is fully grown brings forth death.

James's main teaching here is that the source of our temptation is not from *above,* from God, but from *within* us—from our own desire.

Notice also in this passage the word *own.* In the original Greek language, the word is *idios,* a word from which we get *idiosyncrasy,* something that is unique to an individual. Although everything believers can experience is "common to man" (1 Cor. 10:13), our strong desires are uniquely our own in their strength and combinations. They are as *idios,* or uniquely ours, as are our fingerprints: everyone has them but not in exactly the same patterns.

Because of our ability to learn to lust in unique combinations, we could say we have "designer lusts." Although nothing we wrestle with is new to mankind, no one has desires in exactly the same mixture as the next person. The rebellion of our own way manifests itself differently in each of us. That is why we can observe someone whose own way is different from ours and wonder, "Why would anyone think *that* is so important? It doesn't make any sense." It doesn't make sense to us, but it makes perfect sense to the other person.

To clarify this more in our minds, let us look at some broad categories of rebellion commonly seen in teenagers. These examples do not necessarily represent biblical categories, although we could find biblical characters who fit each description. They are simply observations to help us understand that not all people desire the same things but that all of us are rebels, whichever strategy we adopt. The masks of rebellion may look different from each other, but underlying them is the same face—a demand to have life our own way.

Assertive Rebels

Assertive rebels say, "I won't obey. Nobody is going to tell me what to do." They may do the following:

- Consume drugs or alcohol, smoke, steal, lie, or gamble
- Disobey, break curfews, behave disruptively or violently, bully others, or refuse to study
- Engage in premarital sex, pornography, or other sexual habits
- Dress unacceptably, behave obnoxiously, use bad language, or indulge in fleshly music or movies
- Manipulate, argue, or act defiantly

Assertive rebels are usually not hard to spot. They are often outspoken, and there is no doubt whose way they are demanding. To some assertive rebels, the only evil is getting caught and the only right is getting their own way. Since the 1960s, American culture has tolerated and even encouraged this type of verbal, assertive rebellion. The eventual effect on society will be first anarchy and then totalitarianism to squelch the chaos. No societal unit—family, school, business, church, or country—can survive long when the majority of its members declare, "I won't obey. Nobody tells me what to do."

> *Example:* Craig's parents are at their wit's end. They found pornography on Craig's laptop, and they also strongly suspect he is drinking. He won't come home by his midnight curfew or tell them where he has been or whom he was with. They have tried restricting him, but he defies their word. He speaks to his parents with obvious contempt and constantly asserts that since he is now eighteen, no one can treat

him like a kid any longer. His *own way* is to have autonomy and control of his own life.

Cooperative Rebels

Cooperative rebels are much harder to spot. They quietly decide, "I will obey since it gets me what I want." This mask has two variations.

One type of cooperative rebel is compliant at best: they are obedient but drag their feet, dawdle, are intentionally inefficient, slam doors, punish others by their attitude (pouting, sullenness), and think, "I'll do what I have to do to get what I want, but I don't agree with this and don't want to do it."

> *Example:* Amy doesn't get into any major trouble at home, but for a fifteen-year-old she isn't much help either. She eventually gets her household chores done but usually not without breaking something or causing additional work for her mother in the process. She is never blatantly defiant, so her parents are at a loss about how to discipline her. She is obedient enough to stay out of big trouble but resistive enough to make life miserable for her parents. Her *own way* is to comply while retaining the right to protest.

Another type of cooperative rebel appears to be driven by a sense of duty: as children they are often described as "really good kids," seem to go out of their way to be helpful, never seem to be a problem, are sometimes perfectionistic and legalistic, and think, "I'll do my best because I have learned that life works best this way" or "I'll do my best because I like the image of being a great kid." Perhaps they have seen how authorities respond to assertive rebels and don't want the hassle. They may even enjoy the limelight they get when others compare them to rebellious siblings or peers.

> *Example:* Kevin's own way of making life work is to achieve perfection in everything he does. As a child he was surprisingly obedient. As a teen he thinks that if he doesn't make the top grade or isn't on the starting team, life is not worth living. In fact, if he isn't on top, he often spirals into great despair. Winning is an all or nothing issue with him. What he calls a competitive spirit is nothing more than an obsessive

desire for winning. He has decided he has to have first place and nothing less will do. His *own way* is to ensure success by being the best.

Many of us really try to be good—not because we are allowing God to work in our lives to produce his fruit but because we think life has fewer snags when we stay out of trouble. We often achieve the accolades and image we want. We can become smug around others who aren't doing right and can become easily embittered during the times when we are being good and don't get what we want.

As you can see, "being good" can be just our own way of making life work without God.

Passive Rebels

Lastly, there are those whose *own way* is to passively play the victim. Such rebels may say, "I can't obey," or "I forgot to obey," or "I didn't know to obey." Let's look briefly at three variations of the passive rebel.

"I can't obey" implies powerlessness and shows up in indifference or resistance. Passive rebels of this variety won't get driver's licenses or jobs. They won't try out, reach out, speak out, or move out. They often excuse themselves with "I'm not feeling well" or "I have a disability" or "I'm a victim." He may say, "I'm hurting too much" or "My parents weren't good examples" or "I'm too emotional." They are often stubborn and simply won't be put into a vulnerable position.

Example: Perry's own way of handling life is to avoid anything that would make him vulnerable. He runs from problems, will not try anything unfamiliar, and spends as much time as he can by himself. He calls himself "laid-back" and says he isn't a "people person." Consequently, he is often lonely. His *own way* is to not get involved and not take any risks.

Proverbs calls "being laid-back" by another name—*slothfulness*. The slothful run away from problems instead of toward them (26:13), live in a snooze-alarm mode of procrastination (v. 14), get irritated if someone tries to push them (v. 15), and are seemingly unteachable (v. 16). Their lack of productivity and their lives' deterioration are obvious to any onlooker (24:30–32), but they continue to make excuses (v. 33) that will surely lead to disaster (v. 34).

The second excuse, "I forgot to obey," often indicates laziness and shows up in untidiness and constant sleepiness. These passive rebels conveniently forget chores, responsibilities, and appointments. They often appear absent-minded. Their minds aren't dysfunctional but distracted by some other obsession.

> *Example:* Hannah wants everyone to accept her. She cannot say no to others because she does not want to displease them. Her parents wonder why she always ends up with the wrong friends. They don't know that because of her lust for approval, she has already given up her sexual purity. She is obsessed with her appearance. She spends hours shopping and takes forever to get ready in the morning. She carefully plans her wardrobe so that nothing she wears is repeated within a two week span of time.
>
> Though Hannah is meticulous in these areas and can remember every outfit her friends have worn that week, she cannot seem to remember which days she is supposed to come home right after school to watch her younger brother. She often forgets where her parents told her to be when they come to pick her up after a game, church activity, or shopping trip. She is courteous and helpful at times but has her parents totally baffled. They cannot understand why she is such an airhead when it comes to responsibility. What they don't know is that her *own way* is to have the approval of a select group—nothing else ultimately matters to her.

The last excuse, "I didn't know to obey," is often intentional ignorance. These passive rebels can claim they didn't hear the instructions or didn't think the instructions applied to their situation. A further refinement of this is "I just acted without thinking." They are not, however, acting without thinking. They are acting without thinking about the consequences. They are used to doing what they want without consideration for others.

> *Example:* Josh doesn't seem to be a bad kid—he just always happens to be in the middle of whatever trouble is brewing at the moment.

He loves being a practical joker, even though his pranks have become more daring in recent days and have cost him some money for damages. When confronted about his foolish behavior, he replies, "I guess I just wasn't thinking." His parents are embarrassed by how many times the principal has called them about his class disruptions. They have concluded he is just immature. They are frightened, however, by the thought of how long they may have to wait until he grows up. In the meantime, his upkeep could be costly. Josh's *own way* is to live for the pleasure of the moment with no thought of God or others.

Is There Any Hope for Rebels?

Parents, teachers, or disciple makers who are struggling with rebels like those discussed above may become discouraged when the problems seem to be getting worse. In fact, they may begin to wonder whether such people are beyond help. The Bible assures us, however, that we can have great hope.

The Scriptures teach us that God has a certain kind of change in mind for every believer. In 1 Corinthians 6:9–10, Paul lists a number of behaviors and lifestyles that characterize those who are outside the kingdom of God. Read slowly over these two verses and notice the breadth of perversion mentioned here:

> Or do you not know that the unrighteous will not inherit the kingdom of God? Do not be deceived: neither the sexually immoral, nor idolaters, nor adulterers, nor men who practice homosexuality, nor thieves, nor the greedy, nor drunkards, nor [verbal abusers], nor swindlers will inherit the kingdom of God.

Paul then makes a pretty startling statement in the next verse: "And such were some of you. But you were washed, you were sanctified, you were justified in the name of the Lord Jesus Christ and by the Spirit of our God" (v. 11).

Please don't miss this! Here is a group of people whose designer lusts had taken them to the extremes of wickedness. They were people who did not just occasionally lapse into these sins. The description of their lives of adultery, theft, and other sinful activities suggests that these sins were the habitual patterns of their lives. If any people were going to have a hard time changing, it would be the people in Corinth who had come to Christ out of these lifestyles. Yet Paul did not write them off as hopeless cases. Each one had been fundamentally changed into a "new creation" (2 Cor. 5:17). They were not what they used to be, but they still had much growing to do—hence this letter to the church in Corinth about its problems. They were being *changed* by the Spirit of God!

Let's take a look at one more passage about drastic change. Paul lists the "works of the flesh" in Galatians 5:19–21 (those manifestations of own-way living) and then contrasts them with the "fruit of the Spirit" (vv. 22–23) (the manifestations of living life God's way). Read these over slowly, taking in the full scope of problems listed by the apostle. These too can be changed!

- *Sexual immorality*—adultery; sexual intercourse between individuals married to someone else
- *Impurity*—lewdness; dirty-mindedness
- *Sensuality*—blatant and shameless contempt for public decency
- *Idolatry*—worshipping false gods
- *Sorcery*—use of magical powers, mediums, and occult practices
- *Enmity*—hostile attitude toward others
- *Strife*—contentious spirit; hostile actions
- *Jealousy*—spirit of envy
- *Fits of anger*—explosive, angry outbursts
- *Rivalries*—competition coming from devotion to self
- *Dissensions*—feuding, divisive spirit within the group
- *Divisions*—disunity created by a stubborn opinion
- *Envy*—embittered resentment often manifesting itself in hostile, spiteful deeds
- *Murder*—taking someone's life unlawfully
- *Drunkenness*—intoxication
- *Orgies*—debauched, sensual parties

There is no problem that God's Word doesn't address. All the masks of rebellion and the sinful behaviors and attitudes listed in these Scripture passages can be changed.

In chapter 5 we will look at the dynamics involved in resisting the pull of these desires within us. For now, however, please understand that these attitudes and actions listed in 1 Corinthians 6 and Galatians 5 are customized manifestations of the sinful human heart. We do not all have the same desires to the same degree or in the same combination. All of these, however, are "works of the flesh."

John Owen on Knowing Your Heart

The seventeenth-century Puritan preacher John Owen has written much about the nature of the human heart as revealed in the Scriptures. When warning his readers about the propensity of their heart to certain temptations, he wrote,

> Just as people have differing and distinctive personalities, so they are also affected by distinctive temptations. These relate to their nature, education, and other factors. Unless we are conscious of these propensities, relationships, and dynamic possibilities, temptation will constantly entangle us. This is why it is so important to know ourselves—our temperaments and our attitudes.
>
> If people did not remain strangers to themselves, they would not maintain all their lives in the same paralyzed state. But they give flattering names to their own natural weaknesses. They try to justify, palliate, or excuse the evils of their own hearts, rather than uproot and destroy them ruthlessly. They never gain a realistic view of themselves. Ineffective lives and scandal grow like branches out of this root of self-ignorance. How few truly seek to know themselves, or possess the courage to do so.[1]

We need to heed his words well. We must become accustomed to looking beyond our own behavior and emotions and asking ourselves, "What is the ruling desire in my heart right now that is driving this behavior or emotion?" Once you have read through the following extended case study, set aside a time to prayerfully work through the reflection questions that follow. Perhaps they will help you to determine what is going on in your own heart.

1. John Owen, *Sin and Temptation*, James M. Houston, ed. (Minneapolis: Bethany House Publishers, 1996), 131–32.

A Case in Point

Remember Craig, the assertive rebel mentioned earlier in this chapter? Let's examine the *real* problem in his family.

The Real Problem

Craig defied his parents and was determined that no one would tell him what to do. His folks suspected him of drinking and found pornography on his laptop. Craig's dad, Frank, often remarked to his wife with angry bewilderment, "I can't believe how arrogant that boy is! What that kid needs is a good dose of humility."

Frank was right; his son had an exaggerated sense of his own importance and no concern for others. As Craig's rebellion continued, other problems in the home surfaced. Craig wasn't the only one who needed a "good dose of humility."

Frank, a successful accountant and a leader in the church, seemingly had his act together—at least in public. He appeared godly and disciplined. He never missed a morning for his own devotions and regularly met with his wife and son for Bible reading and prayer. He wouldn't think of arriving at a deacons' meeting late, and every job assigned to him he completed thoroughly and precisely. Although some people thought he was unnecessarily opinionated, he was usually right in the end, so people generally followed his suggestions.

Craig's mother, Susan, was a great asset to the church as well. She was quiet, joyful, and very giving. She could always be counted on to serve extra time in the church nursery and work tirelessly at every banquet or women's retreat. She seemed to be the epitome of a godly, submissive wife.

Craig saw all of this from another angle at home, however. Frank had managed his family through the years with a heavy hand. Craig appeared to be obedient until eighth grade, when he began acting up at school. His public behavior got worse in the next few years. Craig was suspended from his Christian school during his senior year for repeated profanity and then expelled for starting fights in the boys' locker room when others got in his way or didn't agree with him.

Through Craig's growing-up years, his mother often pleaded with her husband, sometimes in front of Craig, to let up on the boy. As Frank grew more irritated and angry over his son's behavior, Susan ached when she saw her husband tear into Craig. Frank told her she was too soft and would ruin the boy with her pampering. She tried to comfort Craig by excusing her husband's reactions. "Your dad had a hard day at work; don't take his words seriously. He really does love you." When her husband took away Craig's phone, Susan let Craig call his girlfriend on her phone when Frank wasn't home. She justified it to herself by thinking that his girlfriend could have a good influence on him.

When Craig got too big to be spanked, Frank became more vicious in his verbal attacks and seemed to gloat over the power he exercised when he placed restrictions on Craig. By the time Craig was eighteen, he was a high school dropout in a constant power struggle with his father.

When Craig's expulsion from school became public, Pastor Williams sat down with Frank and Susan to offer his help. The more they talked, the more the home situation came to light. A conference with Craig later on filled in the rest of the picture. Craig was not the only family member who needed help. Frank admitted he had been out of control with Craig in recent months and had grown to despise his son. Susan revealed that she had let Craig bypass his father's restrictions.

Though these admissions were helpful, Pastor Williams could see there were even deeper problems. Every family member was guilty of trying to make life work his or her own way instead of God's way. Frank's own way was to maintain control of everything by diligent oversight. When things began to go out of control, he threw more power at the problem. After all, as a deacon, he had to manage his own household well (see 1 Tim. 3:12). He frequently complained to his wife, "If you and Craig would only follow my leadership, we wouldn't be in this mess." Susan's own way was to be a peacemaker. She could not stand conflict and did anything she could to smooth over the relationship between her son and her husband. Craig despised his father for his control and lost respect for his mother because of her obvious duplicity. He took advantage of her concessions to his restrictions but never loved her for them. He saw her, rather, as weak and cowering—a stance he despised in people.

The Real Solution

Pastor Williams started in the right place—with the pride at work in each one's heart. The pastor took Frank to Ephesians 4:29–32 and showed him that dealing with his son in anger defied God's instructions to him and was a manifestation of the pride of his heart. How could he have any integrity demanding that his son obey him when he was not obeying his Father in heaven?

Frank began to see how arrogantly he had administered correction. There was no doubt that he had provoked his child to wrath (see Eph. 6:4). He also saw that he had actually taught his son by example that if he had a problem, he should just throw more force at it. His son had learned well and was forcefully pushing back at him. Pastor Williams challenged Frank to take the leadership in his family but in a different direction.

"Frank, God wants you to lead your family, but you need to be the leader in humility first. Your family needs to see you humble yourself before God, before them, and before the assembly at church. You have stepped off God's path of truth. You have been leaning on your own understanding and wise in your own eyes.

"Craig needs to see you get into your place under God. The only way you have sought God is to ask him to help you to get your family under control. God will not help you do that; he wants to break you of your controlling ways. You cannot call Craig to a position of submission to you from your position of rebellion against God.

"If you want to see your family turn around, you will have to be the first one to die. In God's pattern of leadership, you, like Christ, have to be the first one on the cross. From there you can call your family to follow you by dying as well. You must lead in following the Father's will that you humble yourself for others."

Pastor Williams continued, "Susan, you have bypassed God's requirement that you support your husband. You can, and should, make any biblical appeals to him that will help him to be more effective in his ministry at home. But instead you have taught Craig by example that when you do not agree with your leader, you can bypass his commands. Craig didn't need your example to learn how to rebel against authority—that comes naturally for all of us—but your example authorized disobedience in the home."

The Resolution

Susan immediately saw her sin against God and against her husband and asked both to forgive her. Several weeks passed, however, before

Frank was broken enough by his son's continued rebellion to admit to God and others that what had appeared so right to him was actually his own way of controlling life to make it work for him. Frank and Susan would learn much more about humility before they saw their son bow in submission to God and to them eighteen months later.

Pastor Williams could have approached this family's problems from many different angles. Other counselors may have seen this as a communication problem or as a child-rearing problem. Still others may have suggested that Frank and Susan show some tough love. None of these solutions, however, would have addressed the heart of the problem. The contents of three "tea bags" had to be changed before the flavor of the family tasted Christlike.

Not a Pretty Sight

As we saw in the last chapter, a good look at our hearts is often pretty gruesome. As we see our flesh manifesting itself through our designer lusts, which seem so natural to us, we can become even more discouraged. We may think, "There's no hope for me. It looks as though everything I do comes from the wrong motives and desires." There is hope, however. God doesn't show us this picture of ourselves without offering his own wonderful remedy. We will begin to look at that plan in the next chapter. Before going on, however, answer the questions below.

Take Time to Reflect

God says our most basic problem is our propensity to turn "every one—to his own way" (Isa. 53:6). You have seen the examples of several people's own way in this chapter. What are some of the elements that constitute your own way? For further help, complete the sentences below.

- I feel most secure when . . .
- All I want to have/be/do is . . .
- The thing I worry about most is . . .
- The thing that keeps me awake at night is . . .
- I go into a panic when . . .
- I get most angry when . . .
- I tend to get very discouraged when . . .

1. Do you find yourself depicted in any of the three kinds of rebels discussed in this chapter? Rather than trying to find out exactly which kind of rebel you are, identify the ways in which you are most prone to rebel and rebel characteristics that you most identify with. Write out your answers.
2. God exposes the rebellion of our own way by placing us in "hot water." What hot-water situations has God placed you into at this time in order to expose your self-centeredness? (Hot-water situations include physical struggles, struggles with temptations and desires, pressures at home or work, and relational problems with others.)
3. What kinds of wrong responses come out of you when you can't have your own way? How does your self-centered "tea" taste to others around you?

A Word to Disciple Makers

Ruling Desires

James 4:1 teaches us that problems have two levels. First, there is the outward problem, which is easy to recognize and address. In James 4:1, the outward problem is the fighting and warring between two people. Parents and other leaders who address problems only on the outward, visible level are missing important issues of the heart. James says that the underlying problem is hotly pursued desire. The problem is in the heart, not the circumstances.

Warring children, teens, church members, and coworkers need to be confronted about their fighting—but, more fundamentally, they need to be confronted about the underlying desires of their hearts that prompted the fight. It may be a desire to be first (see 3 John 1:9) or a desire to have a possession belonging to someone else (see 1 Kings 21) or a desire to be accepted like someone else (Gen. 4:1–8). Merely insisting that the warring parties get along or separating them for a period of time may stop the fight, but it will not solve the *real* problem—their ruling desires, which are a part of their own way of making life work.

Not only must those ruling desires be identified and confronted in their lives, but the offenders must also ask forgiveness from God and from those they are wronging before lasting biblical change can take place. It is not even enough for individuals to see their ruling desires and acknowledge that they have sinful desires. Unless they repent with the intention of forsaking their sin, fellowship with God remains broken and there will be no lasting change. God warned Israel, "[Do not] follow after your own heart and your own eyes, which you are inclined to whore after. . . . Remember and do all my commandments, and be holy to your God" (Num. 15:39–40).

God was concerned about Israel's heart. Don't miss the heart issues when dealing with the surface problems!

4

GETTING IN YOUR PLACE

Be appalled, O heavens, at this; be shocked, be utterly desolate, declares the LORD, for my people have committed two evils: they have forsaken me, the fountain of living waters, and hewed out cisterns for themselves, broken cisterns that can hold no water. (Jer. 2:12–13)

"MICHAEL! ALL THE rest of you in heaven! Can you believe it? Stop and look down there at Israel. Look at what my people have been doing! Doesn't it make you shudder with terror for them?

"These people of mine have committed two great evils. They first show their rebellion by not coming to drink from my pure springs of water. As if that isn't enough, they further insult me by trying to quench their thirst with the murky runoff water they catch in their makeshift cisterns. What a sad exchange! Israel doesn't have to live that way. They aren't slaves; they aren't captives! They don't have to drink brackish water from such stagnant, leaking basins; I want them to enjoy living water from me. Yet they have brought this on themselves."

God finishes his address to the heavenly beings and turns to Israel:

> Your evil will chastise you,
>   and your apostasy will reprove you.
> Know and see that it is evil and bitter
>   for you to forsake the LORD your God;
>   the fear of me is not in you,
> declares the Lord GOD of hosts. (Jer. 2:19)

Although Scripture is clear that our own way will not work, symbolized by the broken cisterns in the Jeremiah passage, the fact that it won't work is God's secondary concern—the second evil. Forsaking God is the first and the more wicked of the two evils God enumerates here. We must understand that to look to anything apart from God to make life work is to forsake God.

Dependent by Design

Creation inherently demands dependency. Space shuttles, houses, automobiles, and superhighways do not make themselves. Because none is self-created, none is self-sustaining. They depend on their creators to refuel them, service them, and make repairs. Subordination and dependence are inherent for everything that is made by someone else: a river "cannot rise higher than its source."[1]

In the same way, God made us, and we are dependent on him. Adam needed God. He had to be told who he was and what his job was. He had to be told what to eat and what not to eat. Any attempt to make us creatures who can live independently from God is doomed to failure. We can no more joyfully and peacefully live independently from God than we can fly by flapping our hands. God did not create us to be birds but bipeds—by design. He did not make us to be autonomous, self-contained, self-sufficient creatures but to be dependent—by design. Psalm 100:3 says, "It is [the LORD] who made us, and we are his; we are his people, and the sheep of his pasture." The governing principle is that if we needed somebody to make us, we need somebody to maintain us. Trusting in our own way defies the most basic fact of our creation.

Thus, any change that will ultimately help us must move us away from autonomy and toward dependence on our Creator. Any change that gives us the illusion that we are able to make life work our own way makes us only more powerful rebels against God and useless to him. We must face our dependency, repent of our proud attempts to make life work our own way, and submit to the ways of our Creator. God promises satisfaction, hope, security, and joy to those who do so.

A Boy and a Bike

Perhaps a parable can show us how easy it is for us to think we are making life work on our own.

1. A. W. Tozer, *Evenings with Tozer: Daily Devotional Readings* (Chicago: Moody Publishers, 1981), 27.

Johnny approaches his father with a request. "Dad, I'm six now. Can I buy a bike?"

"I'm sure you are old enough to learn to ride," his father replies, "but how are you going to buy a bike?"

"Remember, you give me a quarter every week when I help you wash the car. This week I saved it because I want to buy a bike. I didn't even buy any candy."

"You really are serious about buying a bike! If you think you're ready, go get your quarter and let's go shopping."

After checking out several stores, they find a bike that Johnny really likes. Johnny's father looks at the price tag and calculates that with tax the bike will cost one hundred dollars—a far cry from a quarter.

"Are you sure this is the bike you want?"

"I sure am! I've always dreamed of having a bike like this. This is the one I want—and I've got my quarter!"

"OK then. Wheel the bike up to the counter, Johnny, and let's pay the clerk."

Johnny pushes the bike up to the checkout counter, lays his quarter on the counter, and says to the clerk, "I want to buy this bike."

The clerk smiles at him, winks at his father, and replies, "Sure, you've made a great choice."

Dad turns to Johnny. "Son, take the bike outside and wait for me on the sidewalk. I want to talk to the lady." As Johnny leaves the store, his father pays the full amount, puts Johnny's quarter in his pocket, and then joins his son outside. They load the bike into the car, and on the way home Johnny's father commends him for his choice. "Son, I just want to tell you how proud I am of you today. Every other week you have spent your quarter on candy that would not last. This week you saved your quarter and decided to buy something that would be around for a while. That's a good decision. I can tell you're growing up."

When they arrive at home, they unload the bike, and Johnny runs into the house to get his mother. When she comes outside, Johnny exclaims, "Look at my new bike, Mom! Isn't it beautiful! And I bought it with my own money!"

Someday Johnny will realize that he didn't buy the bike—that his quarter was a mere vote that indicated that he wanted a bike rather than candy. Perhaps this experience will cause him to recognize that he was dependent on his father in ways he never imagined as a six-year-old boy. His dad provided him with a home, food, medical insurance, education, clothing, life skills, and a thousand other things, both tangible and intangible. Without his dad's love, he wouldn't ever have felt that he belonged anywhere. Without his dad's protection, he wouldn't ever have felt really safe. Without his dad's spiritual direction, he might still be lost in his sin. He wouldn't even have life without his father.

Rebels against God's Design

Some children never come to realize their dependence on their parents, and their ingratitude is a grief to their parents' hearts. In the same way, we are dependent on our heavenly Father and owe our gratitude to him—only our dependency extends to far more areas and involves far greater issues than the relationship of a mortal father with his children. Colossians 1:16–17 says,

> For by him all things were created, in heaven and on earth, visible and invisible, whether thrones or dominions or rulers or authorities—all things were created through him and for him. And he is before all things, and in him all things hold together.

These verses and many like them are not just poetry; they are statements of reality. If God were to withdraw his personal superintendence from his creation, it would dissolve into the nothingness from which it was created. It exists only by his continued, wise, powerful, and purposeful will. Hebrews 1:3 testifies that Christ the Creator bears up or sustains the universe by his mighty Word. There is no way that human beings can escape their dependence on God. We can only rebel against it to our own destruction.

The account of Nebuchadnezzar powerfully illustrates the destructive nature of our natural bent toward self-sufficiency. His kingdom of Babylon was at the height of its glory when the following incident took place, as recorded in Daniel 4:29–37.

> At the end of twelve months he was walking on the roof of the royal palace of Babylon, and the king answered and said, "Is not this great Babylon, which I have built by my mighty power as a royal residence

> and for the glory of my majesty?" While the words were still in the king's mouth, there fell a voice from heaven, "O King Nebuchadnezzar, to you it is spoken: The kingdom has departed from you, and you shall be driven from among men, and your dwelling shall be with the beasts of the field. And you shall be made to eat grass like an ox, and seven periods of time shall pass over you, until you know that the Most High rules the kingdom of men and gives it to whom he will." Immediately the word was fulfilled against Nebuchadnezzar. He was driven from among men and ate grass like an ox, and his body was wet with the dew of heaven till his hair grew as long as eagles' feathers, and his nails were like birds' claws.
>
> At the end of the days I, Nebuchadnezzar, lifted my eyes to *heaven*, and my reason returned to me, and I blessed the Most High, and praised and honored him who lives forever,
>
> for his dominion is an everlasting dominion,
>   and his kingdom endures from generation to generation;
> all the inhabitants of the earth are accounted as nothing,
>   and he does according to his will among the host of heaven
>   and among the inhabitants of the earth;
> and none can stay his hand
>   or say to him, "What have you done?"
>
> At the same time my reason returned to me, and for the glory of my kingdom, my majesty and splendor returned to me. My counselors and my lords sought me, and I was established in my kingdom, and still more greatness was added to me. *Now I, Nebuchadnezzar, praise and extol and honor the King of heaven, for all his works are right and his ways are just; and those who walk in pride he is able to humble.*

Nebuchadnezzar "got in his place" when he recognized that he was a creature who was dependent on his Creator. To humble oneself in this way is called *humility*—a topic we must look at more closely.

Humility: The Hallmark of the Dependent Creature

Andrew Murray writes, "Humility, the place of entire dependence on God, is, from the very nature of things, the first duty and the highest virtue of the creature [man], and the root of every virtue. Humility is simply [man's] acknowledging the truth of his position as creature [man] and yielding to God His place."[2] When we finally recognize that we are rebels against God and decide to "lay down our arms," our repentance demonstrates our humility. When we become aware that we cannot make life work our own way but desperately need God, we demonstrate humility by a sense of continued dependence. No one who has been humbled before God is self-justifying, self-protective, or self-confident (see 2 Cor. 3:5; 4:7).

The *International Standard Bible Encyclopedia* says this about humility:

> It by no means implies slavishness or servility; nor is it inconsistent with a right estimate of oneself, one's gifts and calling of God, or with proper self-assertion when called for. But the habitual frame of mind of a child of God is that of one who feels not only that he owes all his natural gifts, etc., to God, but that he has been the object of undeserved redeeming love, and who regards himself as being not his own, but God's in Christ. He cannot exalt himself, for he knows that he has nothing of himself. The humble mind is thus at the root of all other graces and virtues. Self-exaltation spoils everything. There can be no real love without humility. "Love," said Paul, "vaunteth not itself, is not puffed up" (1 Cor. 13:4). As Augustine said, humility is first, second and third in Christianity.[3]

Saint Bernard wisely observed that humility is "the esteeming of ourselves small, inasmuch as we are so; the thinking truly, and because truly, therefore lowlily, of ourselves."[4] Humility is the frame of mind we possess when we are fully aware of our nothingness apart from God and of our sinfulness, which would eternally separate us from God were not God willing to rescue us. It says, "I am sinful and need God's mercy" and "I am insufficient and need God's grace."

2. Andrew Murray, *Humility* (repr., Grand Rapids: Bethany House Publishers, 2001), 16–17.

3. James Orr, ed., *The International Standard Bible Encyclopedia*, vol. 3 (Grand Rapids: Wm. B. Eerdmans Publishing Co., 1956), 1439.

4. Richard C. Trench, *Synonyms of the New Testament* (Grand Rapids: Wm. B. Eerdmans Publishing Co., 1880), 150.

Live the Christian Life the Same Way You Got It

The Christian life starts with this kind of humility (see Matt. 5:3; 18:3–4). To be saved, we must realize we have nothing in ourselves to commend us to God and that we are totally bankrupt before God and unable to do anything about the debt of our sin. We must come to God as broken, needy sinners dependent on God for forgiveness. We bring no personal merit to God to bargain with. Paul describes it this way:

> For by grace you have been saved through faith. And this is *not your own doing*; it is the gift of God, not a result of works, so that no one may boast. (Eph. 2:8–9)

Most Christians understand this and would think it heretical to assume they could do anything to earn God's salvation. They know theirs is the kingdom because they come "poor in spirit" to God (Matt. 5:3). What they are not often ready to accept is that God wants them to have the same dependent attitude *after* salvation. Colossians 2:6 says, "As you received Christ Jesus the Lord, so walk in him." Humility is not only the start of the Christian life; it is the start of everything godly in the Christian life.

Unfortunately, humility is treated as a vice in today's self-assertive, in-your-face culture. In fact, many people would not even know how to describe a humble person. C. S. Lewis puts it this way:

> Do not imagine that if you meet a really humble man he will be what most people call "humble" nowadays: he will not be a sort of greasy, smarmy person, who is always telling you that, of course, he is nobody. Probably all you will think about him is that he seemed a cheerful, intelligent chap who took a real interest in what you said to him. If you do dislike him it will be because you feel a little envious of anyone who seems to enjoy life so easily. He will not be thinking about humility: he will not be thinking about himself at all.[5]

Andrew Murray rightly emphasizes our need for humility in order to fulfill our purpose as image bearers of God.

5. C. S. Lewis, *Mere Christianity* (repr., New York: HarperCollins, 2001), 128.

> Just as Jesus found His glory in taking the form of a servant, so when He said to us, "Whoever wants to become great among you must be your servant" (Matthew 20:26), He was teaching us the truth that there is nothing so divine as being the servant and helper of all. The faithful servant who recognizes his position finds a real pleasure in supplying the wants of the master or his guests. When we realize that humility is something infinitely deeper than contrition, and accept it as our participation in the life of Jesus, we will begin to learn that it is our true nobility, and that to prove it in being servants of all is the highest fulfillment of our destiny, as men created in the image of God.[6]

Notice further our Lord's words about humility as a continuing attitude of the believer.

> Come to me, all who labor and are heavy laden, and I will give you rest. Take my yoke upon you, and learn from me, for I am gentle and *lowly in heart,* and you will find rest for your souls. For my yoke is easy, and my burden is light. (Matt. 11:28–30)

> Whoever would be first among you must be your slave, even as the Son of Man came not to be served but to serve, and to *give his life* as a ransom for many. (Matt. 20:27–28)

> Whoever receives this child in my name receives me, and whoever receives me receives him who sent me. For he who is *least among you all* is the one who is great. (Luke 9:48)

> For everyone who exalts himself will be humbled, and he who *humbles* himself will be exalted. (Luke 14:11)

> Let the greatest among you become *as the youngest,* and the leader as one who serves. For who is the greater, one who reclines at table or one who serves? Is it not the one who reclines at table? But I am among you as the one who serves. (Luke 22:26–27)

6. Murray, *Humility,* 11–12.

> You call me Teacher and Lord, and you are right, for so I am. If I then, your Lord and Teacher, have washed your feet, you also ought to wash one another's feet. (John 13:13–14)

As we said at the start of this book, not just any change will do. The only change that will ultimately be for our good and for God's glory begins with humility. God says, "Likewise, you who are younger, be subject to the elders. *Clothe yourselves, all of you, with humility* toward one another, for 'God opposes the proud but gives grace to the humble'" (1 Peter 5:5).

Being clothed with humility is a concept that most of us have never considered. We do not think of humility as a dominant characteristic of the contemporary "successful person." Today's athletes, entertainers, politicians, businesspeople, and sadly, many church leaders are not known for their humility but for their self-confident arrogance, their control over others, or their self-indulgent lifestyles.

Our aversion to the whole idea of humility testifies to the poverty of our understanding of God's ways. For example, one time I asked a group of college students what had held back them or their friends from submitting to God. Their responses indicated that they felt that if they humbled themselves to submit to God, God would do something to mess up their lives. When I asked for specifics, I received responses like the following:

- I felt that if I surrendered all to God, he would make me be poor the rest of my life. I would not be able to drive a nice car or live in a decent house, and I would have to wear outdated clothes.
- I was afraid that if I made the choice to give my life to God, he would make me confront my friends about their sinful lifestyles. I didn't want to lose the approval of my friends.
- I thought that if I let God run my life, he would make me marry some Christian fanatic whose zeal would always embarrass me or that he would not let me get married at all.
- Having to give up my sensual music and movies kept me from surrendering to Christ. I felt that he was determined to make my life miserable and that I wouldn't have any fun.
- I couldn't imagine what I would do if God were running my life. I thought it meant that I would do nothing but sit around

> reading the Bible all the time. I guess I feared most that he would call me into the ministry or to the mission field somewhere.

The idea that God needs our permission to make our lives miserable is the opposite of the truth. Stop and think about something for a moment. If God were really trying to find some way to mess up our lives, he would not need to wait until we finally surrendered to him to go ahead with his plans for destruction. God doesn't need our permission to mess up our lives. In our wickedness, we believe that *God* is the biggest evil we could encounter and that it is *our* resistance to him that keeps life from charging headlong into misery. What arrogance that is. What corruption within us it reveals.

Actually, the exact opposite is true! Only by "getting in our place" under God can we flourish. David teaches us that the "blessed"—the fulfilled and flourishing ones—are those who seek relationship with God through his Word. Jesus teaches the same truth in his Beatitudes in Matthew 5:1–11. God's Word is filled with his promises to give hope, help, and fulfillment to those who will walk with him in submission and humility.

Because we have not "glorified him . . . as God"—we have not thought of him as worthy of our praise—and have not given "thanks to him," we have become "futile in [our] thinking, and [our] foolish hearts [are] darkened" (Rom. 1:21). This kind of evil thinking leads us to exchange "the glory of the immortal God for images resembling mortal man" (v. 23). We actually make God look evil like ourselves and make ourselves look good like God. No wonder Proverbs warns us that "there is a way that seems right to a man, but its end is the way to death" (Prov. 14:12).

How Does God Humble Us?

Our human limitations and our sinful pride must be exposed; we must be humbled to be changed. But God doesn't humble every person in the same way. He has wrenches of many sizes in his toolbox to fix whatever problem he finds. Let's look briefly at four means God can use to humble us and to bring us to himself in dependence.

The Problems We Can't Handle Expose Our Helplessness

In 2 Kings 5, we read of Naaman, a high-ranking military officer in Syria who contracted leprosy. Through a concerned Israelite slave girl, he learned that the Israelite prophet Elisha could cure him of this horribly disfiguring and eventually fatal disease. But when he approached Elisha's house, he did not find the welcome he expected for a man of his rank and station. Instead of personally greeting Naaman and showing him the customary courtesies of hospitality, Elisha sent a messenger who told Naaman to go to the River Jordan and dip in its murky waters seven times.

Naaman was furious! He wanted a change but on his own terms. He wanted to choose how the message was delivered, and he wanted to choose the means of healing. But finally, persuaded by his servants, he humbled himself and pursued change God's way.

Isn't it interesting that Elisha told him to dip in the water *seven* times! Naaman had to persist in following God's plan even if it didn't seem to be working on the first dip and the second and the third. . . . His biggest need was not to be cured from leprosy but to be delivered from his desire to live life his own way. And thus God did not change just his skin, curing him from leprosy; God also changed his heart. Notice Naaman's response after his healing: "He returned to the man of God, he and all his company, and he came and stood before him. And he said, 'Behold, I know that there is no God in all the earth but in Israel'" (2 Kings 5:15).

Like Naaman, we often come to God with an agenda of our own choosing. We think we know best what changes should occur in our lives and how those changes should be brought about. We believe that the blessings of life will be ours if we can just control the circumstances and people in our lives. The tragedy of this is that the only time we bring God into the picture is when we ask him to help us to make life work according to our own way.

The world around us continually tempts us to think that somehow we have the ability within ourselves to make life work. God mercifully, however, often gives us more than we can handle on our own, to unravel our self-confidence when we have been used to leaning on our *own understanding* (see Prov. 3:5). He has made us dependent by design and must humble us, as he did Naaman. There can be no biblical change without it.

The Commands We Won't Obey Expose Our Self-Centeredness

Another method of teaching humility appears in the account of Israel's prophet Jonah. Second Kings 14:25 tells us that Jonah had announced to

King Jeroboam II that God was going to allow Israel to regain the territory they had lost to their enemies. Jonah enjoyed his popularity as a prophet who delivered the good news of God's deliverance. God knew the stubbornness of Jonah's heart, however, and set out to expose it. Perhaps a conversation like the following went on between Jonah and God.

"Jonah, I see you enjoy delivering messages of redemption to people."

"Oh yes, Lord! You know how much I love to tell people about your great deliverance on their behalf. That last assignment was a sheer delight. I love being your messenger!"

"Good, Jonah, because I have a special message of redemption I want you to deliver to the Ninevites. I want to offer them salvation."

"Salvation . . . to the Ninevites? But they're awful people! They really deserve your judgment, God. Don't you know how brutal they are? When they bring their captives home from battle, they dismember them and pile their body parts outside their city gates just to show everybody 'Ninevites rule!' and 'Nobody messes with a Ninevite!' What if they do the same thing to me? Besides, if I become an ambassador of good will to them, what will my fellow Israelites say? They'll think I've betrayed them! I can't do this, God. This is asking too much!"

"I have spoken, Jonah. Your next assignment is in Nineveh."

Although this dialogue is fictitious, it captures the dynamics of Jonah's situation. God is commanding the prophet to demonstrate love for him by obeying him. God is also commanding the prophet to demonstrate love for his neighbor by doing what his neighbor needs most. Jonah refuses, exposing his rebel heart. Rather than face his assignment and face his rebel heart, Jonah runs.

Nineveh is due east of Israel. Jonah gets on a ship headed for Tarshish, which is due west of Israel, on the coast of Spain—the country farthest west in the known world. For all Jonah knows, the world dropped off on the other side of Tarshish.

Of course, it isn't long before God sends a great wind and shakes up his boat. The mariners finally throw him overboard. God sends a great fish with a sticker on its side that reads, "Have You Hugged a Ninevite Today?" Jonah is not into hugging Ninevites. He wants them damned; he does not want them delivered. After three days and nights in the fish's belly, Jonah surrenders. He tells God he'll go to Nineveh, and the fish spits him up on the shore.

Jonah makes the five-hundred-mile journey from Israel to Nineveh and delivers God's message. To his chagrin, the people repent—from the king down to the most humble beggar. Jonah is outraged! God has extended mercy to this city of barbarians who had terrorized the nations around them with their brutality.

Jonah throws a pity party for himself under a makeshift shelter, perhaps to wait out the forty days God had given the city to repent. God mercifully provides a large plant whose speedy growth entertains the moping prophet and whose shade shields him from the hot Assyrian sun. In one day, however, God sends a worm to cause the plant to wither, then increases the heat until Jonah is about to faint from exposure. Jonah fusses at God for destroying plants. He vents his anger at God and justifies his angry response to everything that is happening. Then God deftly drives home his point that Jonah is more concerned about plants than he is about people and thus exposes the self-righteous pride of the prophet's heart.

Sometimes people ask whether Jonah ever got right with God. I believe Jonah himself wrote this account of his rebellion against God. If that is true, the fact that God used him to write an inspired book and the fact that Jonah was willing to reveal to the world his personal struggle with God are perhaps enough testimony to conclude that he did, indeed, finally humble himself. God often gives us commands that our rebel hearts refuse to obey. We insist on going our own way. God has made us dependent by design and must humble us, as he did Jonah. There can be no biblical change without it.

The Outcomes We Can't Control Expose Our Sinfulness

King David was shocked when he learned that his adultery with his neighbor's wife, Bathsheba, had resulted in her pregnancy (see 2 Sam. 11–12). Her husband had been out of town for months on state business, so it would be obvious the baby was not his. David hadn't counted on this kind of exposure. Everyone thought he was so godly—after all, he had written so many psalms used in the worship of Israel's God. Now everyone would know the wickedness of his secret life. He had to do something! He murdered Bathsheba's husband and waited. But God was determined to expose David. When he did, David was humbled. Sin is pretty heady stuff. We can start thinking that we are invincible, that we can control the outcome of our actions, that we can get away with evil.

God still exposes sin today. Take Jess and Emma, for example. They had grown up together. Even though their parents attended different churches, they saw much of each other since they were neighbors and attended the same Christian high school. When Jess's parents allowed her to have a car her senior year, the friends started driving to school together. Soon the girls became increasingly independent in troubling ways. Their "free spirits" manifested themselves in cheating at school and eventually in shoplifting from stores in town.

That summer after graduation, Emma's family took an early vacation in June to their church's family camp. Emma went reluctantly, consoling herself that she might meet some new boys there. But by Tuesday evening, something happened that neither Emma nor Jess had counted on: Emma came under deep conviction for her rebellion and asked to talk with one of the counselors after the evening service. By Wednesday morning, she had repented of her sin to God, had told her parents everything, and was trying to work out how she would tell Jess. Much of her restitution for cheating and stealing that had to be handled when she got home involved Jess as well; Jess had to be brought into the picture.

To say that Jess was upset was an understatement. She was humiliated and outraged. They had always been careful so that they would never be caught. She refused to go with Emma to talk with the principal about the cheating, and she refused to go with Emma to the stores where they had shoplifted to make restitution. She quit going to church and never talked to Emma again.

Both girls faced an outcome they hadn't counted on. Emma never once thought that God would be able to bring her to her knees with conviction. But her sinfulness was exposed to her own conscience at family camp, and she was humbled. Jess had not anticipated anything like this either. She had not counted on God's reaching the heart of her friend. She was exposed just as much as Emma but refused to repent. God has made us dependent by design and must humble us, as he did Emma and King David. There can be no biblical change without it.

The God We Can't Comprehend Exposes Our Finiteness

A certain man was the envy of every rancher in his part of Kansas. His cattle stock was some of the finest in the country, and his crops never failed to bring in bumper yields. Though a man of means, he never thought of himself as superior or asserted himself as such to his neighbors. In fact, because of his godliness, it was not unusual for him to spend an entire evening with a fellow rancher who needed personal advice about his family or who needed direction about a ranching decision.

Then things changed!

In one evening, a group of professional rustlers stole his entire herd. As if that weren't enough, the same electrical storm spawned a tornado that hit his oldest son's house, killing all the rancher's children, who had gathered there for a birthday celebration. The rancher and his wife had been delayed coming to the party, or they would have been killed too.

The account you just read is fictional but is based on the real-life experience of Job. He too was known for his wisdom and wealth. He too lost all at once everything he had, including his health. Yet he initially responded with unshakable faith in God, saying, "Naked I came from my mother's womb, and naked shall I return. The Lord gave, and the Lord has taken away; blessed be the name of the Lord" (Job 1:21).

By Job 3:11, Job began to question why he had been born, and eventually he demanded an explanation (see Job 23:1–17). He longed for an audience with God to plead his case and to discover why he was enduring such misery.

When enduring great pain, we, like Job, can begin to feel justified in complaining against God and demanding an explanation. We feel certain that God is wrong in allowing particular troubles to come our way. No attribute of God is more emphasized in Scripture than his loving care for his people. Yet no quality of God is doubted more than his love when we are under the burden of a difficult trial. We even begin to feel that if we were running things, we would not let people suffer like this.

Job was not being tried because of his sin, as his friends supposed. His spiritual integrity was being tested by Satan, who had argued that Job served God for personal gain. But when God answered Job, he did not explain the battle going on between him and Satan. Rather, in Job 38–41, he revealed the awesome power of the Almighty. God was very strong in his reply to Job. In essence, he said to Job, "Job, you need to get back in your place. If you think you're so smart and know better how to run this world, let's see how you do on a little quiz about how my world is governed. Where were you when I laid the foundations of the earth? Tell me—if you have so much understanding—have you ever walked on the bottom of the ocean and explored its depths? Have you ever made the sun rise in the morning? Do you know where I keep the treasuries of the ice and snow? Do you know how the stork brings forth her young in the right season?"

For four chapters God questioned Job about the universe around him, periodically asking him how he was doing on the quiz. When presented with the awesome power and wisdom of God in the creation around him, Job took the only action an honest person could do—he humbled himself. Job respectfully replied,

> I know that you can do all things,
> and that no purpose of yours can be thwarted.
> "Who is this that hides counsel without knowledge?"
> Therefore I have uttered what I did not understand,
> things too wonderful for me, which I did not know. (42:2–3)

> I had heard of you by the hearing of the ear,
> but now my eye sees you;
> therefore I despise myself,
> and repent in dust and ashes. (vv. 5–6)

Job was faced not just with circumstances he couldn't understand but with a God he could not comprehend. God exposed Job's finiteness. As a creature, he could never understand the Almighty. In view of the awesome power and wisdom of his God, however, he could—and must—trust him. No other response was worthy of God. The Almighty had made no mistake and deserved no rebuke. The creature could not make demands of the Creator without revealing his arrogance. God has made us dependent by design, and Job learned that the only proper response during the puzzling times of life was humility. There can be no biblical change without it.

What Is Your Next Step?

Is God dealing with your life in one—or more—of these ways? Is he working to expose your lack of humility in the way you handle life? The first step back to God is to repent for going your own way. Note Isaiah's words when he addressed God's people.

> Seek the LORD while he may be found;
> call upon him while he is near;
> let the wicked forsake his way,
> and the unrighteous man his thoughts;
> let him return to the LORD, that he may have compassion on him,
> and to our God, for he will abundantly pardon. (Isa. 55:6–7)

These people once followed God's ways. Then they abandoned him, and God is pleading with them to return. They once knew his fellowship but became wicked and unrighteous by pursuing their own ways and following their own thoughts.

What about you? Do you need to "return" to the Lord? Biblical change starts with "put[ting] off [the ways of] the old self with its practices" (Col. 3:9). The first step toward "putting off" is to repent for "putting on" something God forbids—the garment of self-rule and self-sufficiency instead of the clothing of humility (see 1 Peter 5:5). In light of the patient "mercies of God" toward you, is it not time for you to surrender yourself as a "living sacrifice" (Rom. 12:1)? In the same verse, Paul says it is "your rational service"—it is the least you can do.

As we have seen, this kind of humility—taking our proper place before God—is the hallmark of the dependent creature. It's been said, "There is a God in heaven, and you are not him." Repenting of our self-rule, putting God in his proper place in our heart, and getting in line under his sovereignty are all aspects of the beginning of biblical change and the chief requirements for usefulness to God. Remember the following principle: *Our potential for serving God lies not in our ability, nor in our opportunity, but in our humility before God. God is not impressed with our abilities; they came from him.* He is not impressed with our opportunities; they are gifts from him as well. He is impressed only with our humility; it testifies of our sense of dependency on him.

Take Time to Reflect

1. What application does the parable about the bike have for your dependence on God?
2. Having read this chapter, how would you define humility?
3. Do you have any areas of your life that you are asking God to change? Like Naaman, do you think God ought to be handling a

situation in a different way from how he apparently is? Is he asking you to humble yourself in some way, and are you insisting that change come about some other way? If so, describe what is happening.

4. Jonah apparently felt he was doing pretty well as God's official prophet in Israel—until God exposed his self-centeredness by giving Jonah a command he refused to obey. Is God perhaps doing the same for you at this time? Are there any "Ninevites" in your life—people who are hard to love—whom God is commanding you to love? Are there ministries in your church that you are avoiding because they would involve working with certain children, teens, or adults who are hard to love? Write down examples you can think of and how they are challenging to you.

A Word to Disciple Makers

Don't Be Sidetracked

A HELPFUL QUESTION to ask people you are trying to help is "What is going on between you and God?" If they look very puzzled at your question, ask them to tell you about their closest friends. What do they do together? How long have they known each other? What interests do they share? What are their friends' likes and dislikes? Have they ever been at odds with their friends? If so, what caused the rift? How did they get it resolved? Why do they like spending time with their friends? These kinds of questions show them that they know how to maintain and evaluate relationships with other people. They can evaluate their relationship with God as well.

When holding teens or adults accountable for their spiritual growth, don't be sidetracked by statements such as "I'm really different now; I have done a lot of growing up in the past few months. I realized after all the things that happened to me that I can't be so stubborn." Statements like this do reflect self-evaluation and perhaps the choice to behave less self-destructively. Remember, however, unless people have reconciled with their Creator, they are still at war with God.

Those who decide to change their behavior without changing their fundamental orientation to God may experience a better life in many ways—they may not hurt as many people, they may have more friends, they may be more productive and responsible—but they still are not reconciled to God, and a humbling is probably just around the corner. When it comes, they may be greatly disillusioned and conclude that they have tried doing right but that it "doesn't work" either.

Be sure to differentiate between "adjustments" that people have made to avoid further trouble and the humility of a heart repentance that acknowledges, "I have sinned against God. I need to get in my place and go God's way from here on out."

5

MORTIFYING YOUR FLESH

If you live according to the flesh you will die, but if by the Spirit you put to death [mortify] the deeds of the body, you will live. (Rom. 8:13)

My father, my two brothers, and I were all avid motorcyclists as I was growing up. We rebuilt, tuned, and customized our own bikes. My brother Denny maintained his interest in motorcycles and even became a world-class motorcycle designer and restorer. I could not begin to count the number of bikes that "lived" in our garage through my growing-up years. Although the combined miles we traveled are high, I was the only one to have a serious accident.

On the day of my accident, I was cruising along at a modest speed on a country two-lane highway near our home. A South Dakota tornado had devastated the area. My passenger, Randy, and I were looking over the damage. Distracted by a demolished farm implement dealership on the left side of the road, I did not notice the pickup that had stopped in my lane just yards ahead of me. I noticed him just a split second before I slammed into his tailgate at thirty miles per hour.

I woke up a few minutes later with a badly mangled bike, multiple fractures to my right wrist, and damage to my neck. I had flipped over into the pickup bed and landed on the back of my head. Had I not been wearing a helmet—a requirement of Dad's—I would have been dead. Randy, of course, followed me into the pickup bed and landed on top of me. He walked away without a scratch.

Mortifying a Motorcycle

Had I seen the pickup a few seconds earlier, I probably could have avoided the accident. Stopping a motorcycle involves combining three actions in various ways, depending on the circumstances:

1. Let up on the throttle to cut down on the amount of fuel to the engine.
2. Apply the brakes to reduce forward motion.
3. Disengage the clutch to prohibit the engine's power from driving the rear wheel.

Had I had enough time to initiate these actions, I would have *killed* the force of the engine that was propelling me to destruction. I would have been able to halt all forward motion and come to a resting stop a few feet behind the pickup. The engine would have still been idling, but its ability to ruin me would have been *killed*. If I were using Elizabethan terms, like those we find in the King James Version of the Bible, I could say that I had "mortified my motorcycle" or, more specifically, "mortified my motorcycle's forward motion."

Mortification of the Flesh

Today we use the word *mortify* only to indicate a strong measure of embarrassment. We might say, "When Joe told that story about me, I was mortified. I could have died!" The apostle Paul uses the word translated "put to death" or "mortify," however, to indicate a process of deadening the power of the flesh. Literally, he means that we are to drain the life out of the flesh through the Holy Spirit's assistance. Notice how Paul uses this word *in the following passages*:

> If you live according to the flesh you will die, but if by the Spirit you put to death ["mortify," KJV] the deeds of the body, you will live. (Rom. 8:13)

> If then you have been raised with Christ, seek the things that are above, where Christ is, seated at the right hand of God. Set your minds on things that are above, not on things that are on earth. For you have died, and your life is hidden with Christ in God. When Christ who is your life appears, then you also will appear with him in glory.
>
> Put to death [mortify] therefore what is earthly in you: sexual immorality, impurity, passion, evil desire, and covetousness, which is idolatry. (Col. 3:1–5)

A derivative of the word *mortify* is also used in Hebrews 11:12 when it speaks of the physical impossibility of Abraham's fathering a son at the age of one hundred. The writer of Hebrews comments that Abraham's body was "as good as dead"—it was mortified. It was weakened to the extent that it had no more power. Its potency was killed by age. That is the flavor of this word *mortify*.

We need to look more closely at the word *flesh* as well. The word *flesh* refers to the indwelling sin principle that remains in believers after they are saved, although its absolute power over them is broken—as we shall see later in this chapter. In Romans 8:13, Paul seems to equate *flesh* with "deeds of the body," implying that *flesh* could mean both the *source* of evil (indwelling sin) and the *manifestation* of evil (deeds of the body).

Perhaps his meaning is much the same as ours might be if we saw one of our children about to strike a sibling. We might say to our spouse, who is standing near the children, "Honey, stop Johnny!" Do we mean for our spouse to stop the boy or stop his actions? We mean both, because they are inextricably linked in practice.

It is in this broader, practical sense that I use the word *flesh* in this book. I believe that is the way Paul uses it in his epistles. When we mortify the "deeds of the body"—kill their action by dealing with the indwelling sin that motivates them—we have mortified the flesh or killed its influence, not its existence, on us at that moment.

Mortify is not the only biblical term that shows the proper response to the flesh. There are several parallel designations for indwelling sin and several parallel terms that describe various aspects of the biblical response to it. Take a moment to look them over.

1. The *flesh*—and its resulting deeds—must be *mortified* (see Rom. 8:13; Col. 3:5).
2. *Self* and its "ungodliness and worldly passions" must be *denied* (Titus 2:12; see also Luke 9:23).
3. The deeds of the *old self* must be *put off* (see Eph. 4:22; Col. 3:9).
4. The indwelling *sin nature* must *not* be *served* (see Rom. 6:6, 12–13, 16–19).

The title of this chapter could have come from any of the above statements and meant the same. Instead of "Mortifying Your Flesh," the title could have been "Denying Self," "Putting Off the Deeds of the Old Self," or "Refusing to Serve Sin." The question before us is "How do we mortify the flesh?" If we answer that question, we really address all the statements above. Thankfully, God has given us much help in this matter. The most detailed instruction on this issue is given to us in Romans 6, so it is to that chapter we will turn next.

Before we actually discuss the chapter's details, however, I would encourage you to do two things.

First, after you finish this section, stop reading this book, pick up your Bible, and read the entire chapter of Romans 6. Notice especially the summary of the chapter in verse 22.

Second, take some time to identify the battles you are facing right now. Perhaps write them down. It is important for you to have specific struggles of the flesh in mind when you go through this chapter. Note especially those battles that seem persistent or deeply entrenched. As David did, ask God to search you to see if there is any "grievous way" in you (Ps. 139:24). Or if you are discipling someone else, you may want to keep his or her besetting sins in mind as you study this chapter so that you will know how it applies to those struggles. The list could include sins such as worry, deception, lack of endurance, destructive bodily habits, anger, a critical spirit, discontent, profanity and other sins of the tongue, bitterness, laziness, rebellion to authorities in your life, greed and materialism, gambling, or immoral sexual behavior or fantasies. Of course, the list of possibilities is almost endless. The main point to keep in mind is that none of these sinful attitudes and activities is outside the scope of what is being addressed in Romans 6, no matter how strong their pull or how long-standing their practice.

With that in mind, read Romans 6, make your list, and then continue with the rest of this chapter.

1. We Have to *Know* Some Things

To stop my motorcycle, I need to know some things. Knowing how to apply the brakes is helpful, but braking is only a part of the stopping process. There are other facts I need to know—such as how to disengage the engine using the clutch and how to cut the fuel to the engine to slow it down. I would be in big trouble if I didn't know these things or if I didn't apply them.

Romans 6 deals with an important doctrine—or teaching—of the Christian walk. Bible teachers have called this doctrine by various names, the most common being *our union with Christ, our identification with Christ,* or *our co-crucifixion and co-resurrection with Christ.* Please understand that trying to resist the flesh without knowing and applying this basic doctrine is like trying to stop a speeding motorcycle by putting on the brakes while leaving the clutch engaged and the engine running full throttle. Many believers try to do just that. They try to resist the force of indwelling sin by sheer willpower and self-discipline.

Motorcycle brakes that are applied when the engine is still running eventually overheat and give out. The power of the engine must be disconnected from the wheel assembly. Its connection must be broken so that it no longer influences the motorcycle's forward motion to destruction.[1] In a similar fashion, Christ has made a way for us to break the pull of indwelling sin so that it does not have to affect the way we live.

Before our salvation, we had no choice but to obey the sinful pulls within. It was as if we were riding a motorcycle without a clutch. The engine was always running, and the wheels were always turning. There was no way to disconnect the engine. The back wheel was a slave to the engine. It had to turn when the engine turned. Romans 6:22 teaches us, however, that because of Christ's death and resurrection, we have been "set free from sin." We no longer *have* to obey its pull to go our own way.

How is that possible? Follow Paul's teaching here carefully because this is an especially important doctrine for breaking the power of sin in your life.

Paul says in Romans 6:3 that "all of us who have been baptized into Christ Jesus were baptized into his death." Baptism here is not referring to the church ordinance of water baptism. Rather, it is referring to what the Holy Spirit does for us at the moment of our salvation. The word *baptism* means to "place into" or "immerse." Paul says here that we are immersed or included in all the activities of Christ's death, burial, and resurrection. The actual details of how that takes place will be a mystery until we reach heaven. The implications now for us as believers, however, are staggering. We are recipients of every benefit of his death,

1. This illustration has its limitations, as do all illustrations. Technically, you can slow a motorcycle down faster by leaving it in gear while cutting the throttle. Other discrepancies abound if you take this illustration too far.

burial, and resurrection. He considers it as having happened to us—and wants us to consider it the same way.

This means that when Christ died, *we* died. When he was buried, *we* were buried. When he rose from the dead, *we* were raised to "walk in newness of life" (v. 4). Paul continues, "We know [remember, Paul wants us to know something] that our old self was crucified with him in order that the body of sin might be brought to nothing [its absolute power killed], so that we would no longer be enslaved to sin" (v. 6).

Before our identification with Christ in this way, we, in these earthly bodies, were *required* to serve the flesh. If our sinful bent was better served by lusting, we lusted. If it was better served by lying, we lied. We were truly the "slaves of sin" (v. 20). Paul tells us, however, that the control of that indwelling sin over us has been destroyed or nullified. Our flesh itself is not destroyed in our co-crucifixion with Christ, but just as a dead corpse is powerless to respond to anyone's will, so our flesh's absolute power over us has been broken, "for one who has died has been set free from sin" (v. 7).

During the first year of our marriage, I worked in a funeral home. I assisted the drivers as they picked up bodies from the morgue or from a nursing home and then helped later with the family visitation times. The loved ones of the deceased—most of whom were not believers—despaired because the deceased no longer responded to them. No matter how much they cried and grieved, the deceased would not speak to them, hold their hands, or try to comfort them in any way—they were dead! Their power to respond was destroyed.

This is the picture Paul wants us to have in Romans 6—dead people don't respond! We no longer have to respond to the pull of the flesh within; we now have a choice. We are free from sin's absolute rule—its dominion. We are now free to respond to the Holy Spirit who lives in us. We shall not only "live with him" (v. 8) in heaven later, but we can experience a "newness of life" now (v. 4).

To illustrate this further, let's say that you have been renting a home from a man named Mr. Brown. On the first of every month he comes to your door to collect the rent. Last month Mr. Brown sold the home to Mr. Smith. To your surprise, when the rent is due this month, Mr. Brown shows up at your door again to collect the rent. In months past you were required to pay Mr. Brown. You were under his power. When he sold the house, however, his power to collect the rent was broken. You can pay him if you want, but you don't have to. You are now required to pay the new landlord, Mr. Smith.

In the same way, we are no longer required to obey the flesh: "For [indwelling] sin will have no dominion [control] over you" (v. 14). The flesh's power to demand your obedience has been broken. You can obey it if you want to, but your life is under new management. You are no longer under the power of sin. A new landlord has taken over. A new set of requirements from a new Lord is in place—the law of God (see Rom. 7:25). You are a servant to a new Master.

Paul says, "This is something you need to know!" Resisting the indwelling power of sin starts here. As I mentioned earlier, you cannot stop a motorcycle by merely applying the brakes. Your brakes of self-discipline will give out. The strain will be too much, and you will crash anyway. The power of the engine must be broken. It must be disengaged from the rear wheel. You have to know this if you are going to "mortify your motorcycle"—kill its forward motion toward destruction.

2. We Have to *Consider* Some Things

Paul finishes telling us the facts we need to know about our union with Christ and begins explaining to us the implications of those facts in Romans 6:11. He says, "So you also must consider ["reckon," KJV] yourselves dead to sin and alive to God in Christ Jesus." Paul is saying, "God knows you have been freed from the requirements to obey indwelling sin. Now *you* need to take it personally and quit living as if you *had* to obey it; start living to God."

We need to understand that if we pay Mr. Brown, we choose to do so. We may have grown used to him and his ways. We may have felt that the rent was too much at times and that his demands were unpleasant, but we were bound by law to pay him. The fact, however, is that our house is under new management. We must now consider that to be true.

We consider things every day. When we drive along the highway, we see a sign that says "Speed Limit 55." We are expected to consider that sign to be binding for us. We are to believe that it is an accurate statement of the government's expectations on that highway and that it applies to us. We are then to apply it to our lives. That is an act of faith.

If we don't believe that the law exists and we are accountable to it, we will be duly reminded of both with a speeding ticket. We will be held accountable. Paul says, "God considers it to be true, and you *likewise* need to consider yourself to be dead indeed to sin." You do not have to obey its urges and pulls.

You may protest, however, "I don't feel free. When sinful impulses arise in my heart, I feel as though I have to obey." You are going to have to take it by faith that these facts are true no matter how you feel. It may feel as though you have to give in, but you need to know better because God said otherwise to "consider [yourself] dead to sin" (v. 11).

Many people fail right here. They make decisions about what they will or will not do based on how they feel at the moment—not by the facts God has given us. They don't consider things to be true because God has said they are true. They consider a thing to be true only if it feels to them as though it might be true. The result of this kind of living is instability. Such people are up and down, moody, and unpredictable.

They are the kind of person James describes as "double-minded" (James 1:8). Such a person is "minding" the flesh and his feelings one moment and "minding" God and his truth the next. James says this person is "like a wave of the sea that is driven and tossed by the wind" (v. 6) and warns him not to expect "anything from the Lord; he is a double-minded man, unstable in all his ways" (vv. 7–8).

You cannot afford to let your ways be determined by the skewed view of reality that your flesh and its feelings give you. Paul said that before any of us were saved we "all once lived in the passions of our flesh, carrying out the desires of the body and the mind" (Eph. 2:3). That was the only way we could live. We no longer have to fulfill those desires—those feelings of our flesh and minds. Don't give in to feelings that are generated by fleshly, selfish thinking. They will not give you an accurate picture of reality. They will keep you trapped in a fantasy world. You must "consider [yourself] dead to sin" (Rom. 6:11).

Not only must we know some facts about our identification with Christ in his death, burial, and resurrection and consider those things to be true for us, but, as Paul tells us, we must also yield to the right Master as a result of what we know and consider. Let's look at what it means to "present," or *yield*, ourselves to God (v. 13).

3. We Have to *Yield* Some Things

You may again find yourself at this point protesting and saying, "I'm just not good at yielding. That comes hard for me. I'm not sure I know how to yield." Paul reminds us, however, that we are all experts at yielding. We have done it for years—only, to the wrong master. We are skilled at yielding our bodily "members to sin as instruments [weapons] for unrighteousness" (Rom. 6:13). We therefore know what it is like to be "slaves of sin" (v. 17). The result of presenting ourselves to sin is the "fruit . . . of which [we] are now ashamed" and whose "end . . . is death" (v. 21).

After Paul reminds us that we have had much practice yielding to a master, he says, "For just as you once presented [yielded] your members as slaves to impurity and to lawlessness leading to more lawlessness, so now present [yield] your members as slaves to righteousness leading to sanctification" (v. 19). The "fruit you get" as a result "leads to sanctification and its end, eternal life" (v. 22).

So we are now at a point of decision about how we will respond to whatever pull the flesh has on us at the moment. Are we going to deny God—say no to him—or deny self? Are we going to mortify the flesh or indulge the flesh? Are we going to walk after the flesh or walk after the Spirit? Are we going to obey God or obey indwelling sin? The choice to obey God (yielding) is a twofold responsibility to resist obeying the flesh and to stop feeding it. Let's look at these two responses.

Don't Obey the Flesh

We would like to think that in this or that sin, we have been defeated. The humbling reality is that we have been disobedient.

The Christian life is not an easy life to live because of the sinfulness that wars within us. Though it isn't easy, it isn't complicated. Complications are usually the natural consequences of our going our own way. But even at that, the way out of those complications is always a series of simple choices: "In this thing or that thing before me, am I going to please God or please myself?"[2]

Paul defined the Christian life as one of obedience. He says,

2. See the chart "God's Love versus Self-Love" on pages 281–83 for examples of both fleshly self-serving living and godly self-denying living.

> Do you not know that if you present [yield] yourselves to anyone as obedient slaves, you are slaves of the one whom you obey, either of sin, which leads to death, or of obedience, which leads to righteousness? But thanks be to God, that you who *were* once slaves of sin *have become obedient* from the heart to the standard of teaching to which you were committed. (Rom. 6:16–17)

Don't miss the point here. Paul does not prescribe some long, convoluted series of therapy steps. He says, "You got yourself into this mess by obeying your flesh and denying God, and the only way out is to start denying the flesh and obeying God." Paul is clear—the flesh *can* be denied, and it *must* be denied!

Kirk was a twenty-five-year-old shipping clerk for a local truck line. He came to me for help about his continual tardiness to work in the mornings. He was consistently thirty minutes late. His boss appreciated Kirk's high level of competence and commitment on the job but was growing increasingly frustrated by his late arrivals. Kirk had been given a verbal warning and knew he must take action about his habitual failure in this area.

Kirk told me that his alarm was set each morning for half past six, that he activated the alarm every night, and that it wakened him every morning. He said that he had even placed the alarm on the dresser across the room so that he would have to get out of bed and walk across the room to turn it off.

Kirk revealed with great embarrassment, however, that once he had turned off the alarm, he went back to bed. He would sleep until about half past seven and then make a frantic attempt to arrive at work by eight o'clock. Of course, he never made it on time. I asked him, "Kirk, on the way from the alarm clock back to your bed, do you ever get under conviction from God about staying up instead of going back to bed?"

Kirk replied, "Oh yes! Every day while I shuffle back to the bed, I am convicted about it. God reminds me that I should not go back to bed."

I asked him very pointedly, "Kirk, if I come to your apartment for the next couple of weeks, awaken you at half past six and tell you to stay up, will you stay up?" Kirk's face became very serious as he assured me that if I were to awaken him and tell him to stay up, he would do it. He would not let me down if I tried to help him that way. I then pointed out to Kirk the real issue. He had just revealed that if I spoke to him, he would stay up, but if God spoke to him, he would go back to bed.

The important issue to see here is that what we often call a lack of self-discipline is actually a lack of obedience to God. His Spirit is at work convicting and leading, but we often aren't obeying. I told Kirk that if he wanted to become disciplined in this area, he needed to let the Holy Spirit disciple him. If he would obey God's Spirit, he would end up being a disciplined person. This is what Paul meant when he spoke about yielding or presenting ourselves to God. Instead of obeying the flesh's cry to postpone responsibility, Kirk needed to obey the Holy Spirit's conviction to resist the flesh.

Don't Feed the Flesh

Although the flesh must be restrained instead of indulged at the point of temptation, further probing into Kirk's lifestyle revealed other, more grievous matters. When I asked Kirk about his evening schedule, he told me that in addition to his eight-hour day job, he also worked an evening part-time job until half past nine. After work he would go out for coffee with a couple of his coworkers and arrive home about eleven o'clock. Since he felt he owed himself a little pleasure to make up for the day's rat race, he would usually watch a movie for another couple of hours. He often fell asleep on the couch and dragged himself to bed when the movie was over at about one o'clock.

You can now understand why getting up at half past six was hard for Kirk. A major component in his early morning struggle to get out of bed was obviously the fatigued state of his body, but the effect of his lifestyle on his soul was even more destructive. Kirk was feeding his flesh in several ways throughout his daily routine and then was discouraged because he could not overcome his flesh in the morning.

To begin with, his soul was worn down daily by the wickedness of the people around him at work. He was daily exposed to ungodly attitudes, conversations, values, and temptations. Like Lot, "day after day," Kirk was "tormenting his righteous soul" over the "lawless deeds that he saw and heard" (2 Peter 2:7–8). God is clear in this passage that believers who are exposed to the "sensual conduct of the wicked" (v. 7) will be worn down as they see and hear their "lawless deeds." If believers are exercising their will against these influences, they will not be nearly as affected by them. If, however, they are at all passive to these influences, the result is clear—they will be worn down. Kirk never witnessed to his lost coworkers and never challenged their shameless, sensual talk. He never resisted the evil around him.

Since Kirk was in a weakened spiritual condition, he was not enjoying fellowship with God and constantly felt guilty about his walk with the Lord. Consequently, his work was not a source of joy to him. Rather than punching out at the end of the shift satisfied that he had done his best for Christ that day and grateful for the opportunities for spiritual witness, he was constantly reminded of his disobedience to promptly testify to Christ. The conversations at the coffee shop with his coworkers after work would always drag him further down. He would return home feeling guilty for his participation in their filthy talk.

Not wanting to go to bed feeling so down, he would watch a movie. Usually the movie was laced with profanity, adult themes, or violence. Often its content was gratuitously violent or filled with raw nudity and sex. Of course, feeding his flesh in this way sabotaged any hope of resisting its pull in such a small matter as getting out of bed in the morning.

I think the picture here is clear for us. If you wish to restrain the flesh as God commands, you would be foolish to feed it. Peter warned earlier, "Abstain from the passions of the flesh, which wage war against your soul" (1 Peter 2:11). Paul said,

> Do not be deceived [in other words, "Don't kid yourself!"]: God is not mocked, for whatever one sows, that will he also reap. For the one who sows to his own flesh will from the flesh reap corruption, but the one who sows to the Spirit will from the Spirit reap eternal life. (Gal. 6:7–8)

We will discuss in part 2 of this book how to "sow to the Spirit." In this part, however, we are discussing how to stop sowing to the flesh. Paul says, "Stop being deceived! This will be your ruin."

We have to exercise self-denial by saying no to the promptings of the flesh, but we also have to say no to any pull to feed the flesh and make it stronger. Every time we feed it in one area of life, we make it harder to say no to it in any area. Its pull and control are stronger. As with the motorcycle we are trying to mortify, it is no use for us to merely put on the brakes; we must cut the fuel to the engine. Most believers forget they have a clutch—they don't have to obey the flesh—and try to stop the bike with the brakes while feeding more fuel to the engine. Cut the fuel! Even then, since the flesh is always with us this side of heaven, the engine never stops. At best, it is idling; at worst, it is racing.

I have noticed a puzzling phenomenon in Christian circles. As culture declines and social values change, many believers adopt the world's idea that restraint, self-denial, and discipline are passé. In the name of Christian liberty, they indulge in all sorts of flesh-feeding activities, scoffing at the idea that any behavior could be considered worldly, while at the same time claiming a new freedom in Christ. The final result is always tragic: destruction. God promised that it would be so in Galatians 6:7–8 above.

Whether or not the modern church is concerned about the effect of the world on believers, God is concerned. Carefully consider 1 John 2:15–17. Personal separation from the elements of believers' environments that feed their flesh is not optional; it is critical! The more corrupt our culture becomes, the greater our need for personal separation from the world. Personal separation from the world does not mean *isolating* ourselves from the world but rather *insulating* ourselves from its toxic, fleshly effect on our souls. Let me illustrate it this way.

Today we are more careful about protecting ourselves from viruses and other germs because our awareness of them has increased enormously due to the COVID pandemic. Signs remind us to wash our hands, hand sanitizer is ubiquitous in public places, and hospitals encourage visitors to wear face masks. We are not less careful because "we live in a modern age." We are more careful because we have been reminded that we live in an age where illnesses spread more rapidly than ever across the globe. In the same way, believers who are concerned about their spiritual health will be more careful in this increasingly corrupt culture. There are more dangers to their souls—not fewer. The pagan, sensual, materialistic environment around them is more contaminated with ungodliness. The need for circumspect living is greater today—not less.

When you seem to be susceptible to every fleshly "bug" in the atmosphere, it is probably because your spiritual immune system isn't functioning. You have been quenching the Spirit by indulging in the flesh. You can never get well until you stop your contact with contaminating elements around you. That may mean your entertainment habits, online scrolling, or personal friendships must change. Whatever is dragging you down must be put off. In addition, your immune system must be built up. Our Lord is serious about our avoidance of fleshly indulgence.

Many in our society who are watching their weight try to eat low-fat foods. They can even become rather obsessed with counting how many grams of fat they intake and how many calories they burn in exercise. To paraphrase a Scripture text, their life verse could be, "Make no provision for fattening foods lest you put on the weight thereof."

Oh, that there would be even a fraction of that kind of concern in believers to be living "flesh-free" as much as is possible in this world. We are told to "make no provision for the flesh, to gratify its desires" (Rom. 13:14). Yet Christians consume the world's entertainment and philosophies and embrace its goals and attitudes; consequently, Christians are powerless to make any impact on the world around them.

The Seat Belt of Self-Denial

When we don't obey the flesh and don't feed the flesh, the Bible calls our restraint *denying self*. Jesus said in Luke 9:23, "If anyone would come after me, let him deny himself and take up his cross daily and follow me." Like seat belts, the restraint of self-denial protects us from danger. Seat belts protect us from bodily injury if we are involved in an automobile accident. Self-denial protects us from the danger of giving in to the urges of the flesh. A seat belt, to be effective, must be worn anytime we are riding in an automobile. We are never too young or too old to wear a seat belt. A seat belt is always needed because the danger is always present.

In the same way, we are never too old to be practicing self-denial. Since the flesh is always with us, self-denial is always needed because the danger is always present. There is an unbiblical idea today that the more mature people become in age or in spiritual growth, the less they need to deny themselves. I have had unmarried teen couples tell me that the closer they get to the Lord, the more physically involved they can become with one another because they can handle the temptation better. Their thinking was that only weaker Christians need to establish personal dating standards. Others in the Christian world feel the same way about their music and entertainment standards. Supposedly, the more believers grow spiritually the more liberty they have to do what they want. They can expose themselves to more of the world's toxicity because they are more immune. The result is unbridled indulgence in the flesh in the name of Christian liberty.

In actuality, when believers are walking in the Spirit and the Spirit is bearing fruit in their lives, they will have *more* love, *more* joy, *more* peace, and *more* self-control—not less! As believers mature, they will have more freedom to do what they were intended to do—to fellowship with God unceasingly and to obey God willingly, unhindered by the flesh.

I hope you can see by now that you have to be alert to any manifestation of the flesh in your life. Be familiar with the catalog of the "works of the flesh" in Galatians 5:19–21. Colossians 3:5–9 and Ephesians 4:25–31 discuss many other ways the flesh manifests itself. Don't forget the reason for this abstinence from the flesh: "You are a chosen race, a royal priesthood, a holy nation, a people for his own possession, *that you may proclaim the excellencies of him who called you out of darkness into his marvelous light*" (1 Peter 2:9).

Back to Mortifying

How then do you weaken the flesh? How do you mortify it? Cut the fuel to the "engine" by not feeding the flesh. Disengage the clutch—the power of the engine doesn't have to drive the wheel. The power of indwelling sin has been overruled by Christ; consider it to be so for you. Lastly, put on the brakes. Deny self! Say no to the flesh.

Please understand, however, that all of this merely gets the motorcycle stopped; it doesn't make it useful in any way. It just keeps it from destroying you. There is much more to be learned than how to "put off [the deeds of] the old self" (Col. 3:9). We must next learn how to be "transformed" or changed into something useful by the "renewal of [our] mind" (Rom. 12:2) so that we can demonstrate Christlikeness by having "put on the [lifestyle of the] new self" (Col. 3:10). Such is the subject of our study in parts 2 and 3. Stay with me; we have much ground yet to cover.

Take Time to Reflect

How flesh-free is your lifestyle? Meditate on David's prayer for God's searchlight to expose corruption in his heart. Here is what David asked for in Psalm 139:23–24:

> Search me, O God, and know my heart!
> Try me and know my thoughts!
> And see if there be any grievous way in me,
> and lead me in the way everlasting!

Spend some time (I recommend a couple of hours) reviewing your schedule and lifestyle. Are there elements in any of the following areas that need to be put off because they are high in flesh content?

1. Is your entertainment flesh-free? Examine
   - the *content* of the movies and shows you watch
   - the *style* and *content* of the music you listen to
   - the *atmosphere* of your favorite places to spend leisure time
   - the *values* you absorb while watching or participating in your favorite sports or browsing social media
   - the amount of *time* you spend in these kinds of pursuits
2. Is your pursuit of possessions flesh-free? Examine
   - the appeal to your *pride* in being socially correct with the group you wish to impress
   - the *stumbling block* you are to others who are trying to impress you in the same way
   - the *sexual* appeal in the way you dress or present yourself
   - the *values* you absorb when studying the latest fashion, lifestyle, sports, and consumer trends to make sure you are current
3. Are your friendships flesh-free? Examine
   - the *content* of your conversation—sexual, crude, materialistic, or obsessive
   - the physical *contact* with others—arousing desires in them and in you that cannot righteously be gratified
   - the iron-sharpening-iron *influence* on each other for godliness (living as though God is all that matters) or for worldliness ("living as though this world—*our* world—is all that matters"[3])
   - the *attitudes* that are fostered by your friends—submission to authority versus rebellion, order versus chaos and disorder, or other attitudes that are not Christlike

3. Erwin W. Lutzer, *How in This World Can I Be Holy?* (Chicago: Moody Press, 1974), 26.

A Word to Disciple Makers

Doctors, Wear Your Gloves!

LASTING CHANGE IN those you disciple comes only when the flesh is being exposed and restrained. God is very clear about this matter. A quick review back through part 1 of this book will refresh your mind about the nature and extent of indwelling sin. Be sure, however, when discipling someone about the necessity for self-denial, that you do not leave the impression that spirituality is measured by what we don't do. If that were the case, the most godly people would be the ones already in the cemetery—they *don't* do anything! Restraining the flesh merely keeps the sin nature that is within us and the sinful world that is around us from corrupting us any further.

A doctor's surgical gloves serve only to keep her from contamination. Although they do not make her a skillful surgeon, they are necessary. What would you think of a surgeon who told you, "I won't wear surgical gloves. After all, I'm a surgeon because of my love for medicine, because of my medical training, and because of what I do in the operating room—not because I wear gloves. These rules about wearing gloves are just bureaucratic. Gloves are just for those who need something outward to show they are doctors. *Real* doctors don't wear gloves!"

A doctor with this attitude is showing either her arrogance—thinking herself invincible—or her ignorance about why she needs to wear gloves. She is so lost in her supposed love for medicine and being a *real* doctor that she is oblivious to the danger lurking around her in the form of viruses and other contaminants. She would destroy herself and unwittingly infect her patients—all while feeling confident that she is a good doctor. In the end, she would be only a transmitter of death, not a saver of life.

Restraining the flesh by imposing restrictions on ourselves or others doesn't make us holy, just like wearing gloves doesn't make someone a good doctor. But that doesn't mean restraining our flesh is useless. So don't forget your gloves, and teach your medical students to wear gloves! But also don't forget to drive home to them why they need to wear gloves. Gloves aren't the badge of some elite group. They are lifesavers for everyone in a life-threatening world.

Part Two

RENEWING YOUR MIND

Be renewed in the spirit of your minds. (Eph. 4:23)

6

GETTING IN TOUCH WITH REALITY

In him we live and move and have our being. (Acts 17:28)

IF, AS WE saw in part 1 of this book, the *own way* tendency of indwelling sin is our real problem, what then is the real solution? We ought to be convinced by now that the solution does not lie within us. We *are* the problem.

The world says, and sadly many Christians say, that biblical solutions will not work in the real world. The irony of their complaint is that the Bible *alone* gives the only true picture of the real world. Far from being unable to function in the real world, those who immerse themselves in Christian teaching are the few on the earth who *understand* the real world.

Reality—the truth—is that there is a God in heaven. Reality is that he made us and we are accountable to him. Reality is that this God has spoken and what he says matters—eternally. Reality is that without his salvation, we are doomed to eternal torment. Reality is that God's Son, Jesus Christ, has died for the sins of the world, that he has risen again, and that whoever believes on him is given eternal life.

This is the *real world,* and only believers who are walking in fellowship with their Creator and Redeemer can understand it. Everyone else in the world is experiencing a break with reality. Romans says that those who do not know God "by their unrighteousness suppress the truth" (1:18). They are not walking in truth—which is to say they are not living in reality. No wonder those who do not know Christ—as well as believers who are ignoring God's Word—live and act as if they have gone mad. The only world they *can* know doesn't make sense. The reality of life is that life isn't supposed to make sense or bring any lasting peace and satisfaction as long as we live without God.

An Amazonian in Times Square

Imagine an Amazonian tribe is discovered whose people have never seen an outsider and do not understand the language or the ways of the outside world. Suppose a researcher brings one of these nationals out of the heart of the Amazon and abandons him, untutored and unaccompanied, in Times Square in New York City. This poor Amazonian will have experiences that are entirely outside his frame of reference. As he tries to survive and find food and shelter, he will endure many unsettling events.

In his own country, this man may have enjoyed a measure of security, peace, and productivity, but Times Square presents him with a reality he does not understand and therefore cannot function in effectively. Nothing he attempts to do works as it did back in his homeland. He is not be able to communicate clearly or easily, and the behaviors of the people around him do not make sense to him. As a result, he experiences fear, anger, frustration, confusion, possibly depression. He may even become violent out of desperation.

In short, the Amazonian tribesman soon shows many of the emotional disorders we see in today's society. For although he is out of touch with his newfound reality, most of the rest of those in Times Square are just as out of touch with a much greater reality—God—and are experiencing the same emotional struggles and destructive behaviors but for a different reason.

For the tribesman to be at peace in his New York environment, he needs someone to coach him. The more he learns about his environment and brings himself into line with its nature, the freer he will be from the mental and emotional anguish he initially experienced. He cannot try to solve his New York problems his own way, because the Amazonian way will not work in New York. By the same token, humanity's own way will not work in God's world, and those—both believers and unbelievers—who attempt to live independently of the knowledge and ways of God are experiencing a break with reality.[1]

1. The illustration of the Amazonian is an expanded adaptation of a similar illustration in *Knowing God* by J. I. Packer (Downers Grove, IL: InterVarsity Press, 1973), 19.

How do we come in line with reality? Having a renewed mind—the theme of part 2—is not just memorizing a few Bible verses about a problem you are having, although that may be a start. It is not just becoming familiar with Christian principles and convictions about godly lifestyles. Having a renewed mind involves a relationship with your Creator that actually changes you because of your exposure to his deity.

More than Relief from Problems

The Christian life is first and foremost about God. Christianity is primarily a relationship with the Creator, not merely a means to escape from everlasting torment or get deliverance from life-dominating sins or unsettling emotions. Every trial that ever burdened a mortal man or woman, every temptation that ever stormed a human heart, and every blessing that ever delighted a needy soul have been skillfully designed by the Creator for one purpose: to draw us to himself. God created us to be most satisfied, most joyful, and most useful when we have an ongoing, dependent, obedient, life-giving personal relationship with our Creator.

In Luke 10:38–42, Jesus makes this point very strongly while visiting his friends Lazarus, Mary, and Martha. Martha feels that Mary should be more involved in getting the house and the meal ready for their guest. She even fusses at Jesus for engaging Mary in conversation that keeps her sister from helping with the chores. Jesus kindly rebukes Martha for her preoccupation with doing things for the guest when, like Mary, she should be preoccupied with the guest himself. Mary knows that her greatest need is to know God.

Most of us have experienced a lost connection between our telephone and that of a friend we were talking to. We redialed the number, and the connection was restored. Fellowship with God is blocked by our sin of going our own way in some aspect of life (see Isa. 59:1–2). The connection is restored when we repent. Once restored to fellowship with God, we have the opportunity to develop a dependent, personal relationship with God.

Unfortunately, once the connection is restored with God, many people do not know what to say to the person on the other end of the connection. They do not know how to *develop* their relationship with God. Let's explore the dynamics involved in any relationship to help us see what needs to happen between God and us.

More than Being on Speaking Terms

We were made to function well only when in fellowship with our Creator. Fellowship, in this context, means more than just confessing all known sin. Having "nothing between my soul and the Savior"[2] or "a clear conscience toward both God and man" is a crucial starting point (Acts 24:16). But there must also be *much going on* between my soul and the Savior. The apostle John instructs us to "abide in the vine" (John 15:4) and to "walk in the light" (1 John 1:7). Paul also describes our relationship as a "walk" (Eph. 4:1; 5:2, 8) and as being "filled with all the fullness of God" (Eph. 3:19).

A married couple may live in the same house, get along pretty well with each other, and even have great respect for each other. In this sense, they are friends who share mutual interests—buying a house, raising a family, getting ahead at work. But marriage the way God planned it includes so much more than mutual interests, goals, and respect. God intends for a couple to become "one flesh" (Eph. 5:31). He wants them to develop such a like-mindedness with each other that they enjoy each other's mutual devotion, admiration, and dependence. This kind of relationship is more than just accomplishing goals with each other's help. This kind of relationship is, first and foremost, about each other. Each finds his or her greatest joy to be the *joy of the other.*

Marriage was created by God to mirror the kind of relationship he wishes to have with us. Intimate fellowship with God, as we can see, is more than just being on speaking terms. The kind of relationship he has in mind for us means that both the Creator and the creature find their greatest joy in the joy of the other. As David wrote, "You make known to me the path of life; in your presence there is fullness of joy; at your right hand are pleasures forevermore" (Ps. 16:11).

Anyone who has read the Bible very much is aware that certain Bible characters stand above their peers in their relationship with God. For example, Abraham is called "a friend of God" (James 2:23). Moses spoke with God "face to face, as a man speaks to his friend" (Ex. 33:11). Genesis 5:24 tells us that "Enoch walked with God." God himself called David "a man after his own heart" (1 Sam. 13:14). Their relationships with God were not unique experiences that cannot be

2. Charles A. Tindley, "Nothing Between," 1905.

duplicated by anyone else. Such a relationship is available to all who believe.

Perhaps we can explain the kind of relationship these men had with God by examining what happens in a dating experience.

One of the blessings of working in a college environment is seeing God drawing couples together into a dating relationship and eventually into marriage. I often notice a couple sitting together in class but will not think anything about it until I see them consistently walking to and from the class together. They talk to each other in low tones, almost oblivious to the people around them. There is an obvious admiration for each other in their faces, and most of their conversation is about each other. They discover something else about the other person and then comment on and compliment what they see in that person. They explore each other's opinions, likes, dislikes, family backgrounds, interests, and knowledge about various topics. They seem never to have enough time to be with each other, and they plan times when they can see each other again. In addition, they show their affection by giving each other small gifts. Some of the gifts may have no meaning to onlookers but have great personal significance to both of them.

Relationships like this are characterized by continual personal interaction. At first, each may pursue the relationship because of the delight each one receives from the other. As godly love becomes central in the relationship, each will become increasingly motivated by how to be a delight to the other. If they truly delight in each other, they will not be able to keep their joy a secret. They will praise their friend to roommates, family, and anyone else who will listen. In fact, anyone who has much contact with either of them can see that there is something going on between them.

A relationship with God includes the same basic elements of learning *about* him (revelation), followed by much personal interaction *with* him. Knowing God in a personal way requires two initial elements.

1. Knowing God Requires That We Have a Desire for God

Our greatest need is for God, yet because of our sinful bent (which is still a part of us, even after salvation), we often resort to going our own way. That path leads us directly away from God. God reminds us that the "way that seems right to a man" leads to "death" (Prov. 14:12).

Fortunately, God places within those of us who are his children a desire for a relationship with him. This is not something we work up ourselves; it is the work of God. Philippians 2:13 says, "It is God who works in you, both to will and to work for his good pleasure." He is at work in every believer, creating a will and an ability to do what is "his good pleasure." In Jeremiah 31:3, God speaks of his initiative in drawing people to himself: "The Lord hath appeared of old unto me, saying, Yea, I have loved thee with an everlasting love: therefore with lovingkindness *have I drawn thee*" (KJV).

E. M. Bounds quotes David Brainerd, who testified of the desire God placed within him: "Of late God has been pleased to keep my soul hungry almost continually, so that I have been filled with a kind of pleasing pain. When I really enjoy God, I feel my desires of Him the more insatiable, and my thirstings after holiness more unquenchable."[3]

In Revelation 3:20, Christ is portrayed as standing outside the door of the believing church of Laodicea, knocking. It is clear that Christ, not the believers in the church, is taking the initiative for the relationship. Moses told the children of Israel that God was at work in their hearts to draw them to himself: "The LORD your God will circumcise your heart and the heart of your offspring, so that you will love the LORD your God with all your heart and with all your soul, that you may live" (Deut. 30:6). Just as God sought Adam and Eve in the garden of Eden in order to continue fellowship with them (see Gen. 3:8–9), so God continues to seek us in order that we can have a personal, dependent relationship with him.

In his account of the battle between his flesh and his spirit, Paul writes, "I have the desire to do what is right" (Rom. 7:18). This continual desire to do right is the work of the Spirit of God and an evidence of salvation. Paul states in the next chapter that "all who are led by the Spirit of God [away from the flesh] are sons of God" (8:14). In the next verse, he says that the Spirit of God creates in us the cry of adopted children for their new Father. In this way, Paul says, "The Spirit himself bears witness with our spirit that we are children of God" (v. 16).

3. E. M. Bounds, *The Weapon of Prayer* (repr., Radford, VA: Wilder Publications, 2008), 74.

God has created in us the desire for himself and has offered himself as the object of our desire. He is the only one sufficient to fill the God-shaped hole within our souls. Augustine wrote, "You made us for yourself, and our heart is restless, until it rests in you."[4]

Psalmists described God's work in their hearts in the following ways:

As a deer pants for flowing streams,
  so pants my soul for you, O God.
My soul thirsts for God,
  for the living God. (Ps. 42:1–2)

O God, you are my God; earnestly I seek you;
  my soul thirsts for you;
my flesh faints for you,
  as in a dry and weary land where there is no water. (Ps. 63:1)

Whom have I in heaven but you?
  And there is nothing on earth that I desire besides you.
My flesh and my heart may fail,
  but God is the strength of my heart and my portion forever. (Ps. 73:25–26)

My soul longs, yes, faints
  for the courts of the LORD;
my heart and flesh sing for joy
  to the living God. (Ps. 84:2)

God is glorified when we take our place of joyful, grateful dependence because then God is exalted as the only worthy, all-sufficient object of that dependence. David testifies of it this way: "The sorrows of those who run after another god shall multiply" (Ps. 16:4), but "I have set the LORD always before me; because he is at my right hand, I shall not be shaken" (v. 8).

Make no mistake about it. If you are God's child, he has placed within you a desire for himself. If your only desires in life are for yourself

4. John K. Ryan, trans., *The Confessions of Saint Augustine* (New York: Doubleday, 1960), 1.

and for relief from your problems, and you experience no desire whatsoever for a relationship with God, your first step needs to be a very careful examination of whether or not you even belong to him. Those who are truly members of his family experience a God-given desire for intimacy with their Father. If you are a true believer, along with your desire to have deliverance from whatever problems seem to plague your life, you will have a desire for a better relationship with God. In fact, you may experience a great deal of frustration that the kind of relationship with him that you desire seems so elusive. Unbelievers never experience that kind of frustration. They may know they do not have fellowship with God, but it does not bother them. They are content to seek their own solutions to their own problems—apart from God.

The desire for God is, first, an assurance that we are his children. It is, second, the sign that he is at work in our lives, since a desire for God cannot be generated by us on our own. It is also the indication that he is intending to do more in us for our good and for his ultimate glory. Jesus said in the Beatitudes, "Blessed are those who hunger and thirst for righteousness, *for they shall be satisfied*" (Matt. 5:6). When God takes the initiative to create in us a hunger and thirst for righteousness, he intends to satisfy those desires with himself. He promises we shall be filled.

Paul's chief prayer for the Ephesian church was that they would be "strengthened . . . in [their] inner being" (Eph. 3:16) as they allowed Christ to "dwell in [their] hearts through faith" (v. 17). The word *dwell* has the idea of permanence. It has the idea of becoming an intimate part of the family by moving in and settling down. As the Ephesians increased their personal interaction with Christ, they would be able to understand and experience "the breadth, and length, and depth, and height" (v. 18) of Christ's love for them. The result of that increased intimacy with him would be that they would "be filled with all the fullness of God" (v. 19).

Please understand that the information in this chapter is not incidental to, but is the heart of, biblical change. Any attempt to solve the problems of life apart from a dependent relationship with God is both arrogant and, in the long run, ineffective. When Jesus sought to help the adulterous woman at the well in Samaria, he did not offer a recovery program from sexual addiction. Her greatest problem was not her present immorality. Her greatest problem was that she sought to fulfill the longing in her soul with something temporal—relationships with mere men. Jesus offered her a relationship with her Creator that would have permanent impact on her thirst for intimacy with another person. He said in John 4:13–14, "Everyone who drinks of this water will be thirsty again, but whoever drinks of the water that I will give him *will never be thirsty again.*"

Knowing God requires that we first have a desire for God. If you are truly his child, he has already placed within you a "hunger and thirst for righteousness" (Matt. 5:6), which he promises to fill.

Knowing God requires something else, however.

2. Knowing God Requires That We Seek Him

God promises that those who respond to the desire he places within them by seeking him will not be disappointed.

> And without faith it is impossible to please him, for whoever would draw near to God must believe that he exists and that he rewards those who seek him. (Heb. 11:6)

> You will seek the LORD your God and you will find him, if you search after him with all your heart and with all your soul. (Deut. 4:29)

The Search for God Must Be a Passionate, Whole-Hearted Search

A common complaint about modern Christians is that they are apathetic. That is not entirely true. They are very passionate people—passionate for sports, entertainment, leisure, adventure, fashions, sex, wealth, and achievement. Everyone is passionate!

We either love ourselves (and are thus passionate for those things that please ourselves), or we love God and our neighbors. Apathy toward God is the result of being passionate toward something or someone else. Jesus was clear on this issue. "No one can serve two masters, for either he will hate the one and love the other, or he will be devoted to the one and despise the other" (Matt. 6:24). If someone considers God and his interests a small thing—another way of saying he despises them—it is because he is passionate about something else.

Jesus directly confronted Peter about his misdirected passion.

> But he turned and said to Peter, "Get behind me, Satan! You are a hindrance to me. For you are not setting your mind on the things of God, but on the things of man."
>
> Then Jesus told his disciples, "If anyone would come after me, let him deny himself and take up his cross and follow me. For whoever would save his life will lose it, but whoever loses his life for my sake will find it." (Matt. 16:23–25)

Jesus said in the Beatitudes that only the "pure in heart" could "see God" (Matt. 5:8). "Pure in heart" does not mean sin is absent, although that is a part of the meaning. It refers to an undivided heart, a heart free (or pure) from other conflicting priorities. God takes our double-mindedness very seriously. He likens himself to a spouse with an unfaithful partner and likens the believers whose first love is not for Christ to the spouse having an illicit sexual affair.

> You adulterous people! Do you not know that friendship with the world is enmity with God? Therefore whoever wishes to be a friend of the world makes himself an enemy of God. . . . Draw near to God, and he will draw near to you. Cleanse your hands, you sinners, and purify your hearts, you *double-minded*. . . . Humble yourselves before the Lord, and he will exalt you. (James 4:4, 8, 10)

We can have a personal, dependent relationship with God if we are willing to seek him and forsake all other loves. No young woman who is being sought out by a young man will be impressed by his proposal of marriage if he insists on continuing to date other women. If the relationship is to be lasting and meaningful, each must love the other exclusively and wholeheartedly. Similarly, as Creator and sustainer of all, God deserves first place in our lives—and demands it—if we are to know him in any kind of personal, intimate way.

The Search for God Must Be a Search for a Person

Seeking God is not just an exercise in exploring Bible content or studying systematic theology. Those pursuits play an important part in knowing God but are only means to an end—never ends in themselves. The following dialogue illustrates the proper approach when seeking to know God.

Phil played first string on the soccer team for his Christian high school. One day after soccer practice, Phil jogged over to the bleachers and sat down on the bench next to his coach. They exchanged greetings and talked briefly about the scrimmage the team had just finished. Finally, Phil posed a question.

"Coach, I've been struggling with something in my spiritual life recently and wonder if I could talk to you about it."

"Sure, Phil, what's up?"

"Well, since my decision at summer teen camp to live for the Lord, I have really made an effort to be faithful in reading my Bible and spending some time in prayer every day. It hasn't been easy, but I've been pretty faithful."

"If it's any encouragement to you, Phil, the difference in you this year is noticeable. You used to be far more uptight about things that didn't go your way. I have really been encouraged."

"Thanks, Coach, but I really feel that something is still missing. In addition to my regular devotions, I volunteered to lead singing when the youth group does the Wednesday night service at the rescue mission, and I started the Thursday morning prayer meeting for the seniors before first-hour class. But even with all these things going on, I still feel as if my heart is cold toward God. I'm doing a lot of the right things now, and I really am glad I'm doing them, but there has to be something more to the Christian life."

"Phil, let me ask you a question about the time you spend reading your Bible each day. When you open your Bible to read every day, what are you looking for?"

"Well, I have been reading through the New Testament, and I usually try to find something that will encourage me for the day or a principle that I can apply."

"That's fine, Phil, but do you have any idea why God gave us the Bible in the first place?"

"I guess he gave it as a guidebook for life?"

"It does teach us how to live, Phil, but it is far more than that. First John 5:9 says, 'This is the testimony of God that he has borne concerning his Son.' Your Bible is first and foremost a revelation from God about his Son. There is a person at the center of everything you read in the Bible. If you merely look for principles and encouraging passages, you will find what you are looking for, but you will miss God in the process."

"I've never thought about it that way before, Coach."

"Let me give you an example. Since you have been reading in the New Testament, you have probably read the account of Jesus feeding the five thousand in John 6."

"Yes, I read that sometime last week. I'm almost through the four gospels now."

"God did not put that account in the Bible as an explanation of how we ought to feed large numbers of people when we have a church picnic. It was given to reveal something to us about God's Son, Jesus Christ. You have to stop and ask yourself, 'What does this passage reveal about Jesus Christ?' In fact, you may want to make yourself a bookmark for your Bible with that question on it. You have to look for a person in the Scriptures if you are to have a personal relationship with God. When it becomes just a source of principles to you, then you will find your heart cold. This account in John shows us Jesus's great compassion for people in need and his great ability to meet that need. It also shows us that he purposefully arranges situations to test the faith of his disciples.

"His compassion and power are two of his attributes. You might stop right there and ask yourself further, 'What is compassion? What else do I know about God's compassion? Who else in the Bible experienced it? Who else in the Bible demonstrated it? How has God personally demonstrated compassion to me? Since I am called to be Christlike, how am I doing at displaying compassion? If it has been lacking in my daily contacts with people, what have others been seeing in me instead of the compassion that would have been Christlike in those situations?'

"You might spend thirty to forty-five minutes on this one attribute, taking notes, praying for God to 'search' you and 'try' you as David prayed in Psalm 139:23 and thanking him for showing you more about himself. You might make a list of people whom you tend to shun—maybe here at school, maybe at your youth group, or maybe at the rescue mission.

"You might jot a note after each name, spelling out what you could do to make a difference in each life by showing compassion in some way as Jude 1:22 teaches. You could then spend time praying that God would use you as a channel of his love to them to draw them into a more personal relationship with God as well. You would want to thank God for showing you more of himself, and you would want to express to him that it is this kind of excellence in him that makes you glad that you are his child. You could tell him about the delight that these verses have been to you as you have meditated on them. You might even want to write out a special prayer of thanksgiving in a journal to remind you of what you have told him."

"Wow, Coach! I never thought of my daily devotions like that before; that's pretty exciting! I can see how it makes everything more personal, and it would certainly change me more."

"Phil, what I have just described to you is what the Bible calls meditation. It is not merely studying the Bible to learn more principles, although they are important. It is studying the Bible to learn more about a *person*—God himself. The principles you find along the way are manifestations of his character. If you don't see the person behind the principles, you have missed God's intention for his revelation. Of course, you probably can't take an hour every day for this kind of study, but you should consider setting aside a significant block of time on the weekend that you will spend seeking the Lord in this way. It won't be long before you are looking for ways to spend more time like this with him throughout the week in addition to your daily Bible reading and prayer. Your daily devotional time becomes an extension of the larger chunks of time you are spending with God on the weekend. Think about the words of William Longstaff's hymn 'Take Time to Be Holy.' The second stanza says,

> Take time to be holy; the world rushes on.
> Spend much time in secret with Jesus alone.
> By looking to Jesus, like him thou shalt be.
> Thy friends in thy conduct, his likeness shall see.[5]

"You really can't find lasting joy or peace any other way. You have to take the Bible *personally* and treat God like a *person* before your heart will be warmed."

5. William Longstaff, "Take Time to be Holy," 1882.

"Thanks, Coach! You've given me a lot to think about. I'll change my approach and let you know in a few days how things are going."

Phil's coach is right. He described to Phil a relationship with God based on fellowship—personal interactions with God. This kind of interaction with God delights him because we are finding our delight *in* him.

Note the comments of these disciples who walked with Jesus on the way to Emmaus in Luke 24:27–32. They said, "Did not our hearts burn within us while he talked to us on the road, while he opened to us the Scriptures?" (v. 32). They experienced just the opposite of Phil's cold heart. If you look back at verse 27, you will find out what they saw in the Scriptures that made their hearts burn. Luke says, "Beginning with Moses and all the Prophets, he [Jesus] interpreted to them in all the Scriptures the things concerning himself." The disciples were talking about the person and work of the Messiah. Jesus Christ is central to the Scriptures. If we miss him in the process of reading the Bible, we have missed the whole purpose of God in giving us the Scriptures. The Scriptures are about a *person!*

One theologian summarized the truths of the coach's conversation with Phil this way: "Our aim in studying the Godhead must be to know God Himself the better. Our concern must be to enlarge our acquaintance, not simply with the doctrine of God's attributes, but with the living God whose attributes they are. As He is the subject of our study, and our helper in it, so He must Himself be the end of it. We must seek, in studying God, to be led to God. It was for this purpose that revelation was given, and it is to this use that we must put it."[6]

A Letter to John

I want to share with you an actual letter from a mother to her son. She knew he would never read it; he had died in an accident on a farm three years before she wrote the letter. She wrote it as a testimony of how she had come to really know God since her son's death.

Dear John,

It's been three years since that night when God called you to

6. J. I. Packer, *Knowing God* (Downers Grove, IL: InterVarsity Press, 1973), 23.

heaven. We have missed you so much, and I'm sure we will until we are together again.

At the time of your death, there was such a searching going on in your heart. I remember our long discussions and your attempts to make us understand what you were looking for. You were searching for a depth that was missing in your life. You had wisdom and insight in your youth. Some of the things you talked about, things that we didn't understand, have become clearer to us. You remarked about the students at college who were so busy serving the Lord yet lacked a personal relationship with him. In fact some of them with whom you talked couldn't say for sure they were saved. At the time your daddy and I talked with you I don't think we even understood, but I remember your saying that you wanted something "earthshaking" to show us. Well, when you died it was earthshaking. It tore our very foundations away. I feel that I, especially, took up your searching. I believe the Lord answered your prayer. I don't know why it had to be through your death. I'll never understand that, but through it I have discovered that my foundation was built on a creed more than on a person. I had accepted the Lord as my Savior, but I was living my life by self-effort. When you died, everything I believed fell apart. I didn't turn from God, but I started questioning what I believed because your eternity rested on what we had taught you to believe. Was it right? Is there a God? Do I believe the Bible? Does God love me, really love me? Is there a heaven? Are you there with God? What is it like where you are? What are you doing now? Will I really see you and know you in heaven?

I can't say I've gotten all the answers to all my questions, but let me tell you some of the things that have happened. In my searching I have come across some of the things you were struggling with. The Bible is more than just a book of rules. It presents a God who wants to have fellowship with us. We do have a personal relationship with the God of the Bible. As you said, we do need to see our sins as God sees them. When we see God for who he is, then we can see our sins as he sees them. Then we can realize the full impact of what it meant to have those sins forgiven through the cross. Also our emotions do have a part in our Christian life. The Bible says that we worship the Lord "in spirit and in truth." If we don't let our total being become involved in worshiping the Lord, we hinder the Holy Spirit, and we cannot truly worship God. We are to love God with our whole being—body, soul, and spirit. We can know his Spirit's presence. God can be alive to us. We can know his presence in our daily lives. We can have this while we are still here on earth. We can come before his throne and worship him and in a real sense, be in his presence. I feel that is what you are doing now. Maybe that's why I have a yearning to do the same thing even while I'm still on earth. . . .

Since your death, things have become very simple in my life, and I believe in your daddy's life too. The things we thought were so necessary are unimportant. To get to the basics of who God is and my relationship with him is most important. After all, I really want to know the person who is now taking care of my son. How well I live by the rules we as Christians have laid down is not so important now. There was a lot of self-effort in my Christian life. God didn't save me by faith and then expect me to live the Christian life by self-effort. I think you were struggling to establish a relationship with God. You had accepted Christ as your Savior and always lived above reproach as a Christian, but you were wanting a real, personal relationship with God. In heaven you have that relationship now, but I'm still here on earth struggling. I always tried to live right, but it was very "legalistic." I'm afraid that is how we taught you and your sister to live. We taught you how to accept Christ as Savior apart from works but then led you to believe that the Christian life was lived by self-effort, doing everything right. I believe that the element of love was left out of our teaching—accepting God's unchanging love and loving him with your total being. This should come before works and lead to good works which are done out of a heart full of love for him.

I'm writing this "open letter" to you as a testimony of an answer to your prayer, even after your death. If there is anything I have learned, it's that no matter how straight the line we walk in our Christian life is, it is empty self-effort without an attitude of worship and without allowing the Spirit of God to involve our total being in a loving relationship with him. Out of that love will flow good work, a desire to fellowship with him, a desire to please him and serve him. His love will compel us to be witnesses of his love to others. As the saying goes, I think I've had "the cart before the horse" by trying through self-effort

> to please the Lord and serve him without letting his love fill my being in a very real, everyday sense. This realization is just beginning. Now I have to let it become an experience in my life. My prayer is that now I will live what I have learned.
>
> Remember when I used to take you by the shoulder, tell you to look at me, and then say, "I love you, John"? I remember the sheepish look you would give me when I said that. Well, John, I still love you very much.
>
> Your Mother

This mother picked up her son's search for a relationship with his Creator. She sought her God and was not disappointed. She was in touch with reality. May it be true for all of us.

Living in the Real World

The dictionary defines *reality* as follows:

1. The quality or state of being actual or true.
2. One, such as a person, an entity, or an event, that is actual. . . .
3. The totality of all things possessing actuality, existence, or essence.
4. That which exists objectively and in fact.[7]

The real world ("that which exists objectively and in fact"), as we have just read, is one that is created by and for the pleasure of the God of heaven. Those who are not seeking God ("a person, an entity, . . . that is actual") and who consequently are not seeing God, are living in the world without a full picture of reality ("the totality of all things possessing actuality, existence, or essence").

Paul instructed the pagan philosophers on Mars Hill in Athens about the real (true) God:

> God . . . made the world and everything in it, . . . [and] gives to all mankind life and breath and everything. . . . For

7. The American Heritage Dictionary of the English Language, s.v. "reality (*n*.)," accessed June 19, 2023, https://www.ahdictionary.com/word/search.html?q=reality.

> "in him we live and move and have our being";
>
> . . . Now he commands all people everywhere to repent, because he has fixed a day on which he will judge the world in righteousness by a man whom he has appointed; and of this he has given assurance to all by raising him from the dead. (Acts 17:24, 25, 28, 30–31)

Ignorance of this truth—this reality—is not only eternally fatal but also a guarantee that life itself will be filled with emptiness, restlessness, and frustration.

The book of Ecclesiastes presents a powerful argument for precisely this point. Solomon said that God has "put eternity into man's heart, yet so that he cannot find out what God has done from the beginning to the end" (3:11). This verse teaches that God has created within all people a desire to know the end from the beginning (the eternity) of everything they see, yet God has withheld the solutions to the mysteries. Solomon learned that he cannot control life (vv. 1–10) and that he cannot even comprehend life (v. 11). God's purpose in human limitations is "that people fear before him" (v. 14). Unless we, with our natural, sinful bent, experience some mysteries beyond our comprehension and some experiences beyond our power, we begin to think that we are pretty much in control of our lives, and in the process we forget God. That is a dangerous break from reality. God mercifully prompts us to return to reality.

When a person I know is experiencing a particularly difficult trial and is asked how he is doing, he often replies, "I'll be OK once I take some time to argue myself back to reality." It is very easy when in a trial to get a distorted view of reality. It may appear that God isn't concerned or that he isn't able to keep his world running on schedule for us. Those are illusions. They are not true. They are not reality. This is why Peter warns those experiencing difficulty to "prepar[e] [their] minds for action" (1 Peter 1:13). Like Greek warriors who tied their loose skirts tightly around their waists so that they would not impair their movement, believers who are enduring trial must restrain all sloppy thinking about life and about God during those times of difficulty. They must argue themselves back to reality. They must renew their minds about the central part God plays in every aspect of life.

Conclusion

Living in the real world requires us to know the God who has revealed himself to us. We cannot create within ourselves a desire for God. *God* must take the initiative if we are to know him. The good news is that God *has* taken the initiative—he has revealed himself to us and created within us a desire to know him. For this reason, we are able to know him and his truth and thus to live in the real world. Renewing our minds starts right here—with God.

Take Time to Reflect

We so easily become consumed with our own problems and obsessed with the search for the things we have decided we must have to make life work. In the process, we abandon God. That is a great evil, according to Jeremiah 2:13. Put God on the forestage, and turn the spotlights on him! He is all that matters and the only one who can help.

The old hymn writers had a keen sense of their need for God and of his all-sufficiency. Find a church hymnal or a website that contains the following songs and meditate on their words. Make them a part of your personal praise to God by singing them to the Lord. Begin building your relationship with him by putting him into the center of your thoughts. The words of these hymns will help you.

- "Constantly Abiding," by Anne S. Murphy
- "Draw Me Nearer," by Fanny J. Crosby
- "Fairest Lord Jesus," author unknown
- "How Sweet the Name of Jesus Sounds," by John Newton
- "I Am His, and He Is Mine," by George W. Robinson
- "I've Found a Friend," by James G. Small
- "Jesus, I Am Resting, Resting," by Jean S. Pigott
- "Jesus Is All the World to Me," by Will L. Thompson
- "Jesus, Lover of My Soul," by Charles Wesley
- "Jesus, the Very Thought of Thee," by Bernard of Clairvaux
- "Near to the Heart of God," by Cleland B. McAfee
- "Nothing Between," by Charles A. Tindley
- "Oh, to Be Like Thee!" by Thomas O. Chisholm
- "O Thou in Whose Presence," by Joseph Swain
- "'Tis So Sweet to Trust in Jesus," by Louisa M. R. Stead

Write out your observations about the thoughts and desires for God expressed in these hymns. Do any of them reflect your own thirst for God? Do the ambitions of these hymn writers seem too lofty, or are they expressing something that any child of God can know? Do they stir you to have a greater desire for God, or do they discourage you? Summarize your thoughts on paper.

A Word to Disciple Makers
Resting in God's Fatherly Care

In the Creator-creature relationship, which we explored in part 1, we see an immense distance between the essential nature and power of God and that of his creatures. That realization spawns *humility* in the creature. Part 2 of this book describes how to develop a personal relationship with God and how to be changed by exposure to him.

The New Testament introduces us to the reality that God is the Father of those who believe on him: once we have faced our sinfulness and come to God in humility and repentance, we become "children of God" (John 1:12). As a Father, he is our source of life and likeness, but the New Testament writers also use this term to teach us his tender care for his children. In the Father-child relationship, we have a nearness that fosters *security*.

This powerful, sovereign Creator is also our loving and wise Father. We can speak to him intimately and call him "our Father in heaven" (Matt. 6:9). Jesus said that in his Father's house he is preparing places for us in which we will dwell with him forever (see John 14:2). In the meantime, God deals with us as children—disciplining us (see Heb. 12:5–11), addressing us as "little children" who need to heed his instruction and admonition (see 1 John), and constantly prompting us to "grow up" to be like our elder brother, Jesus Christ (Eph. 4:15; see also v. 13).

As believers understand the Father's complete and perfect love for his children, they will experience a growing sense of security. The apostle Paul assures us that in place of the "spirit of slavery" and "fear" we had before salvation, we have "received the Spirit of adoption as sons, by whom we cry, "Abba! Father [Daddy]!" (Rom. 8:15). John testifies of this security when he says that "perfect [mature] love casts out fear" (1 John 4:18). The security extends not only to our eternal home with the Father but also applies to our temporal walk in the Father's ways in this life. As a loving Father, he gives both protection and direction to his children. Believers who are plagued by fears, anxieties, worries, obsessions, addictions, and other dependencies has not yet learned the liberating truth of the Father's love for his children. They have not learned the goodness of God.

Please note here that many say they have a hard time accepting God's fatherly care for them because they have never had a good father. We often hear that people's view of their own fathers shapes their view of God. We need to understand what is true and what is false about this idea.

First, our view of our fathers does not necessarily shape our view of God. We are not without a basic view of a good father, or we would not have a standard in mind against which we compare our experience with our own fathers. We cannot know if our own fathers were bad if we do not know what a good father is like. More likely, we do not have a good view of God because we have not learned from the Scriptures who God is and what he is really like. In addition, we can have the best of earthly fathers and still not know what God is like if we have not been exposed to biblical teaching about him.

Another likely dynamic involved in the I've-never-had-a-good-father-so-I-can't-understand-how-God-is-good rationale is the propensity of our hearts to make excuses for our own misbehaver—a strategy that started in Eden—and our arrogant habit of prejudice. By *prejudice* I mean our inclination to prejudge everyone in a certain category by our experiences with a representative of that category. A bad experience with a father can easily prejudice us against all those who fit that description, including God.

That said, it is also quite possible that those who have not had the blessing of loving relationships in their homes have never learned how to respond to love. They perhaps have learned to view every kindness as a step of manipulation. For example, an abused daughter soon learns that any special attention and kindness from her dad means that he is setting her up for another sexual favor.

Individuals may also be threatened by genuine acts of love and goodness to them because such acts require some sort of response from them—one with which they are yet unfamiliar because they were not taught at home how to graciously receive and respond to kindness.

Therefore, they are threatened by any expression of love toward them. They can be taught from the Scriptures what a proper response to God's loving-kindness is.

The crucial need in any case is for believers to learn from God himself what he is like. Jesus presented to the Jews a totally new concept of God when he presented God as his Father and the Father of those who followed Christ. His Sermon on the Mount in Matthew 5 through 7 introduced an entirely new dimension of relationship with God that was different from any they had previously known. In the Old Testament, God called himself the Father of Israel. In the New Testament, he called himself the Father of individual believers. Study the gospels, especially Matthew and John, and 1 John to see this relationship of believers to their Father. The result is a great sense of security at being objects of the Father's love and a great devotion to the one who has loved us so.

7

BECOMING LIKE CHRIST

With you is the fountain of life; in your light do we see light. (Ps. 36:9)

SINCE THIS BOOK is about biblical change, you may be asking right now, "How does a search for God and a study of his attributes change me and make me more like Christ? What does this have to do with renewing my mind?" Those are good questions that are at the heart of what this book is all about. Exposure to God brings about profound change in believers—the kind of change to Christlikeness we need.

More about God's Attributes

To understand biblical change, we must understand the biblical doctrine of illumination. We will look at it in some detail in this chapter. But first we will learn how God's attributes fit into our study of sanctification.

Some theologians divide God's attributes into *communicable* and *noncommunicable* attributes. We use these two terms more commonly to talk about diseases. A communicable disease, like measles, is one you can get from someone else. A noncommunicable disease, like cancer, is one that cannot be passed from one person to another through normal contact. A noncommunicable attribute is one that no creature of God can get. These attributes include the following:

- *Omnipotence*. God is all-powerful.
- *Omniscience*. God innately knows everything.
- *Omnipresence*. God is everywhere at all times.
- *Immutability*. God's nature will never change.
- *Transcendence*. God is distinctly different from his creation.
- *Eternality*. God has no beginning or end.

Being like Christ does not involve acquiring any of the attributes above. That would be impossible. Rather, being Christlike means acquiring his communicable attributes—those generally known as the "fruit of the Spirit." Galatians 5:22–23 lists several of the Spirit's fruit.[1]

- *Love*—genuine self-sacrifice for the good of others
- *Joy*—a feeling of great pleasure and delight in who God is and in what he has provided
- *Peace*—a sense of well-being; rest; tranquility; contentment
- *Patience*—stability under pressure; self-control under provocation from people
- *Kindness*—reasonableness; flexibility
- *Goodness*—benevolent thoughts and actions toward others; generosity
- *Faithfulness*—reliability
- *Gentleness* ["meekness," KJV]—humility; trusting submission to God's wise and fatherly choices for our lives
- *Self-control*—governing one's passions

These are all communicable attributes of God. That means that God possesses these qualities, that Jesus's life on earth was characterized by them, and that all believers can also possess them as they are controlled by the Holy Spirit. These are what comes out of the "tea bag" of Spirit-filled believers when they are put in hot-water situations. Those who manifest these characteristics on a consistent basis, even under pressure, can be said to have Christian (Christlike) character.

Changed by His Glory

Second Corinthians 3:18 is a key verse for understanding biblical change: "We all, with unveiled face, beholding the glory of the Lord, are being *transformed* ["changed," KJV] into the same image from one degree of glory to another. For this comes from the Lord who is the Spirit." In the verses preceding this one, Paul shows the benefits of the new life in Christ as opposed to the former life of the Jews under the law

1. The list in Galatians 5:22–23 is representative, not exhaustive. Other passages that outline godly qualities include Matthew 5:1–12, 1 Corinthians 13:4–8, 2 Peter 1:3–11, and James 3:17–18.

of Moses. He says that those who insist on remaining under the Jewish system of laws in order to try to please God are spiritually blinded (see also 2 Cor. 4:3–4). It is as though they have veils over their faces.

He teaches that, by contrast, believers have *open* or *unveiled* faces—that is, the veil of blindness has been lifted, and they can perceive what God's Spirit wants to teach them about himself (see 1 Cor. 2:9–16). As God shows them his glory in his Word, they experience a very specific change. By God's Spirit, they display an ever-increasing reflection of those glories in their own lives.

God's glory is the manifestation of his many-splendored excellencies. It was shown in the Old Testament as a *shekinah*—a radiant reflection of God's nature that was too brilliant for any mortal to view directly. It was the overwhelming presence of his perfection.

When we look up at the sun, we see its white light—all its colors mixed together. If we look at sunlight through a prism, we see the white light broken up into its individual colors of the rainbow. When the apostle John saw the "white light" of God's glory, he was almost blinded by the manifestation, as if looking at the sun directly, and fell on his face in stunned humility (see Rev. 1:12–17). When Ezekiel the prophet told of the experience later, he almost stammered as he tried to come up with words to describe the experience. He said,

> Above the expanse over their heads there was the *likeness of a throne,* in *appearance* like sapphire; and seated above the *likeness of a throne was* a *likeness with a human appearance.* And upward from what had the *appearance of his waist I saw as it were* gleaming metal, like the *appearance of fire enclosed all around. And downward from what had the appearance of his waist I saw as it were the appearance of fire, and* there was brightness around him. Like the *appearance of* the bow that is in the cloud on the day of rain, so was the *appearance of the brightness all around.*
>
> Such was the *appearance of the likeness of* the glory of the LORD. And when I saw it, I fell on my face, and I heard the voice of one speaking. (Ezek. 1:26–28)

Most people in the Scriptures who saw God, however, did not have a blinding vision of the Lord. Rather than the white light of his glory, they saw individual colors—individual attributes. God revealed some aspect of himself by giving certain people a name for him that stood for some part of his character. Sometimes he dealt with the nation Israel or with an individual by showing some part of himself—perhaps his faithfulness, his compassion, his power, his mercy, his covenant love, and so forth. His law given to Moses revealed the holiness of his nature. The behavioral codes of the Pentateuch showed aspects of his righteousness and his wisdom.

In the New Testament, God's specific glories or attributes were demonstrated more clearly in the earthly life of Jesus Christ. John 1:14 says, "The Word [speaking of Jesus Christ] became flesh [came to this earth] and dwelt among us, *and we have seen his glory, glory as of the only Son from the Father,* full of grace and truth."

Second Corinthians 3:18 tells us that we are "changed" when we are exposed to God with an "unveiled face" (unobstructed contact). Paul is saying that no one who is exposed to the glories of God as they are revealed by God's Spirit through the Scriptures will remain the same.

Illumination: When God Turns on the Light

Let's look at the actual process of this change more closely. We must not think that *reading* the Bible alone changes us. God's Spirit must personally show the realities of God to us as we ponder the Scriptures. This divine work is called *illumination.* Let's look at a couple of biblical examples of this experience.

In Matthew 16:13, Jesus asks his disciples, "Who do people say that the Son of Man is?" They reply that some think he is John the Baptist and that others think he is one of the prophets—perhaps Elijah or Jeremiah. He asks them a more pointed question in verse 15: "But who do you say that I am?" Peter answers with a powerful statement of reality: "You are the Christ, the Son of the living God" (v. 16). Jesus's reply to Peter is instructive. Our Lord says, "Blessed are you, Simon Bar-Jonah! *For flesh and blood has not revealed this to you, but my Father who is in heaven*" (v. 17). He says in effect, "Peter, you have experienced something that is not common to all. You cannot learn what you learned by natural means. My Father himself showed you this truth. He opened your eyes and you were illuminated."

Read Luke 24 and note the accounts of the resurrected Christ's appearances to the two disciples traveling on the road to the city of

Emmaus in verses 13 through 35 and to a larger group of disciples in verses 36 through 48. You will find that the disciples did not understand the significance of his death, burial, and resurrection until they were illuminated. Jesus reminded them of "'everything written about [him] in the Law of Moses and the Prophets and the Psalms. . . .' Then he opened their minds to understand the Scriptures" (24:44, 45).

Here is how C. H. Spurgeon described illumination when commenting on Psalm 36:9: "In your light do we see light."

> Purify flesh and blood by any educational process you may select, elevate mental faculties to the highest degree of intellectual power, yet none of these can reveal Christ. The Spirit of God must come with power, and overshadow the man with His wings, and then in that mystic holy of holies the Lord Jesus must display Himself to the sanctified eye, as He doth not unto the purblind [blinded] sons of men. Christ must be His own mirror. The great mass of this blear-eyed world can see nothing of the ineffable glories of Immanuel. He stands before them without form or comeliness, a root out of a dry ground, rejected by the vain and despised by the proud. Only where the Spirit has touched the eye with eye-salve, quickened the heart with divine life, and educated the soul to a heavenly taste, only there is He understood.[2]

A. W. Tozer expresses the same thought this way:

> For millions of Christians . . . God is no more real than He is to the non-Christian. They go through life trying to love an ideal and be loyal to a mere principle. . . . [But] a loving Personality dominates the Bible, walking among the trees of the garden and breathing fragrance over every scene. Always a living Person is present, speaking, pleading, loving, working, and manifesting Himself whenever and wherever His people have the receptivity necessary to receive the manifestation. . . .
>
> If we cooperate with Him in loving obedience, God will manifest Himself to us, and that manifestation will be the difference between a nominal Christian life and a life radiant with the light of His face.[3]

2. Charles Haddon Spurgeon, *Morning and Evening* (Peabody, MA: Hendrickson Publishers, 1991), 619.
3. A. W. Tozer, *The Pursuit of God* (Camp Hill, PA: Christian Publications, 1993), 48, 60.

Tanned by the Sun

Change into Christlikeness is not something we do to ourselves. It is something that happens supernaturally through the agency of the Holy Spirit when we expose ourselves to God's Word and he reveals to us his glory. We might think of it in terms of tanning. Light-skinned people who would like to get a (true) tan can do only one thing—spend more time in the sun. In fact if a dark tan is truly important to them, they will not watch the clock to see whether their fifteen minutes in the sun is up; they will watch their skin to see whether it has the color they want. If they want a darker tan than their time in the sun permits in one day, they will look at what they have to do tomorrow to see whether they can delay or eliminate anything so that they can spend more time in the sun.

In the same way, believers who are not manifesting godliness in some area of their lives can do only one thing—spend more time in the Word, asking God to illuminate their minds and hearts. Believers who have very little "tan" reveal their limited exposure to the glory of God.

We are called by God in 1 Peter 2:9 to "proclaim the excellencies [attributes] of him who called [us] out of darkness into his marvelous light." If we aren't spending time walking "in the light," our untanned—unchanged—lives show that our walk has been mostly "in darkness." If we truly want more change in our lives, we will look at what is on our agenda today to see whether anything can be postponed or eliminated so that we can spend more time being exposed to the glory of God. We won't be watching the clock; we will be watching for the effect of the glory of God on our lives.

Youth directors and pastors are aware of a phenomenon common to young people who go to a summer Bible camp and make decisions for the Lord. The decisions to give up their ungodly friends, habits, music, and so forth seem to last for only a couple of weeks before their desires and resolves weaken over time. Many teenagers eventually return to their former lifestyles very discouraged and perhaps even cynical because they lose hope that change is possible for them. Unfortunately, many adults (and consequently, many teens) come to expect this phenomenon—an attitude that betrays a shallow understanding of biblical change.

Suppose we were to take the same attitude toward a coworker who came back from a vacation at the ocean three weeks ago. She came back very tanned because of the time she spent in the sun, but now her tan is fading. We would not look scornfully at her and chide her for her vacation tan. We wouldn't say that the tan she had when she returned wasn't real because it didn't last! We would understand that unless she keeps up the same level of exposure to the sun that gave her the tan in the first place, she will not keep the tan.

Rather than looking contemptuously at teens (or even adults) who make "camp decisions," we who understand how the Christian life works should immediately get involved helping them to structure their lives to include generous amounts of time exposed to God's Word, while we pray that the Holy Spirit will continue to illumine their hearts.

Evidences of Exposure to God

All of us know the most obvious effect of time spent in the sun—darker skin—but what happens when we are exposed to the glory of God? What are the effects of illuminated truth on believers? Not all the effects we will discuss are present in the same proportion every time for every person who is illuminated, but there *will* be some effect. No one can see God or his truth and be unaffected by it. The person who sees God will be moved in some way by the experience.

Illuminated Truth Moves the Believer Intellectually

Often when God's Spirit illumines some Scripture passage, believers see afresh the *validity* of the truth. They are moved to have a steadfast confidence, an inner assurance. They say to themselves, "This is right; I must believe it!" Illuminated believers are divinely persuaded that they have seen something from God and that what they have seen is right. They will boldly defy every assault of hell and will burn at the stake if necessary before they will deny the truth of what they have seen and know to be true.

Although illuminated believers are intellectually convinced of the truth, they are also humbled by the experience. They are not cocky or arrogant in their knowledge. Everyone in the Bible who truly saw some aspect of God and his nature was found "on his face" (Gen. 17:3; see also Ezek. 1:28; Acts 9:4; Rev. 1:17). Whenever we see some area of our own life in contrast to God's nature, we see our own great deficiency and rebellion in that area. We will be humbled and repentant.

At a teen leadership camp, the teens were given an assignment to memorize and meditate on Philippians 2:3–16 to learn about the servant nature of their Lord. They were challenged to look at how Christ denied himself in order to be a servant to others. Jesus did not concern himself about his reputation among his peers. He obeyed his Father to take the lowest form of created, rational beings. He further obeyed his Father and submitted to his human authorities to the point of death, even death by a humiliating and excruciating form of Roman torture—crucifixion.

Later, one teen shared how God had humbled him as he spent several hours during the week meditating on the text and thinking of its ramifications for Christ and for himself. As part of the exercise, Karl was to list seventy-five ways he was selfish at home, at work, and at school. It was humbling enough for Karl to see how much he looked out for himself at the expense of others; it was painful for him to realize his own selfishness compared to the self-sacrifice of his Lord on his behalf. He sought the Lord's forgiveness and was ready for help on how to be more like Christ at home. He had been humbled when his illuminated heart saw the glory of the Lord.

When we behold the glory of God and see some aspect of his nature, we learn what that virtue truly looks like. Karl had thought he was a pretty good teen. In fact, his parents and youth director would have called him a model teen. He was leader of the youth group and had a good testimony at home and at school. Without doubt, Karl had been responsive to his earthly authorities and to God in the areas he knew about, but it was not until he was exposed to this aspect of the glory of God that he learned what self-sacrificing love really looks like. When he saw it manifested in the person and works of God's Son, he was shown a new, higher standard. Compared to the teens around him, Karl always came out on top. When he considered the self-sacrificing humility of God's Son, Karl realized how much further he had to go to be Christlike.

Jesus taught his disciples a similar lesson when he washed his disciples' feet. Peter thought he was doing pretty well until he was exposed to this level of servant activity by his Master. After his actions, Jesus instructed them.

> When he had washed their feet and put on his outer garments and resumed his place, he said to them, "Do you understand what I have done to you? You call me Teacher and Lord, and you are right, for so I

> am. If I then, your Lord and Teacher, have washed your feet, you also ought to wash one another's feet. For I have given you an example, that you also should do just as I have done to you. Truly, truly, I say to you, a servant is not greater than his master, nor is a messenger greater than the one who sent him. If you know these things, blessed are you if you do them." (John 13:12–17)

Not one of us can be proud of our level of spiritual maturity or theological understanding when we have been exposed to God's nature. We "all have sinned and *fall short of the glory of God*" (Rom. 3:23). We may have made some progress on our spiritual journey, but we will quickly be taught by the glory of God that we have many more miles to cover before we can say we have arrived.

Such are the impressions on the intellect of those who see God. They are at the same time taught, humbled, and made bold. How can it be otherwise? They have seen God!

Illuminated Truth Moves the Believer Emotionally

Illuminated believers who view the glory of God see the *beauty* of the truth. They declare, "This is wonderful; I must praise it!" The Word becomes attractive to them, and they find themselves admiring it. It may even be breathtaking to them. They discover a new loveliness and worthiness about the truth. They cherish it and delight in its splendor. Emotionally, the result is twofold.

First, there is great joy within illuminated believers. Notice how the psalmist almost explodes with delight over the law of God in Psalm 119. He sees the glory of the Word, loves its taste, and praises its beauty. He sees the excellency of it. Peter called the effect "joy that is inexpressible and filled with glory" (1 Peter 1:8). Illuminated believers drink deeply of this wellspring of joy, and others look with envy on their continual feast of joy. Sometimes they are overwhelmed by the hymns they sing. The truth of the words reminds them of what they have seen from God himself, and they experience a silent sense of camaraderie with the hymn writer who, they know, has truly seen God himself. This joy of which I speak is far more than the lightheartedness of a naturally exuberant, bubbling personality. It is the effect on the soul of an illuminated believer who has seen the glory of God.

Second, there is a great peace in illuminated believers. Seeing God brings a great stability and steadiness to the soul. Those who are seeing truth illuminated by the Spirit of God are not agitated, restless, irritable, worried, or moody. They are at rest! They have seen God, and that is enough. They are satisfied that nothing shall separate them from the love of their God (see Rom. 8:35–39) and that God will use his power on their behalf as he wisely sees fit. Paul called it the "peace . . . which surpasses all understanding" (Phil. 4:7).

Joy and peace melt together to show an effect in believers greater than the sum of its two parts. Illuminated believers are satisfied. They are like a person who has just pushed his chair back from the Thanksgiving dinner table at his grandmother's home after stuffing himself with turkey, dressing, gravy, sweet potatoes, hot rolls, cranberry sauce, and pumpkin pie; he cannot be tempted with an invitation to eat a bologna sandwich. He is just too full to eat anything else.

God made us to be completely satisfied with himself. Believers who are beholding the glory of the Lord finds "fullness of joy" (Ps. 16:11). Such was the experience of the psalmist David. He was a "satisfied customer" because he had tasted and seen "that the Lord is good" (Ps. 34:8).

Many Christian organizations and churches are filled with discontented, frantic believers. Many of them are driven, perfectionistic, controlling people who never seem to be able to get everything checked off their lists. There is always something more to do. They never experience any real peace or rest because there is always something else out of control at the moment. If for some reason life quiets down for a few moments, they worry about what could go out of control if they don't keep an eye on everything. It is not long before these on-the-go, high-energy people turn into relational terrorists. When they are irritated, people keep their distance.

This sad state of affairs is a revelation that these believers have not spent much time "in the sun." Here's how our Lord expressed this in Matthew 11:28–30:

> Come to me, all who labor and are heavy laden, and I will give you rest. Take my yoke upon you, and learn from me, for I am gentle and lowly in heart, and you will find rest for your souls. For my yoke is easy, and my burden is light.

Jesus made it quite clear that people who spend time learning about him will be people who are known for the peace in their souls. Prayerful reflection on God's wisdom, power, and sovereignty calms the heart. Peter reminds us that "grace and *peace* [are] multiplied to [us] in the knowledge of God" (2 Peter 1:2). A person without peace—constantly agitated or restless—does not know God well (see Ps. 119:165).

Centuries ago, the prophet Isaiah promised that those who would "seek . . . the Lord while he may be found" would "go out in joy, and be led forth in peace" (Isa. 55:6, 12). Illuminated truth surges with an unspeakable joy and an unquenchable peace that totally satisfies believers. How can it be otherwise? They have seen God!

Illuminated Truth Moves the Believer Volitionally

When God's Spirit illumines the mind with truth, believers are shown the *urgency* and the *responsibility* of the truth. They cry, "This is compelling; I must do it!" They are energized and motivated. They immediately wish to become witnesses of these things. They have something to testify about—they have seen God! The prophet Isaiah, when he saw God, exclaimed, "Here I am! Send *me*" (Isa. 6:8). The apostle Paul, upon beholding the glory of God, asked, "Lord, what wilt thou have *me* to do?" (Acts 9:6 KJV).

Karl's response at camp, when he saw the Lord's humility and obedience, was to humble himself in repentance, ponder how Christ's humility would look if manifested in his life, and cheerfully throw himself into whatever service for others he could find around him. The attitude of willing service is the natural result of seeing the glory of God. There is no grudging service here—no clock-watching laborers—only a burning passion of believers to "present [their] bodies as a living sacrifice, holy, acceptable unto God." They feel it is their "spiritual worship" (Rom. 12:1). How can it be otherwise? They have seen God!

This Is Revival!

This effect of illuminated truth on the hearts of believers is the essence of revival. When the Holy Spirit reveals the glory of God to us, our response is always, "This is right; I must believe it! This is wonderful; I must praise it! This is compelling; I must do it!" When we are moved in this manner by what we see of God, we are being revived, and others cannot help but notice the profound change. Those around us see our "light shin[ing] before others, so that they . . . see [our] good works and give glory to [our] Father who is in heaven" (Matt. 5:16). The change in us is the direct work of the Spirit of God on the souls of those who are seeking God in his Word.

Believers must take the time and effort to hike into the forest of God's Word and harvest the logs of truth from that massive timberland. They must by reflection split the logs and stack them in the fireplace of their own heart while they pray for the illumination from God to set the logs ablaze. The resulting fire will provide the light that directs their paths and the heat that fuels their passion for God.

Unfortunately, most people accumulate only a few sticks of kindling from their pastor's Sunday sermons—not because he doesn't present great truths from God's Word but because they think little about those truths, even during the message. Even when God does ignite those splinters of truth, their fire blazes only momentarily because there is so little truth for the Holy Spirit to burn.

Solomon's burden in Proverbs 2 is that we would embark on this earnest and diligent search for truth. He says that those who will do so will "find the knowledge of God" (v. 5). They are the ones who God says will "*receive* my words and *treasure up* my commandments" (v. 1). They will make their ears *attentive* and *incline* their hearts to God (see v. 2). They will "*call out* for insight" and "*raise* [their] voice for understanding" (v. 3). They "*seek* [wisdom] like silver" and "*search* for [wisdom] as for hidden treasures" (v. 4). This is no casual I'll-pursue-God-if-I-have-the-time-and-if-I-remember-to-do-it attitude. It is the wholehearted pursuit of God within his revelation that is rewarded with a view of God himself!

This is revival! This is the crying need of our day! Our preaching, counseling, and writing must point people to the God whose glories fill eternity. We must teach people to pursue *him* in the Word while they beg the Spirit of God to illumine their eyes so that they can be "transformed into the same image from one degree of glory to another. For this comes from the Lord who is the Spirit" (2 Cor. 3:18).

The Right Diagnosis

When we look around us, we can see so many disheartening problems. Violence, crime, poverty, and educational deficiencies grieve any sensitive person. The family, which should be the greatest refuge for children, has become a domestic battlefield where children are often caught in the crossfire of their parents' warfare. The time and energy that should be spent giving children the direction and training they need to prepare for life are drained by each spouse's preoccupation with protecting his or her "territory" from the other spouse.

At the same time that social ills and marital troubles are escalating, we witness an increase in the personal instability of even the average middle-class citizen. Attempts to achieve emotional stability, recover from disorders, fix the family, restructure society, upgrade education, eliminate poverty, and rehabilitate criminals continue to fall short of their intended goals because they don't address the root cause of the problem—humanity is estranged from God and, therefore, out of touch with reality.

Sadly, even those who have experienced God's salvation from eternal torment are ignorant of most of reality as God defines it because they do not know God well. Most believers know God only as well as tourists in their destination's airport know the country they are visiting. They may know more *about* the country than they did before their arrival, but they don't really *know* the country. They have not explored its coasts, set foot on its mainland, and gazed on its natural beauty. Tourists who don't leave the airport are poor tourists indeed.

In much the same way, many believers simply do not know God in any kind of personal, ongoing, intimate relationship. Their hearts are, for the most part, unilluminated. Consequently, they are not "transformed into the same image" (2 Cor. 3:18). Biblical change starts with God, is orchestrated by God, and is accomplished by his Spirit entirely for the glory of God.

What Is Your View of God?

In this chapter, we have touched very little on the actual disciplines involved in beholding the glory of God. We will devote more time to discussing those elements in chapters 8 and 9. For now, it is crucial that you at least understand the importance of beholding the glory of God as he illuminates his truth by his Spirit. We cannot change to Christlikeness without it. To further impress this truth on our minds, I will conclude this section with a quotation from A. W. Tozer.

> What comes into our minds when we think about God is the most important thing about us. . . .
>
> Were we able to extract from any man a complete answer to the question, "What comes into your mind when you think about God?" we might predict with certainty the spiritual future of that man.
>
> All the problems of heaven and earth, though they were to confront us together and at once, would be nothing compared with the overwhelming problem of God: That He is; what He is like; and what we as moral beings must do about Him.[4]

If our view of God is not right, nothing can ultimately be right in our lives. For us to live in the real world, God must be central in our thoughts. We must embrace Paul's perspective of God's role.

> For by him all things were created, in heaven and on earth, visible and invisible, whether thrones or dominions or rulers or authorities—all things were created through him and for him. And he is before all things, and in him all things hold together. And he is the head of the body, the church. He is the beginning, the firstborn from the dead, *that in everything he might be preeminent.* (Col. 1:16–18)

Take Time to Reflect

I'm sure by now you realize that you cannot change any part of your life without a growing relationship with your Creator. You must first be reconciled with and submissive to God. In addition, something must be "going on" between you and God for any real progress to be made.

Everything God allows in our lives is designed by him to draw us to himself in humble submission and dependence. You grow only when you are moving toward that end.

Furthermore, you cannot help others to come to know God in this way if you are not walking in this kind of fellowship yourself. If you have not seen much progress in your own walk with Christ, let me suggest that you plan to take a day or weekend off and spend it alone with God. Remove yourself from daily distractions so you can devote your thoughts and attention to God and your relationship with him.

4. A. W. Tozer, *The Knowledge of the Holy* (New York: Harper & Row, 1961), 1–2.

If your responsibilities will not allow you to take an entire weekend away, at least plan for quarterly outings with God. For example, arrange to free up several hours of a Saturday. Pack a lunch and drive to a place where you will not be around many people, such as a local or state park. Take your Bible, a notebook, your prayer list, a hymnal, and perhaps a devotional book. Spend your time reading lengthy sections of the Scriptures and writing down what you are learning about God or about your own heart condition. Allow God to bring to your mind any matters that need to be reconciled with him or others. Write down the names of the people you need to see to make reconciliation so that you do not forget to do so once you return home. Confess your sin to God and praise him for the promises of his forgiveness.

Take some time to sing praises to him out of your hymnal. (Go ahead and sing out loud if no one is around, even if you can't carry a tune.) If you absolutely cannot sing, read the words out loud slowly and reflectively so that their meaning can sink into your heart. If you play a portable musical instrument, take it with you to accompany yourself, but don't get sidetracked by getting caught up on practice time or performing for anyone close by who might hear you. If it will distract you in any way from your worship of God, leave it home.

Set aside some time to get caught up on your intercessory prayer for family members, coworkers, spiritual leaders in your life, missionaries, and those who are enduring great affliction because of illness or disaster. Make note of any "errands of mercy" you could do for them when you return home or spend a few minutes writing a letter of encouragement right then.

Choose a Scripture passage of several verses and meditate on it using "The MAP Method of Meditation" study sheet in appendix A of this book. Memorize the passage and spend time prayerfully reflecting on its meaning and application for you. Write out what changes you will need to make in your life to carry out what you learned from God's Word. You must take time for God to speak to you. Ask him to illumine you by his Spirit. Listen to him and reflect seriously on what he says.

Finally, as fuel for your devotions, consider these admonitions from twenty-year-old C. H. Spurgeon as he began his Sunday morning sermon at the New Park Street Chapel on January 7, 1855:

It has been said by some one that "the proper study of mankind is man." I will not oppose the idea, but I believe it is equally true that the proper study of God's elect is God; the proper study of a Christian is the Godhead. The highest science, the loftiest speculation, the mightiest philosophy, which can ever engage the attention of a child of God, is the name, the nature, the person, the work, the doings, and the existence of the great God whom he calls his Father. There is something exceedingly improving to the mind in a contemplation of the Divinity. It is a subject so vast, that all our thoughts are lost in its immensity; so deep, that our pride is drowned in its infinity. Other subjects we can compass and grapple with; in them we feel a kind of self-content, and go our way with the thought, "Behold I am wise." But when we come to this master-science, finding that our plumb-line cannot sound its depth, and that our eagle eye cannot see its height, we turn away with the thought, that vain man would be wise, but he is like a wild ass's colt; and with the solemn exclamation, "I am but of yesterday, and know nothing." No subject of contemplation will tend more to humble the mind, than thoughts of God. . . .

But while the subject humbles the mind it also expands it. He who often thinks of God, will have a larger mind than the man who simply plods around this narrow globe. . . . The most excellent study for expanding the soul, is the science of Christ, and him crucified, and the knowledge of the Godhead in the glorious Trinity. Nothing will so enlarge the intellect, nothing so magnify the whole soul of man, as a devout, earnest, continued investigation of the great subject of the Deity. And whilst humbling and expanding, this subject is eminently consolatory. Oh, there is, in contemplating Christ, a balm for every wound; in musing on the Father, there is a quietus for every grief; and in the influence of the Holy Ghost, there is a balsam for every sore. Would you lose your sorrows? Would you drown your cares? Then go, plunge yourself in the Godhead's deepest sea; be lost in his immensity; and you shall come forth as from a couch of rest, refreshed and invigorated. I know nothing which can so comfort the soul; so calm the swelling billows of grief and sorrow; so speak peace to the winds of trial, as a devout musing upon the subject of the Godhead.[5]

5. C. H. Spurgeon, *The New Park Street Pulpit* (repr., Grand Rapids: Zondervan, 1963), 5–6.

A Word to Disciple Makers
How God's Attributes Affect Christian Standards

As we saw in chapter 7, we cannot know God on the run any more than we can know any other person that way. Personal relationships are not built efficiently. Enormous amounts of time must be devoted to interacting with the other person. As you put in the time, you will find that a special retreat with God will have a significant effect on your regular, daily devotional time with him. When you spend time with him each day, though it be only thirty to forty-five minutes, the depth and quality of the interaction with God will be profoundly different. When you sense shallowness creeping back in, schedule another day with God along the lines described on pages 140–41.

You cannot become an effective disciple maker of others if you do not spend good quality time with God on a regular basis. You will soon lose sight of the place God must play in your ministry to others. You will not be passionate about their need for God since you are experiencing no passion for God yourself. You will not know how to help others to develop their relationship with God since you have not done it yourself. Nor will you have a strong understanding of how the character of God ought to shape your behavior and that of those you are discipling.

Every *precept*, or specific command from God, is a revelation of his nature. He commands us to be holy because he is holy. He commands us to be merciful because he is merciful. We are to forgive others because he has forgiven us. He commands husbands to love their wives because Christ loved the church. Behind each of his commands is a specific concept about God's nature that compels him to issue that command. We will honor his commands if we honor him as a person.

The same is true for every *principle,* or general law, we find in the Scriptures. For example, we are to do everything "decently and in order" because God is a God of order and design (1 Cor. 14:40). He does everything according to plan and on time. He does not do anything haphazardly or halfheartedly.

From these precepts and principles, which are based on God's *attributes,* we form *convictions*—personal beliefs about how an attribute of God relates to us. As a result of the principle of God's orderliness and purpose that we see in his creation and in his redemptive works, we might come to the following conclusion: "Since I want to be like God, I must strive to have an affinity for order and stop living chaotically. I must start planning what I am going to do with my time instead of impulsively doing whatever comes to my mind and appeals to my flesh at the moment."

The application of that newly formed conviction shows up in various *standards,* or personal guidelines, we might impose on our lives. To apply the conviction for order in the previous paragraph, we might come up with the following plan: "I will establish and maintain a personal budget so that my spending reflects godly priorities instead of impulse buying. I will sit down on Sunday afternoon and decide how I will spend my evenings during the coming week. I will keep a running list of jobs that need to be done around the house or for others, and I will work on these a little bit at a time instead of letting them pile up while I vegetate on the couch watching television every night."

Again, it takes reflective time to go through this process, but it is the only way to bring your life into conformity to the nature of God. Remember, this whole process starts with meditation on the attributes of God and a study of the Word that highlights for us his precepts and principles. Precepts and principles come from God and are the products of God's revelation to us. Convictions and standards come from the time we spend with God as we meditate on his Word and ask him to show us how his revelation should affect our daily lives.

We need to be sure that we do not merely pass on our *standards* to those we are discipling. We must take the time to show them the biblical *precept* or *principle* behind the *conviction* and *standard,* and, even more important, we must show them the *God* behind the precepts and principles.

8

SEARCHING FOR WISDOM

Have this mind among yourselves, which is yours in Christ Jesus. (Phil. 2:5)

The beginning of wisdom is this: Get wisdom, and whatever you get, get insight. Prize her highly, and she will exalt you; she will honor you if you embrace her. (Prov. 4:7–8)

We have looked at how we are changed into the image of Christ by beholding the glory of God. There are still a few gaps that must be filled in, however, if we are to have a working understanding of how this change takes place as God's Spirit uses God's Word to renew our mind.

Part 2 of this book is titled "Renewing Your Mind." Another title for this section could have been "Developing the Mind of Christ." It could also have been called "Getting Wisdom from God," since the Old Testament forerunner and equivalent to Christlikeness is wisdom. In fact, Jesus Christ is called "the wisdom of God" (1 Cor. 1:24). Many Bible teachers believe that Lady Wisdom in Proverbs 1:20–33 and Proverbs 8 is a personification of Christ. Furthermore, the fruit of the Spirit and the characteristics of wisdom are the same. That shouldn't surprise us, since they have the same source. A study of how we become wise, therefore, will clarify many of the basics of how we become Christlike by renewing our minds.

A Call to Hear and Do

In the first sermon of his public earthly ministry, Jesus himself preached that we must have two specific heart responses to his call to be wise.

> Everyone then who hears these words of mine and does them will be like a wise man who built his house on the rock. And the rain fell, and the floods came, and the winds blew and beat on that house, but it did not fall, because it had been founded on the rock. And everyone who hears these words of mine and does not do them will be like a foolish man who built his house on the sand. And the rain fell, and the floods came, and the winds blew and beat against that house, and it fell, and great was the fall of it. (Matt. 7:24–27)

These final words of his sermon have several important implications for believers that will be the focus of our study in this chapter and the next.

First, Jesus teaches that wisdom is found in the context of a relationship with him—the hearers' response to his words. These are not the words of a fellow mortal. They are the words of the living God. We cannot have a take-it-or-leave-it attitude about anything God says without significantly affecting our relationship with him.

Second, this passage teaches which responses to Jesus's words will make us wise. Jesus clearly defined two: hearing and doing. We will see later how these two responses must become habitual practices in order for our hearts to remain fertile soil for truth. They are the primary disciplines of wisdom and thus of a Christlike, renewed mind.

Third, Jesus made it clear that whether we respond by hearing and doing determines the usefulness of our lives to God. Foolish people who ignore his words will come to a predictable end: instability and uselessness. A house that cannot withstand the pressures of a storm is useless as a shelter. In the same way, those who are unstable and inconsistent are useless as servants of God. Conversely, believers who faithfully hear and do Jesus's words will have the stability of life to be useful to their Master, just as a solidly built house is useful to the owner.

Jesus's closing remarks to the Sermon on the Mount concisely and powerfully state the nonnegotiable, bottom-line requirements for acquiring wisdom—the mind of Christ. They are not at all like the lengthy and contradictory teachings of the religious leaders of Jesus's day. Imagine how his audience of ordinary people must have felt after hearing his words. Now anyone—young, old, blind, poor, unlearned, man or woman alike—would be wise. No wonder "the common people heard him gladly" (Mark 12:37 KJV). Jesus's simple requirements should put hope in our heart as well. We too can be wise.

What Is Wisdom?

Before we look at the actual disciplines of wisdom—hearing and doing—we need to have a good idea of what wisdom is. We especially want to avoid some misconceptions about it.

The View from the Helicopter

Some people have the idea that to possess wisdom is to have some kind of bird's-eye view of all that God is doing in the world—and particularly in their own lives. They think of wisdom as the view of the rush-hour traffic snarl from the traffic helicopter. From that vantage point the pilot and news broadcaster can view the whole area and see the exact cause and effect of every automobile's activity. These people think that, with wisdom, life should be equally understandable. It is not uncommon for people who believe that wisdom is a helicopter view to become quite discouraged when they come to a crisis and cannot see the whole picture.[1]

Carolyn was distraught when complications developed during her infant son's surgery to correct a birth defect. Her anxiety went beyond the normal motherly love and concern for her baby. She began to question her own walk with God. She was known in her circle of friends as a spiritually minded woman and seemed to know how to interpret the circumstances of life to know what God was doing. She said, "I could see how God was using my own illness last year to teach me more of his love and care, but I can't see any good that will come out of this for little Timmy. What is he going to learn? He's only eight months old. And why would God do something to Timmy to teach me anything? It seems that God should be doing something to *me*—not my son—if he wants to teach me something."

We can all understand Carolyn's concern for her son's welfare and perhaps even identify with her questions. Part of Carolyn's struggle, however, is a result of her faulty view of wisdom and godliness. She truly

1. The two descriptions of wisdom (helicopter here and dashboard in the next section) are adapted from concepts suggested by J. I. Packer in *Knowing God* (Downers Grove, IL: InterVarsity Press, 1973), 91–93.

believes that if she is walking with God she will understand the whys and wherefores of everything that happens in her life. If she cannot figure out how "all things work together for good" (Rom. 8:28) in her life, she feels that somehow she has disqualified herself from God's inner circle where he shares all the secrets of his providence.

A quick survey of the Scriptures will reveal, however, that most of God's saints never knew much of his plan at all. That was the case with Abraham, who was told to leave home and just follow God. It was the experience of Joseph, Daniel, Job, and hosts of others as well. Very seldom did they have a big picture of God's providence. Wisdom, then, is not the view of the road from the helicopter *above* the traffic snarl.

The View from the Dashboard

A more fitting illustration of wisdom is to view it as the skill exercised by the drivers who are caught in the middle of the traffic snarl. They must know the next right response when someone slams on the brakes in front of them or cuts them off unexpectedly or when a child in the back seat lets out a bloodcurdling scream. Their responses to dilemmas like these reveal their real skill (wisdom) as drivers. They do not have to know why their car blew a tire at that time, but they need to know how to skillfully get their disabled vehicle off to the side of the road without injury to people or property. They do not have to know why the lane ahead of them is barricaded, but they must know how to skillfully merge with the cars in the lane next to them.

In Genesis 39, Joseph did not know why he had to spend time in prison on a trumped-up charge of attempted rape, but he knew and practiced responses that kept him usable to God anyway. The patriarch Job never knew why all his children and properties were wiped out in God's providence, but he knew and practiced responses that kept him usable to God anyway. The apostle Paul never knew why God refused to remove his "thorn . . . in the flesh" (2 Cor. 12:7), but he knew and practiced responses that kept him usable to God anyway. The important lesson here is that wisdom is not having God's perspective of the whole matter before us, but having God's perspective about what next response will honor him while keeping us still usable to him.

The goal of safe driving is to stay on the road in order to reach the destination. Skillful drivers know how to do that in most of the conditions that may confront them. Similarly, the goal of the Christian life is to stay on the path of usefulness to God no matter what the circumstances. Christians who are thrown off the road of usefulness by indulgences in their own flesh or by ungodly reactions to calamity or to the fleshly actions of others are not living wisely.

Incidentally, parenting, as well as any other discipleship effort, is essentially this kind of spiritual driver's training—teaching and training that prepare children to stay on the path of usefulness to Christ no matter what comes from without or within. The goal is not to rear "good kids" or have students who are excelling academically. The goal is to equip these young saints "for the work of ministry" (Eph. 4:12) to help them to stay on the road of usefulness. If, in the end, they are unusable to Christ— they are not handling life wisely—both we and they have failed.

A Day of Judgment Is Coming

We must not forget how critical this matter of *usefulness* is to God. Many Christians today have the idea that they will appear at the judgment seat of Christ to be judged for their sin. That is not the case. All our sin—past, present, and future—was judged at Calvary. The total payment was made and the wrath of God was propitiated by Christ's atonement.

The judgment seat of Christ will be an examination of our usefulness, or fruitfulness, for God. Our works—not our sin—will be exposed as either "good or bad" (2 Cor. 5:10 KJV). The word *bad* in this verse does not mean ethically *evil*—our evil has been punished at the cross. It means "useless" or "good for nothing" in the practical advancement of Christ's kingdom. Since Jesus fully paid our sin debt and bought us for himself, he is entitled to a full measure of usefulness from us. That is why we are called his servants.

The whole point of our Lord's teaching about abiding in the vine in John 15 is that he is interested in our fruit-bearing ability. He said, "You did not choose me, but I chose you . . . *that you should go and bear fruit and that your fruit should abide*" (v. 16). He is speaking here of the fruit of our service (converts) and of our sanctification (Christlike character). In the Sermon on the Mount, he expresses his plan that we be the "salt of the earth" (Matt. 5:13). He warned that if we lose our "taste"—our saltiness—we are "good for nothing" (v. 13) as far as use to his kingdom is concerned. He further states that we are to be the "light of the world" (v. 14), but that we will be useless unless the light can be seen. It does no good to be hidden. Believers who are out of fellowship with God because of unconfessed sin in their lives are contributing to the darkness around them. Their lives have no redemptive influence. Since they are not working "with" the Lord in his purposes, Jesus said they are actually "against me" (Matt. 12:30). Our Lord is serious about our usefulness to him.

Believers who practice already-paid-for-sin disqualify themselves from usefulness because they are grieving the Spirit of God, who must empower them for service. They will be held accountable for that good-for-nothing condition—not for the sin that disqualified them from that usefulness. That sin was judged fully and forever at the cross.[2] Walking in wisdom, as the Bible defines it, is the only way for us to be useful to God. It is the only way we avoid "shrink[ing] from him in shame at his coming" (1 John 2:28) when we shall stand before him to give an account of our usefulness.

The Path to Wisdom

As we have seen, Jesus set forth the twin disciplines of hearing and doing as foundational to the acquisition of wisdom. His statement at the end of the Sermon on the Mount is not the only passage where God links these two disciplines together. Consider carefully the following passages:

> The king of Assyria carried the Israelites away to Assyria . . . because they did not obey the voice of the Lord their God but transgressed his covenant, even all that Moses the servant of the Lord commanded. They neither *listened* nor *obeyed*. (2 Kings 18:11, 12)

> And they come to you as people come, and they sit before you as my people, and they *hear* what you say but they will not *do* it; for with lustful talk in their mouths they act; their heart is set on their gain. And behold, you are to them like one who sings lustful songs with a beautiful voice and plays well on an instrument, for they *hear* what you say, but they will not *do* it. (Ezek. 33:31–32)

2. For teaching about the judgment seat of Christ see Romans 14:12; 1 Corinthians 3:13–15; 2 Corinthians 5:10; and 1 John 2:28; 4:17.

> But [Jesus] answered them, "My mother and my brothers are those who *hear* the word of God and *do* it." (Luke 8:21)

> But be *doers* of the word, and not *hearers* only, deceiving yourselves. For if anyone is a *hearer* of the word and not a *doer,* he is like a man who looks intently at his natural face in a mirror . . . and goes away and at once forgets what he was like. But the one who looks into the perfect law, the law of liberty, and perseveres, being no *hearer* who forgets but a *doer* who acts, he will be blessed in his doing. (James 1:22–25)

God's concern is that his people often fail to *hear* his words, or they hear but fail to *do* them. This twofold responsibility is the foundation for usefulness in God's plan for us.

Study carefully the chart below so that you can see where our study in wisdom is headed. Make sure the map is clear in your mind before we start the journey. We divide each of the two master disciplines of hearing and doing into two more basic disciplines so that we can look at them more closely. We call these components of wisdom disciplines to underscore the need for them to become habitual responses of life. They are developed on purpose and with diligent practice. They are developed in submission to God with a dependence on God to carry them out. We call hearing and doing master disciplines in order to show their higher order in relationship to their basic components (attention, meditation, and so on). The rest of this chapter will be spent discussing the master discipline of hearing. Chapter 9 will cover the master discipline of doing. Now that you know where we are headed, study the chart carefully, and let's get started.

The Goal: Wisdom (The Mind of Christ)				
The Master Disciplines	Hearing		Doing	
The Basic Disciplines	*Attention*: Choosing to listen to God	*Meditation*: Choosing to think like God	*Obedience*: Choosing to obey God	*Endurance*: Choosing to persevere for God

The Master Discipline of Hearing

One of the first parables our Lord tells focuses on the importance of hearing. In Luke 8:4–15, he sets forth what has been called "the parable of the sower" or, more accurately, "the parable of the soil." He tells how a farmer who spreads seed on the ground can expect various results depending on the condition of the soil. Only one kind of soil is truly productive and bears fruit. Each soil represents a different kind of hearer.

Indifferent Hearers

The soil "along the path" (v. 5) refers to the footpath that borders the field. It is packed hard because of constant traffic and frequent rains, and the seed is left exposed to wild birds that quickly devour it. The hearts of such hearers are totally unreceptive to truth—indifferent. It bears no fruit and is useless to the farmer.

Impulsive Hearers

The soil in this part of the field is shallow because of underlying bedrock. The heat of the sun quickly bakes the seed, and it does not bring forth any fruit. The hearts described here are emotional and insincere. These hearers do not count the cost of receiving the Word and are unwilling to pay the price. Initially they seem to be open and receptive, but the tests of life reveal that no seed has really taken root. Their reaction often is, "All that sounds good to me, but not if I have to . . ." An underlying bedrock of stubbornness keeps God's Word from deeply penetrating the soil of their hearts. This ground too is basically useless to the farmer because it bears no lasting fruit.

Infested Hearers

Fruit does not grow well in the third soil because it is infested with weeds that crowd out the seed. Such hearers seem receptive to the Word but are unwilling to weed out the distractions that consume their lives—anxieties, riches, pleasures. Like the previous type of soil, this soil is almost useless to the farmer because its yield is almost nonexistent.

Ideal Hearers

The good soil receives the seed and produces "a hundredfold" (v. 8). It is the heart that hears the Word and keeps it. Jesus said it is "honest" (truthful with itself) and "good" (v. 15). *Good* here does not mean morally good but means "free from defects." It is a heart that has not let anything crowd out or hinder the growth of the seed of the Word. Such hearers are the Marys who sit at Jesus's feet, the Corneliuses who wish to "hear all . . . commanded by the Lord" (Acts 10:33), and the Bereans who "received the word with all eagerness, examining the Scriptures daily" (Acts 17:11). This kind of soil keeps the Word. This heart goes to whatever extent necessary to nurture the seed to fruit-bearing maturity. This kind of soil is truly useful to the farmer.

In this parable, Jesus admonishes his audience, "He who has ears to *hear*, let him *hear*" (Luke 8:8). A few verses later, he says, "Take care then how you *hear*" (v. 18). Notice that he places the main responsibility for fruitfulness on the condition of the soil. The sower, here speaking of Christ, always does his part.[3] The seed is always of highest quality. The only deciding factor is the soil—the human heart.

What does it mean, therefore, to hear?

The Basic Discipline of Attention

In Scripture, the word *hearing* describes a high quality of attention and retention. Biblically, hearing means first of all choosing to listen to God. As we said earlier, wisdom is found in context of a relationship with Christ. His words are not the words of a fellow mortal. They cannot be ignored or disobeyed without seriously changing our relationship with the speaker. It is fitting that the book of Proverbs should open with the statement "Let the wise hear" (1:5).

Spiritual Junk Mail?

Imagine that you have received an oversized envelope in the mail soliciting your subscription to a national news magazine. You open the envelope, briefly scan the offer, and throw the whole thing into the trash can. As far as you are concerned, your actions are appropriate because you have decided you do not need that subscription. You do not for a moment imagine that four weeks later an executive in the magazine's

3. While Christ is here referring to himself as the sower, he commissioned all believers to be his agents in spreading the truth of the gospel to every creature (Matt. 28:19–20).

publishing headquarters will be distraught as he ponders, "I sent one of our packets to [your name], and an entire month has gone by without a response. I wonder what I did wrong. Did I offend him in some way? Why would he ignore me this way? Why doesn't he respond?"

The scene, of course, is ludicrous. We don't expect any publishing executive to be upset over our failure to reply. There is no personal relationship involved. The scenario is entirely different, however, if the piece of mail we received four weeks ago was from a parent or from a grandparent. Ignoring *their* letters will certainly have an effect on the relationship.

By now I'm sure you see the application to our walk with God. Too often we hear the words of our God and ignore them. We don't respond in any particular way to him, and then we wonder why there seems to be so much distance between us and God. The answer is simple: his words to us demand and deserve an appropriate response. His words cannot be ignored or discarded as if they were a piece of junk mail.

The Christian life is not merely about maintaining biblical rules but about maintaining a relationship with God. Jesus said, "Everyone then who hears these words of mine" can be wise (Matt. 7:24). Godliness is not the result of responding to biblical principles but the result of responding to a person. That is why Solomon says, "The fear of the *Lord* is the beginning [the choicest part, the foundation] of wisdom" (Prov. 9:10). Those who are not in their proper place of reverence for and submission to God cannot be wise. They can listen only to their own sinful hearts or to the sinful hearts of others and will become greater fools.[4]

Adam was not created autonomous. He was designed to listen to someone for direction in life. That direction was to come from God as Adam fellowshipped with him in the garden. When he stopped listening to God and listened to the serpent, the sinful desires of the serpent's own nature were implanted within him, furnishing him with a constant flow of information antagonistic to God.

This is not a new theme to us since we have studied the sinful bent of the human heart in part 1 of this book, but it has important

4. For a more thorough study of the fool as he is described in the book of Proverbs, see "Fools by Default" in appendix B.

implications for us here. If we are to move out of the foolishness of our own hearts and develop renewed minds, we must make it a habit of life, a discipline, to listen to God rather than to our own hearts. Notice how often Proverbs directs the attention of learners to our God and to our elders—whatever spiritual leaders God has placed over us.

> Hear, my son, your *father's* instruction,
> and forsake not your *mother's* teaching. (1:8)
>
> *Wisdom* [Christ himself] cries aloud. . . .
> . . . .
> "Turn at my reproof." (1:20, 23)
>
> My son, . . . receive *my* words,
> and treasure up *my* commandments with you. (2:1)
>
> For the *Lord* gives wisdom;
> from his mouth come knowledge and understanding. (2:6)
>
> *He* [God] stores up sound wisdom for the upright. (2:7)
>
> My son, do not forget *my* teaching. (3:1)
>
> Trust in the *Lord*. (3:5)
>
> Be not wise in your own eyes;
> fear the Lord. (3:7)
>
> Hear, O sons, a *father's* instruction. (4:1)
>
> Hear, my son, and accept *my* words. (4:10)
>
> My son, be attentive to *my* words;
> incline your ear to *my* sayings. (4:20)
>
> My son, be attentive to *my* wisdom;
> incline your ear to *my* understanding. (5:1)

My son, keep your *father's* commandment,
and forsake not your *mother's* teaching. (6:20)

My son, keep *my* words
and treasure up *my* commandments with you. (7:1)

And now, O sons, listen to *me*,
and be attentive to the words of *my* mouth. (7:24)

Does not *wisdom* [Christ himself] call?

. . . .

"Hear, for I will speak noble things." (8:1, 6)

Wisdom has built her house.

. . . .

"Come, eat of *my* bread.

. . . .

Leave your simple ways." (9:1, 5, 6)

The list could go on, but I think you get the point. Never in Proverbs is a man advised to listen to his own heart or to the heart of his peers. He is warned not to listen to seductive women, to crowds and mobs, to companions bent on destruction or waste, or to evil men. He is exhorted often to listen to his God and to his elders. Understand then that the cornerstone of wisdom is a dependent and submissive heart that shows itself by giving its attention to God and to spiritual leaders—primarily our godly parents and our pastors.

The Basic Discipline of Meditation

In addition to calling us to listen to God, Proverbs exhorts believers to retain the words of God and of their elders. The goal is to think like God. We are to make these words a permanent part of our lives so that they actually direct our steps, preserve us from evil, and make our lives fruitful. Notice Solomon's exhortation toward this end.

Forsake not your mother's teaching. (1:8; see also 4:2, 6)

> *Inclin[e]* your heart to understanding. (2:2)
>
> My son, do not *forget* my teaching. (3:1; see also 4:5)
>
> *Let not steadfast love and faithfulness forsake you;*
> bind them around your neck;
> write them on the tablet of your heart. (3:3)
>
> My son, *do not lose sight of these—*
> *keep* sound wisdom and discretion. (3:21)
>
> Let your heart *hold fast* my words. (4:4)
>
> *Keep hold* of instruction. (4:13)
>
> *Let them not escape* from your sight;
> *keep* them within your heart. (4:21)
>
> *Bind* them on your heart always;
> *tie* them around your neck. (6:21)
>
> My son, *keep* my words
> and *treasure up* my commandments with you. (7:1)
>
> *Bind* them on your fingers;
> *write* them on the tablet of your heart. (7:3)

Again, the list could go on and on. These words from God must become so much a part of us that we do not forget them in the day-to-day activities of life. They can then dictate the next right responses we must make to life's challenges.

Some Things You Just Don't Forget

Many believers become concerned at this point and protest that they have bad memories. I would assert, however, that they can remember anything that is important enough to them if they have rehearsed it enough times or if a relationship is important enough to them. Suppose that a man discovers that the woman he is dating is allergic to daisies. That bit of information about her nature becomes a governing principle for him. It dictates his actions toward her. If he wishes to show her his affection through a gift of flowers, he will not do so with a bouquet of daisies. If he truly cares about protecting her, and if he values his relationship with her, he will always remember to bring her something other than daisies.

If I can say it reverently, God is allergic to some things too. His Word teaches us what he loves and what he hates—his laws and words reflect his nature. In order not to violate his relationship with God, David was intent on knowing what God had said. In these familiar verses from Psalm 119:4–16, which is traditionally attributed to David, notice the psalmist's concern for the personal relationship he had with God.

> *You* have commanded *your* precepts
>   to be kept diligently.
> Oh that my ways may be steadfast
>   in keeping *your* statutes!
> Then I shall not be put to shame,
>   having my eyes fixed on all *your* commandments.
> I will praise *you* with an upright heart,
>   when I learn *your* righteous rules.
> I will keep *your* statutes;
>   do not utterly forsake me!
>
> How can a young man keep his way pure?
>   By guarding it according to *your* word.
> With my whole heart I seek *you*;
>   let me not wander from *your* commandments!
> I have stored up *your* word in my heart,
>   that I might not sin against *you*.
> Blessed are *you*, O Lord;
>   teach me *your* statutes!
> With my lips I declare
>   all the rules of *your* mouth.
> In the way of *your* testimonies I delight
>   as much as in all riches.
> I will meditate on your precepts

and fix my eyes on *your* ways.
I will delight in *your* statutes;
I will not forget *your* word.

Much of our motivation to remember the words of God is tied to the kind of relationship we have with him. If we view his words like the words of our state's highway department printed in a motor vehicle manual, we may have a difficult time being motivated to remember them. If, however, we view the words of God as the self-revelation of one we love, our motivation to know and keep them increases dramatically. We want to know how the one we love thinks so that we can become like-minded with him.

We cannot soon forget the words of one in whom we take delight. If our relationship with God drives our desire to know his words, their mastery will be neither tedious nor burdensome. Without this relationship, however, the knowledge of the Word becomes merely an academic pursuit or an exercise in duty-driven self-discipline.

How to Remember Not to Forget

James tells us that when trouble comes we are to be "quick to hear, slow to speak, slow to anger" (1:19). It is so easy when pressures mount for us to be quick to speak, quick to blow off steam, and very slow to listen to God. Peter, James's copastor of the church in Jerusalem, had similar words for this congregation. He told them that in times of trial they must be diligent in "preparing [their] minds for action" (1 Peter 1:13). Pressured times are not the times to give in to sloppy thinking. Yet those are the times when it is especially easy to forget what kind of next right response keeps us usable to Christ during the trial.

After admonishing us to be "swift to hear," James outlines for us the procedures to master the Word, or rather, to let it master us.

> Therefore put away all filthiness and rampant wickedness and receive with meekness the implanted word, which is able to save your souls.
>
> But be doers of the word, and not hearers only, deceiving yourselves. For if anyone is a hearer of the word and not a doer, he is like a man who looks intently at his natural face in a mirror. For he looks at himself and goes away and at once forgets what he was like. But the

> one who looks into the perfect law, the law of liberty, and perseveres, being no hearer who forgets but a doer who acts, he will be blessed in his doing. (1:21–25)

The last verse in this passage tells us how to avoid being a "hearer who forgets." It says we are to look "into the perfect law, the law of liberty" (v. 25), which refers to the Word itself. It is the liberating "truth [that] will set you free" (John 8:32).

The word *looks* is the operative word in James 1:25. The Greek, *parakupto,* means "to bend over (to see something better)."[5] If you have ever been around someone who has lost a contact lens on the carpet, you can understand the force of this word. There your friend is, on all fours, his eyeballs only inches from the floor scanning the carpet. He is *peering intently* at the carpet, systematically covering a section at a time, trying to catch a glimpse of his lens. He is careful to ward off others who would come near the search site lest they step on his contact. He has one goal—find the contact! This is no casual, haphazard glance at the floor from a standing position. This word communicates the kind of single-minded, systematic search for something valuable that has us bending over in order to see better.

This illustrates as well the force of Proverbs 2, where we learn the normal means of getting wisdom. Proverbs 2:2–6 says,

> Making your ear attentive to wisdom
> and inclining your heart to understanding;
> yes, if you call out for insight
> and raise your voice for understanding,
> if you seek it like silver
> and search for it as for hidden treasures,
> then you will understand the fear of the LORD
> and find the knowledge of God.
> For the LORD gives wisdom;
> from his mouth come knowledge and understanding.

5. Walter Bauer, William Arndt, and Wilbur Gingrich, *A Greek-English Lexicon of the New Testament and Other Early Christian Literature* (Chicago: University of Chicago Press, 1979), 624.

Notice again the intensity and the single-mindedness of this search. This is what is involved in biblical meditation.

Single-Minded Meditation

Meditation is not hard to understand. Anyone who knows how to worry knows how to meditate. Worriers take one thought—"I just know I'll never get married," "I'm afraid my husband will leave me," "We don't have any money left"—and look single-mindedly at that thought from every possible angle, examining every possible personal implication and application of that thought. Worriers are skilled in the meditation process but are meditating on the wrong kind of thoughts.

Biblical meditation involves the same process, but the reflective thought must be on the truth from God and not on a lie from our own hearts or from Satan. We must start with truth revealed to us from the Word and then examine it from every possible angle, asking God to show us its implications and applications for us and our relationship with him. We will "bend over to see it better."

This kind of reflection does not necessarily follow the same pattern for every believer. For some, that means looking up the verses in commentaries or studying the individual words in Bible dictionaries or word studies. It may mean looking up cross-references to other passages in the Scripture that shed more light on the passage being studied. For those who know Greek or Hebrew, it means examining the words in their original languages.

Above all, it means participating in an ongoing interaction with God himself, asking him to reveal to us the truth he wants us to know and practice so that our fellowship with him can increase and our fruitfulness for him can grow.

God will most often respond to us first by convicting us of unconfessed sin. Psalm 119:130 says, "The unfolding of [his] words gives light," and the light will expose our sin. Notice the sequence in Proverbs 1:23: "If you turn at my reproof, behold, I will pour out my spirit to you; I will make my words known to you." Remember, the aim of our meditation is to help us to behold our God and think like him so that we can know and therefore "do what pleases him" (1 John 3:22). The barriers that hinder our fellowship with him must be removed before he reveals his words.

Continual Meditation

The passage in James 1:25 that exhorts us to look into the "perfect law, the law of liberty" says we are to continue in it. How long do we continue peering intently into the Word? A clue to the twofold answer is found in the next phrase: each one of us is not to be a "hearer who forgets but a doer who acts." We are to continue as long as it takes to make sure we do not forget what we have heard.

This often means meditating on the same passage—studying and reflecting on it—for several weeks. That doesn't mean we can't read other passages or keep up with a through-the-Bible-in-a-year schedule, but it does mean that our focused attention must continually come back to the passage at hand until it becomes a permanent part of our thinking.

That is not as impossible as it seems. The Holy Spirit wants to teach the Word to us. In addition, the constant repetition and concentration of the meditation process firmly entrenches God's words in our hearts.

The second indicator of the thoroughness of our meditation is when we actually become doers who act. We are to continue our meditation as long as it takes to actually begin to show a difference in our lifestyle and practice. Here is how Paul describes it in 1 Timothy 4:15–16:

> Practice these things, immerse yourself in them, *so that all may see your progress*. Keep a close watch on yourself and on the teaching. Persist in this, for by so doing you will save both yourself and your hearers.

The Fruit of Meditation

Psalm 1 testifies of the fruitfulness and stability that meditation will produce in the life of a believer who continually reflects on God's Word.

> Blessed is the man
>   who walks not in the counsel of the wicked,
> nor stands in the way of sinners,
>   nor sits in the seat of scoffers;
> but his delight is in the law of the LORD,
>   and on his law he meditates day and night.
>
> He is like a tree
>   planted by streams of water

> that yields its fruit in its season,
> and its leaf does not wither.
> In all that he does, he prospers. (Ps. 1:1–3)

This, then, is the first discipline of wisdom—hearing the Word of God. We must choose to listen to God instead of our own hearts or others who listen to their own hearts. In addition, we must choose to think like God. The time we spend in reflection will yield a lasting like-mindedness with God that increases our affection for him and controls our decisions. We will know the next right response in any given circumstance because we are beginning to have a renewed mind—the mind of Christ.

Take Time to Reflect

Ask yourself whether you have developed the habit of hearing in the attentive, biblical sense. The most searching tests of your willingness to learn are threefold. Do you have a regular time of Bible reading, meditation, and prayer? Do you regularly attend a Bible-preaching church? Do you willingly receive instruction and correction from the spiritual leaders in your life? Proverbs depicts the fool as one who will not listen to God, to rebuke, or to reason. Be brutally honest with yourself on this point. Do you listen on purpose to God and to the elders in your life?

Now ask yourself whether you have developed the habit of remembering what you are told. Wise people figure out ways to make sure they do not forget what is important. The sluggard in Proverbs offers many reasons why he does not have the time, opportunity, or inclination to work his field so that his crop will grow. He comes to spiritual poverty while the wise man flourishes (see Prov. 24:30–34).

Earlier in this chapter you were exposed to a brief portion of Psalm 119 with the second-person personal pronouns (*you, yours*) italicized. If you emphasized the italicized words as you read the passage, you saw that the psalmist took his relationship with God very seriously. Psalm 119 is the lengthiest chapter in the Bible, but it is also the most instructive about the kind of attitude we should have toward the words of our God.

Take a pen, colored pencil, or highlighter (or use the tools on an electronic device) and shade or underline the second-person personal pronouns for the entirety of Psalm 119. Once you have done this, read the passage reflectively and audibly (if possible) as a prayer to God, affirming your desire to hear and heed his words.

Another project that will reinforce your need to hear God's Word in order to be wise is to go through the book of Proverbs and mark or underline the words *wise* and *wisdom*. Study the context of each occurrence to see the benefits of wisdom and to learn the process of acquiring it.

Finally, to further reinforce the truths you have studied in this book so far, go back and reflect on the "Take Time to Reflect" section at the end of each chapter. Systematic and purposeful review will help to solidify in your mind the truths you have studied. Wisdom does not come when you merely desire it. It takes diligent effort to know God and his ways. Note the warning in Proverbs 13:4: "The soul of the sluggard craves and gets nothing, while the soul of the diligent is richly supplied."

A Word to Disciple Makers

You Are Being Watched

When it comes to learning how to hear the Word of God, you are perhaps the most powerful influence on those you are discipling. Do those who follow you see that you are serious about listening to God? Do they see your regular church attendance? Do they ever see you taking notes during sermons, see you studying the Bible on your own so that you actually think like God, or hear you talking about what you learned from God? When you try to help them to solve a problem, is it obvious that you have scriptural foundations for your advice, or are you just giving them your own ideas? Do your own attendance and participation at church reveal a genuine desire to listen to God and think like him?

Many children reach their teen years without ever being trained to pay attention to anyone, let alone God or their elders, nor have they been taught how to reflect on truth in such a way that they are not a "hearer who forgets" (James 1:25). Without these basic disciplines of hearing, they cannot be wise. It is never too late to start discipling someone in these disciplines, but like any parental training—and discipleship is spiritual parenting—the process will be greatly accelerated if the disciple maker holds the trainee accountable and practices what he or she preaches.

Godly habits of the heart are developed by a combination of example, exhortation, rebuke, and explanation. All these teaching tools are found in the book of Proverbs, and every disciple maker should become proficient in their use.

9

WALKING IN WISDOM

But be doers of the word, and not hearers only, deceiving yourselves. (James 1:22)

The Master Discipline of Doing

In the last chapter, we looked at *hearing*, the first master discipline of wisdom. We learned that hearing consists of the two basic disciplines of attention and meditation. We also saw that Jesus taught in his Sermon on the Mount that *doing* is the second master discipline of those who would be wise. We divided doing into two basic disciplines of obedience and endurance. These are the subjects of our study in this chapter.

Doing versus Being

Though I will say much in this chapter about doing, I want to be sure you understand that Christianity is not made up of just the things we do or do not do. Please don't misunderstand this issue. It should be clear by now that Christianity is essentially a relationship with God, not a system of rules. At the same time, it should be clear that every relationship produces its own rules. We saw that illustrated in the last chapter with the rule "Thou shalt not bring her daisies." Every relationship generates laws that are consistent with the nature of the person we are relating to.

As we saw in chapter 1, sanctification is a cooperative venture between God and us. That is not a human idea and does not in any way detract from God's sovereignty. God set it up that way. We need to get it straight, then, that God himself has determined that those who will be like his Son, and therefore wise, will be doing certain things.

The Key Player

We must remember that we cannot do any hearing unless the Holy Spirit teaches us God's Word as we are bending over, peering intently at it. We see this in 1 Corinthians 2:9–16. The Holy Spirit is the one who illuminates our minds.

Just as the Holy Spirit is the key player in the hearing aspect of gaining the Christlike wisdom of a renewed mind, he is also central to the doing aspect. Our flesh, as we have seen, often begs us to obey its desires. Galatians 5:16–17 captures the nature of that battle:

> But I say, walk by the Spirit, and you will not gratify the desires of the flesh. For the desires of the flesh are against the Spirit, and the desires of the Spirit are against the flesh, for these are opposed to each other, to keep you from doing the things you want to do.

Paul and other biblical writers speak much of doing, but doing is to be a response of obedience to God the Holy Spirit and is to be energized by him. We call this obedience to the Holy Spirit, walking in the Spirit, or being controlled by the Holy Spirit.

We must have a fuller understanding of the Holy Spirit's role in our lives if we are to understand the kind of doing Jesus is calling for in Matthew 7:24–27. There is much confusion today about the Holy Spirit's ministry in our lives.

From the moment of salvation, the Holy Spirit is God's resident agent who personally handles every transaction that goes on between us and God. His continuous presence gives believers the opportunity to fellowship with God at all times. His presence within us is also the permanent seal (mark of ownership) that we are indeed God's children (see Eph. 1:13; 4:30). In addition, his presence within us is the guarantee (down payment) that assures us that God will bring us to the total likeness of Christ when we finally stand in his presence in heaven (see 2 Cor. 1:22; 5:5; Eph. 1:14).

From that base of operation within us, the Holy Spirit convicts us of sin that would hinder our fellowship with the Father (see Gal. 5:17; 1 Thess. 4:7–8). He teaches us more of Christ so that our fellowship with him is enriched, and he assists us in our work for Christ—he is our "Helper" (John 14:26; 15:26). How blessed we are to have within us

God's personal agent who serves as arresting officer, private tutor, and personal assistant or helper in order to carry out his mission of establishing and maintaining our fellowship with God!

There is much more to his work, however. The Holy Spirit's permanent presence not only allows us to continually fellowship with God as we respond to his conviction and heed his teaching but also empowers us to be what we ought to be (sanctification) and do what we ought to do (serve) when he fills us. Just as my grandfather needed the power of the Cat to do his work in the fields, so every believer needs the power of the Spirit to do the work of God and to reflect his nature. Since these cannot be done by us on our own, every Christian needs to understand and practice what it means to be controlled by or filled with the Spirit.

Controlled by the Spirit

The *indwelling* of the Spirit, which is the birthright of every believer, should not be confused with the *control* of the Spirit, which is conditional. All believers have the Spirit's presence in their lives, but not every believer has the Spirit's power.

One of the New Testament expressions of the Holy Spirit's empowering work is found in Ephesians 5:18, which says, "Do not get drunk with wine, for that is debauchery, but be filled with the Spirit." The word *filled* here is not speaking of possessing a certain quantity of the Spirit as we might speak of a glass filled with water. It expresses, rather, the idea of control, as when we speak of people being filled with rage. By that phrase, we mean that anger is such a dominant part of their lives that they are controlled by it. We might speak of people as being filled with fear or filled with lust in the same way. These people are so consumed by their fear or lust that their behavior is noticeably affected.

Paul compares being filled with the Spirit to being drunk with wine. People who are filled with wine to the extent of drunkenness behave differently when they are under the influence of the wine than when they are sober. Alcohol affects every part of a drunkard's life, but in a destructive way. That is why Paul says the effect of drunkenness is "debauchery" (literally *wastefulness*).

Christians who are under the control of the Holy Spirit are also transformed, but in a useful way. They too come under the influence—the controlling influence of the Holy Spirit. It transforms them so that they walk differently. The Bible says that God "works in you, both to will and to work for his good pleasure" (Phil. 2:13). Notice this is a work *in* you, not *of* you. That means it is something the Holy Spirit does.

Notice also that the Holy Spirit does two things in us. First, he creates within us a will—a desire—to do what pleases him. If you have any desire to please God, if you have any desire to do what is right, God's Spirit put that desire there. We have already learned that left to ourselves "no one understands; no one seeks for God" (Rom. 3:11). He *wants* us to please God, and he wants us to *want* to do so as well.

Second, we see that he creates in us an ability to do God's good pleasure. You can be assured that if he puts a desire in you to please God, he is doing so because he expects to enable you to do just that. He doesn't create a desire in us to please him in a way that can't be accomplished. The Greek word for *do* in this verse is the word from which we get the word *energy*. He gives us the divine energy—the power—to please God.

Amazing Grace

This divine help in creating a desire and giving us power to please God is called *grace*. It is his undeserved help to accomplish what pleases him. And what's more, he is willing to give us all the grace—the divine help—we need to do whatever he requires.

Look at Paul's encouraging words in 2 Corinthians 9:8: "God is able to make all grace abound to you, so that having all sufficiency in all things at all times, you may abound in every good work." This is a powerful promise. He will always give us everything we need to do whatever he asks us to do. What battle are you facing with your flesh right now? What habit are you struggling with? What bitterness or anger stays unresolved in your heart? God promises to always give you everything you need to do whatever it is that pleases him in that situation. With his help you can always make the next right response. His grace is mediated to us by his Spirit as we say no to the flesh and say yes to God. Here's how Peter puts it: "God opposes the proud [the one insisting on his own way] but he gives grace [divine assistance] to the humble [the one submitting to God's way]" (1 Peter 5:5).

As long as we are insisting that we have our own way, we can expect God to resist us. When we get in our place as submissive creatures, however, he immediately gives us sufficient grace so that we can always make the next right response of obedience.

The Basic Discipline of Obedience

Let's see how this relationship of obedience to the Spirit of God works out in a real-life situation. Let's suppose that your Christian friend Amelia has been convicted by God from his Word that she must stop lying. It must be put off or laid aside. She realizes that she is especially susceptible to lying when her image before others is at stake.

Suppose Amelia says to herself, "I must stop this bad habit of lying. It always gets me into more trouble than it's worth. I may look better at first, but it seems I always get found out, and I end up looking like a real idiot. Therefore, I must remember not to lie when I am tempted to do so."

Here Amelia is trying to stop lying for the same selfish reason she started lying. Her motive for now telling the truth is as self-centered as her motive for lying in the first place, because her primary concern is still her image. She will not be successful long. In the end she will always choose to do what advances her own cause the most. She will no doubt become discouraged when she can't seem to give up her bad habit.

Your friend Amelia cannot lie without showing enormous disrespect for the very nature of God. Jesus described himself as "the way, and *the truth*, and the life" in John 14:6. The Holy Spirit is called the "Spirit of *truth*" in John 14:17. By lying, Amelia is not showing any concern about how her behavior will affect God. She is thinking only of what *she* likes. Because of his nature, God is "allergic" to lies. Even more fundamentally offensive to God is the whole mindset that Amelia's way (in any part of life) should take precedence over his way, since he is Amelia's Creator and Redeemer.

God dwells within us in the person of the Holy Spirit. He is personally wronged when his nature is violated. That is why Paul warns us, "Do not grieve the Holy Spirit of God" (Eph. 4:30). His work in us is hindered by our selfishness.

Suppose, however, that Amelia desires to be controlled by the Spirit of God. She knows from the Bible that lying is wrong. She has been convicted by the Holy Spirit when she has lied in the past. She says to herself, "I cannot continue to grieve God in this way. My lying shows that I am more concerned about myself and what I want than about God and what he deserves and dfemands." Amelia might then express her heart's desire to God in a prayer like this:

> Dear God, you are so patient with me. You have watched me lie over and over again, and yet you have not dealt harshly with me for violating your very nature of truth. You have faithfully convicted me by your Holy Spirit. I know I have grieved you by my deception. Forgive me for my selfish concern for my own image. I want to be concerned only about how I portray the image of Christ to others through my life.
>
> I will need the help of your Holy Spirit to renew my mind as I meditate on Ephesians 4:15 and 25 and other passages about your hatred for lying and deception. May he enlighten my heart with an understanding of your ways. Continue to convict me by your Spirit and help me to be sensitive to his conviction. Help me to "speak the truth" at all times no matter what the cost. Help me to be willing to deny everything—including a good image before others—in order *not* to deny you what is rightfully yours: a life that represents you well. Help me to that end. In Jesus's name, amen.

When Amelia comes to God with the kind of heart demonstrated in the prayer above, she will receive divine help—grace—from the Holy Spirit to resist the temptation. The Holy Spirit will, in the process, be helping her become a "truth teller."

The key element shown in Amelia's heart is humility. Notice what David says about God's response to humility in Psalm 34 and in Psalm 51, David's psalm of repentance.

> The Lord is near to the brokenhearted
> and saves the crushed in spirit. (Ps. 34:18)

> For you will not delight in sacrifice, or I would give it;
> you will not be pleased with a burnt offering.
> The sacrifices of God are a broken spirit;
> a broken and contrite heart, O God, you will not despise. (Ps. 51:16–17)

God himself showed his high esteem for such a heart in Isaiah 66:1–2. He said that he is not looking for any dwelling that we can build. After all, heaven itself is his throne, and he rests his feet on the footstool of the earth. How can we impress him with anything we can build? He said, however, that there is one thing that always arrests his attention and causes him to look with interest and offer willing assistance—a person who humbles himself before his God, a person who takes his Word seriously. He put it this way:

> Heaven is my throne,
> and the earth is my footstool;
> what is the house that you would build for me,
> and what is the place of my rest?
> All these things my hand has made,
> and so all these things came to be,
> declares the LORD.
> *But this is the one to whom I will look:*
> *he who is humble and contrite in spirit*
> *and trembles at my word.*

The kind of humility reflected in Amelia's prayer showed itself in three ways. Amelia was repentant—she knew she needed God's forgiveness. She was submissive—she knew she needed to subject herself to God and his ways. She was dependent—she knew she couldn't resist sin effectively without supernatural help from God.

At that moment of repentant, submissive, dependent humility, Amelia received God's attention and assistance. The Holy Spirit was pleased—not grieved. The Spirit of God was also now free to give Amelia the power she needed since he did not need to resist Amelia any longer.

That same expression from Amelia's heart will need to be offered to God many times in the days ahead—and many times during each of those days—for Amelia to see any lasting change in her pattern of lying. Amelia is practicing putting off the ways of the flesh, and as she is hearing and doing what the Holy Spirit says, she is developing the mind of Christ. She is being "renewed in the spirit" of her mind (Eph. 4:23). She is handling life wisely. Her life will demonstrate an increasing stability and fruitfulness for Christ.

Biblical obedience is not just compliance with some abstract law or rule. It is the submissive response to the person of the Holy Spirit, who has revealed the will of God to us through his Word. It means saying yes to God as we say no to self. It means denying self instead of indulging self. It means pleasing God instead of pleasing self. It means walking in the Spirit instead of grieving the Spirit. It is the way of wisdom instead of the way of the fool.

Biblical obedience is more than just commandment-oriented living versus desire- or feeling-oriented living, however. Though commands must be obeyed and feelings may need to be ignored, the issue can be more fundamentally stated as a *flesh versus Spirit* issue. We are either obeying our flesh and pleasing ourselves or obeying the Holy Spirit and pleasing God. A love relationship is at the heart of our obedience. As my friend Ken Collier would say, "We will always please the one we love the most." If we love God the most, we will please him. If we love ourselves the most, we will please ourselves.

Deuteronomy 6:5 commands us to love God "with all [our] heart and with all [our] soul and with all [our] might." Paul emphasizes this kind of wholehearted obedience in Colossians 3:23–24:

> Whatever you do, work heartily, as for the Lord and not for men, knowing that from the Lord you will receive the inheritance as your reward. You are serving the Lord Christ.

In the small Old Testament book of Malachi, God confronted the Israelites about their lack of devotion for him. He said, "A son honors his father, and a servant his master. If then I am a father, where is my honor? And if I am a master, where is my fear?" (Mal. 1:6). The people replied with surprise, "How have we despised your name?" (v. 6). God answered that their less-than-wholehearted devotion to him was evidenced by the quality of sacrificial lambs they were bringing to him each day: "When you offer blind animals in sacrifice, is that not evil? And when you offer those that are lame or sick, is that not evil? Present that to your governor; will he accept you or show you favor? says the Lord of hosts" (v. 8).

The Lord's test here is simple and foundational. We will always reserve the best for the one we love the most, whether it be the biggest piece of cake, the foremost position in line, or the most prominent position on a team. When the Israelites reserved the best lamb in the flock for themselves instead of offering it to God, God challenged them about their lack of love for him. He said in essence, "If you offered to your civic leaders the kind of diseased, crippled gifts you give to me, they would throw you out. You are treating your governors better than you are treating your God!" He then pronounced the coming punishment on those who tried to get by with inferior sacrifices. "Cursed be the cheat who has a male in his flock, and vows it, and yet sacrifices to the Lord what is blemished. For I am a great King, says the LORD of hosts, and my name will be feared among the nations" (v. 14).

Anyone who watched an Israelite lead a crippled lamb to the sacrificial altar had every right to judge the devotion of that Israelite to God. His inferior gift to God meant that he was keeping the best lambs at home for himself. It was a simple test: whoever got his best lamb—himself or God—was the one he loved most. Such is the nature of obedience: it reflects the heart.

The Basic Discipline of Endurance

Endurance is continued obedience to God even under pressure. It is the obedience of the heroes of the faith in Hebrews 11, who continued doing right even though it cost many of them their lives. Endurance is the crowning virtue of character. In fact, when we say others "have character," we are usually referring to their endurance in the midst of hardship.

Our Lord himself demonstrated the sustained obedience that lies at the heart of endurance. We find it described in Philippians 2:5–11.

> Have this mind among yourselves, which is yours in Christ Jesus, who, though he was in the form of God, did not count equality with God a thing to be grasped, but emptied himself, by taking the form of a servant, being born in the likeness of men. And being found in human form, *he humbled himself by becoming obedient to the point of death, even death on a cross.* Therefore God has highly exalted him and bestowed on him the name that is above every name, so that at the name of Jesus

> every knee should bow, in heaven and on earth and under the earth, and every tongue confess that Jesus Christ is Lord, to the glory of God the Father.

We looked at this passage in chapter 1 to discover the Christlike humility that God honors. It is a submission to the Father that demonstrates itself in obedience. The obedience, however, is a specific kind of obedience. It is a "death on a cross" kind of obedience. Jesus essentially said, "I'll die before I disobey my Father."

The kind of endurance that the Father honors is not the stubborn self-will of those who refuse to give in because they believe they are right. It is absolute submission to the one who loves us most. It is our refusal as believers to betray the Father by looking out for ourselves. It is the Christlike mindset that denies everything dear to itself—even life—before it would ever deny the Father.

Notice the relationship that drove Christ's loyal endurance:

> My food is to do the will of *him* who sent me and to accomplish his work. (John 4:34)

> For I have come down from heaven, not to do my own will but the will of *him* who sent me. (John 6:38)

> I always do the things that are pleasing to *him* [the Father]. (John 8:29)

> I honor my *Father*. . . . I do not seek my own glory. (John 8:49, 50)

> We must work the works of *him* who sent me while it is day; night is coming, when no one can work. As long as I am in the world, I am the light of the world. (John 9:4–5)

> I lay down my life. . . . This charge I have received from my *Father*. (John 10:17, 18)

> Now is my soul troubled. And what shall I say? "*Father*, save me from this hour"? But for this purpose I have come to this hour. *Father*, glorify your name. (John 12:27–28)

This same response to the Father is the heart cry of the believers who take up the cross of suffering and follow Christ. In its maturity, this "death on the cross" kind of obedience is driven by something that is much deeper than mere duty. It is motivated by the devotion of believers to their heavenly Father. It is the cry of the Savior to the Father in the messianic statement of Psalm 40:7–8:

> Then I said, "Behold, I have come;
>   in the scroll of the book it is written of me:
> I delight to do your will, O my God;
>   your law is within my heart."

You might protest, "God can expect that of his Son, but he cannot expect that of us, can he?" Yes, he can, and he does. This delight to do the will of the Father is what Paul is commanding when he says, "Have this mind among yourselves, which is yours in Christ Jesus" (Phil. 2:5). The kind of endurance that is honored by God in his Son, as explained in Philippians 2, is the same endurance God says he honors in us. "Blessed is the man who *remains steadfast* under trial [of any sort], for when he has stood [passed] the test he will receive the crown of life, which God has promised to those who love *him*" (James 1:12).

Notice the love for Christ, the relationship, that fuels a believer's endurance in a trial. This kind of Christ-centered endurance is what the writer of Hebrews is calling us to when he says,

> Therefore, since we are surrounded by so great a cloud of witnesses, let us also lay aside every weight, and sin which clings so closely, and let us run with *endurance* the race that is set before us, *looking to Jesus*, the founder and perfecter of our faith, who for the joy that was set before him endured the cross, despising the shame, and is seated at the right hand of the throne of God.
>
> *Consider him* who endured from sinners such hostility against himself, so that you may not grow weary or fainthearted. (Heb. 12:1–3)

For examples of many others who have endured this way, study Hebrews 11, the hall of faith. These believers looked beyond the trial to the face of their Master. Moses, one of the heroes listed in Hebrews

11, "endured as seeing *him* who is invisible" (v. 27). He would not let the temptations of affluence and ease or the possibility of persecution and suffering turn his gaze away from God. This "gaze of a soul upon a saving God"[1] is the essence of faith.

All the believers listed in Hebrews 11 kept their faces turned toward God for fellowship, comfort, and strength during difficult times. They would let nothing pull their hearts away from him. This is why they are called heroes of the faith. We could rename them "heroes of the Godward gaze" and mean the same thing. Their endurance—sustained obedience under pressure—was fueled by a sustained look at their God and at things eternal.

Paul also exhorts us to "see" the invisible by faith in order to endure.

> So we do not lose heart. Though our outer self is wasting away, our inner self is being renewed day by day. For this light momentary affliction is preparing for us an eternal weight of glory beyond all comparison, *as we look not to the things that are seen* but to the things that are unseen. For the things that are seen are transient, but the things that are unseen are eternal. (2 Cor. 4:16–18)

This endurance is the fruit of a Christlike, renewed mind. It is more than having a head filled with Bible passages and scriptural principles. A renewed mind must start with that kind of hearing, but it is far more. It is a mind that is beholding "the things that are above, where Christ is, seated at the right hand of God" (Col. 3:1) and is setting its "affection on things above, not on things on the earth" (v. 2 KJV). It is a mind that is "renewed in knowledge after the image of its creator" (v. 10) and that is letting "the word of Christ dwell in [it] richly, teaching and admonishing one another in all wisdom" (v. 16). This is why Paul could exclaim, "And whatever you *do*, in word or deed, *do* everything in the name of the Lord Jesus, giving thanks to God the Father through him" (v. 17).

Endurance with its face toward God and its eye on the eternal is Christlikeness. When listening to God is followed by reflecting on God's words so that we begin to think like God, we are properly hearing. When obeying his words and enduring in them because they are his words

1. A. W. Tozer, *The Pursuit of God* (Camp Hill, PA: Christian Publications, 1993), 83.

drive us to being "faithful unto death" (Rev. 2:10), we are doing his will and are living wisely. There is a certain biblical role God used to describe how all of this blends together into a usable life on this earth. It is a role that describes mature, grown-up Christianity.

Grown-Up Christianity

As we have seen, Christlikeness is not the same as following a moral or ethical ideal. It is not simply possessing more knowledge of the Bible's content or principles. It is not merely replacing old habits with new ones or being and doing good. Furthermore, it is not becoming well-adjusted or recovering from some life-dominating sin. Christlikeness is the manifestation of the fruit of God's Spirit in the lives of believers who behold the glory of God. The result of the process is a person who looks increasingly like Christ—the grown-up Christian.

Paul said God's goal for believers is to come "to the measure of the stature of the fullness of Christ" (Eph. 4:13). In chapter 1, I wrote that while living on this earth, Jesus Christ exemplified the characteristics of a man controlled by the Holy Spirit and abiding in perfect fellowship with God. His submission to and dependence on his Father and his sacrificial ministry to others blended those characteristics into a perfect ideal Paul called "the form [nature] of a servant" (Phil. 2:7). Servanthood is grown-up Christianity.

We will close part 2 of this book with a brief look at how all we have learned about having a renewed mind prepares us to be Christlike servants. The designation *servant* means little to us today, but to a first-century believer the term was filled with meaning. Slaves in the ancient world were valued for two basic qualities, which are also characteristics of our Lord.

First-Century Slaves Were Responsive to the Needs of Others

The concept of being responsive to the needs of others is set forth in the New Testament word *diakonos* (*servant*), which appears over sixty times in the New Testament in its various forms. It is the Greek word from which we get the word *deacon* and describes someone who is actively involved in meeting the needs of others. Jesus used the word in the following passages:

> You know that the rulers of the Gentiles lord it over them, and their great ones exercise authority over them. It shall not be so among you. But whoever would be great among you must be your servant [*diakonos*]; . . . even as the Son of Man came not to be served [verb formed of *diakonos*] but to serve [same word again], and to give his life as a ransom for many. (Matt. 20:25–26, 28)

> The greatest among you shall be your servant [*diakonos*]. Whoever exalts himself will be humbled, and whoever humbles himself will be exalted. (Matt. 23:11–12)

> If anyone would be first, he must be last of all and servant [*diakonos*] of all. (Mark 9:35)

> If anyone serves [verb form of *diakonos*] me, he must follow me; and where I am, there will my servant [*diakonos*] be also. If anyone serves [verb form again] me, the Father will honor him. (John 12:26)

In these passages, our Lord teaches that those who are most exalted in his scheme of events have an attitude that is oriented toward others. Their energies and concerns were not with themselves and how others could serve them but on how they could become a blessing to someone else.

Useful first-century slaves did not hang around in the shadows hoping they would not be called on to perform a task. They were right in the middle of the action—washing feet, filling water pots, tutoring children, working in the fields, and running errands. God's attributes of love, compassion, kindness, patience, and mercy, when manifested in the lives of believers who behold the glory of God, result in Christlike service for others (see John 13:12–17; Rom. 15:l–7). This servanthood is grown-up Christianity!

This aspect of servanthood is familiar to most of us. We admire people who are constantly doing things for others. But if our servanthood is indeed Christlike, it has yet another quality about it.

First-Century Slaves Were Responsive to the Will of Another

Another Greek word, *doulos,* emphasizes the second aspect of slavery—being responsive to the will of another. In the classical world, this word spoke of someone who was enslaved to another. It emphasized the total ownership and sovereignty of the individual by someone else. It is used 125 times in the New Testament and eventually took on a different meaning in the Christian use of the word.

Paul used the word *doulos* in Romans 1:1 and elsewhere when he called himself "a servant of Jesus Christ." John the apostle used it in the same way in Revelation 1:1. These men were stressing their total submission to their Master, Jesus Christ. They were testifying of their responsiveness to his will—to his commands. In fact, Jesus himself said, "Why do you call me 'Lord, Lord,' [implying that I am your Master, and you are my slave], and not do what I tell you?" (Luke 6:46).

This aspect of servanthood is often overlooked in our freethinking, democratic society. By this definition, many believers are not very good servants. They do not respond well to the will of their masters. They do not obey parking restrictions, tax laws, and a host of other civil and institutional laws. They do not cheerfully submit to parents, husbands, employers, church leaders, and other authority figures in their lives. The spirit of our age preaches that if you do not like the will of your master, it is all right to ignore or defy it. Nothing is more un-Christlike! A serious look again at Philippians 2:1–11 shows our Lord's spirit to the earthly authorities who sentenced him to death—"even death on a cross" (v. 8).

Paul gave very serious instructions to the New Testament slaves who made up a large part of his congregations. Many of them were owned by "unworthy" masters who severely mistreated them. Carefully and reflectively note his words to them.

> Bondservants [*doulos*], obey your earthly masters with fear and trembling, with a sincere heart, as you would Christ, not by the way of eye-service, as people-pleasers, but as bondservants [*doulos*] of Christ, doing the will of God from the heart; rendering service [verb form of *doulos*] with a good will as to the Lord and not to man, knowing that whatever good anyone does, this he will receive back from

> the Lord, whether he is a bondservant or is free. (Eph. 6:5–8; see also Col. 3:22–25)

> Let all who are under a yoke as bondservants [*doulos*] regard their own masters as worthy of all honor, so that the name of God and the teaching may not be reviled. Those who have believing masters must not be disrespectful on the ground that they are brothers; rather they must serve [verb form of *doulos*], all the better since those who benefit by their good service are believers and beloved. Teach and urge these things. (1 Tim. 6:1–2)

> Bondservants [*doulos*] are to be submissive to their own masters in everything; they are to be well-pleasing, not argumentative, not pilfering, but showing all good faith, so that in everything they may adorn the doctrine of God our Savior. (Titus 2:9–10)

There was no doubt about the obedience required of first-century slaves. They belonged to other people and were expected to carry out the wishes of their masters without complaint or back talk. They were to submit even to unreasonable masters with a single-minded humility that would "adorn" the gospel they professed. Our Lord himself played by his own rules; he came to this earth and responded to his human authorities the same way.

Christlikeness, then, will be evidenced in doing good for others—but, just as important, it will be evidenced by submission to authority. Those who want the image of being "good Christians" but are not good servants will have a fierce struggle with submission. They will contest that they have learned to think for themselves or will protest that there is no way to succeed in modern times without asserting themselves. Our Lord slashes through all the rationality of every age by reminding us not to call him Lord if we refuse to do the things he says (see Luke 6:46). And he says, "Obey your leaders" (Heb. 13:17; see also Roman 13:1–7; 1 Peter 2:13–17). God takes our disobedience to human authorities personally.

By contrast, Christ's attributes of meekness (willingness to be governed), humility, faith (confidence in his Father), and temperance when manifested in the lives of believers result in a Christlike submission to authority. Here is the testimony of Peter about how Christ suffered at the hands of human authority:

> Christ also suffered for you, leaving you an example, so that you might follow in his steps. He committed no sin, neither was deceit found in his mouth. When he was reviled, he did not revile in return; when he suffered, he did not threaten, but continued entrusting himself to him who judges justly. (1 Peter 2:21–23)

These two issues—being responsive to the needs of others and being responsive to the will of our masters—are the litmus tests of Christlikeness. This is grown-up Christianity. This is why the Father gave the highest commendation to his Son in Matthew 12:18 when he said, "Behold, my *servant* whom I have chosen, my beloved with whom my soul is well pleased." He called his Son a servant because he was responsive to the needs of others. He was known for his sacrifice. He denied himself to stay involved. But he was also responsive to the will of his Father. He was known for his submission. He denied himself to stay in line. May we hear the same commendation when we stand before him: "Well done, good and faithful servant [*doulos*]: . . . Enter into the joy of your master" (Matt. 25:21).

We *will* hear him say those words to us if we "have this mind among [us], which is [ours] in Christ Jesus" (Phil. 2:5). We will become living advertisements of Christlikeness, true servants, when we have renewed minds that hear and do the will of the Father.

Take Time to Reflect

Reflect on the following questions that are based on the four basic disciplines we have studied in the past two chapters. Examine yourself to see whether you are truly hearing and doing or whether you are self-deceived and not becoming truly wise.

1. Do you *listen* to what God says through his Word and through your elders? Or do you more often listen to your own heart or to others who listen to their own heart? Your inclination to listen to God and your elders will be revealed most often by how well you take correction from them. Wise people welcome reproof and instruction

because they want to become wiser. Fools reject correction and instruction and remain fools.

2. Do you *reflect* on and *remember* what God and your elders say? What kind of soil are you? Being good soil is no accident. If you truly are good soil, you should be able to list the things you do on purpose to make sure you "keep" the seed so that it bears fruit. Biblical meditation is one such activity and is not done on the run or on the spur of the moment. If you are truly reflecting on God's Word, you should be able to point to extended periods of time in your schedule that are devoted to time with God.
3. Do you *do* what God and your elders say? Do you find yourself using your mind to think of reasons not to obey God or your leaders? Are you quick to find excuses like the following that justify your lack of compliance? Remember, even obedience can be an act of self-love if you obey to get what you want—esteem in other people's eyes, freedom from hassle, and so forth. If this concept is just beginning to dawn on you, go back and reread part 1 to get a better look at what is really going on in your heart.
4. Do you *persevere* in what God and your elders say? Do you follow through even though you must pay an unexpected price for enduring? An unwillingness to pay the price is most often the reason spouses bail out of marriages, teens bail out of their families, families bail out of their good Bible-believing churches, and employees bail out of their jobs. They encounter difficulties they did not anticipate and eventually decide that they should not have to deny self any longer. They do not endure and, consequently, will not be crowned (see James 1:12). The question is never "What will please me in this decision?" but "What will please the one who loves me most?"

A Word to Disciple Makers

Fostering Obedience and Endurance

Many disciple makers shirk the responsibility of rebuking and disciplining those they are trying to help—even more so in today's individualistic and relativistic culture. The tragic result is that few parents rear truly wise children, few Christian schools develop truly wise students, and few Christian counselors produce truly wise counselees. Rebuke and corrective action are wisdom's training tools. The entire Bible is replete with examples and exhortations that teach the necessity of using these tools.

Obedience is fostered in an atmosphere of loving accountability. Most often that accountability is provided from God-ordained authority in our lives at home, at church, at school, and at work. First Peter 2:13–25 teaches that God sends authorities to (1) "punish those who *do* evil" and (2) "praise those who *do* good" (v. 14). Authorities are to both enforce and encourage.

Think with me about the effect that correction has on people when it is administered in a godly fashion. First, the rebuke or penalty gets offenders' *attention*. Second, with the proper kind of confrontation, it can cause them to stop and think. Third, it reinforces what offenders are supposed to be *doing*. And finally, the surety of a penalty will motivate people to *persevere* in obedience the next time they are tempted to disobey.

Did you notice that in each of these four effects of correction is one of the basic disciplines of wisdom—attention, meditation, obedience, and endurance? Parents, pastors, and others who are unwilling to correct those they lead in a biblical fashion are abandoning one of God's most important tools for developing the disciplines of wisdom. No one becomes wise who has not become skilled in using all these tools through much practice.

Sometimes fellow Christians who refuse to get involved protest, "I didn't want to get him into trouble, so I didn't do anything." Their spirit betrays a faulty view of sin and its effects. Those who are hearing but not doing are already in trouble! The principle of sowing and reaping is already activated. The time bomb is ticking, and their destruction is sure. The involvement of one who will rebuke and chasten is a mission of mercy to rescue those who are already in trouble. Don't let fellow believers continue in their downward spiral of self-deception and destruction. Rescue them by your involvement of rebuke and correction.

Of course it isn't easy, but you have to decide whether you yourself will be a hearer and a doer in this matter of rebuking and correcting. James says that "whoever knows the right thing to *do* and fails to *do* it, for him it is sin" (James 4:17). You are being deceived if you think you do not have to get involved with others. Seriously consider God's mandate for you to get involved restoring a brother or sister "caught in any transgression" (Gal. 6:1).

Continuing to do what is right in the face of pressure to disobey often requires generous doses of encouragement. But again, notice how God encourages. He does not encourage his children by reminding them about something good about themselves. He does not say, "You've been good, so I think things should turn out all right if you just hang in there." Nor does he say, "You haven't done anything wrong that deserves that kind of mistreatment. You don't have to take it from them. Just stand up for yourself." Much so-called encouragement given today is sentimental at best and unbiblical at worst.

God encourages us by revealing to us something good about himself. For example, note these passages:

> Blessed be the God and Father of our Lord Jesus Christ, the *Father of mercies* and *God of all comfort*, who comforts us in all our affliction, so that we may be able to comfort those who are in any affliction, with the comfort with which we ourselves are comforted by God. (2 Cor.1:3–4)

> No temptation has overtaken you that is not common to man. *God is faithful*, and he will not let you be tempted beyond your ability, but with the temptation he will also provide the way of escape, that you may be able to endure it. (1 Cor. 10:13)

> The Lord is not slow to fulfill his promise as some count slowness, but is *patient* toward you, not wishing that any should perish, but that all should reach repentance. (2 Peter 3:9)

Often in the Old Testament, God encourages believers by revealing one of his names or some aspect of his nature. Notice how God does this with Job in Job 38–42 or with Israel in Isaiah 40–66. In the book of Psalms, David often comforts himself with what he knows about God. Study these passages and meditate on the names of God so that you can comfort and encourage others with some truth about him.

Part Three

REFLECTING YOUR LORD

Put on the new self, created after the likeness of God in true righteousness and holiness. (Eph. 4:24)

10

BEING A GOD-LOVING EXAMPLE

You shall love the LORD your God with all your heart and with all your soul and with all your might. (Deut. 6:5)

Where We Have Been

Congratulations on coming this far in your study of biblical change. We have seen that we have three basic personal responsibilities in the sanctification process. These are summarized for us by the apostle Paul in Ephesians 4:22–24. I want to review the first two briefly for you so that you can see where we have been.

The first was the responsibility to restrain the flesh through the enablement of the Holy Spirit. We learned how to recognize the evil within us (chapter 2), how to identify our own way of making life work (chapter 3), how to get into our place of submission to God (chapter 4), and how to mortify the flesh (chapter 5).

Second, Paul taught us that we are changed when our minds are illuminated and renewed by the Holy Spirit as he teaches us from God's Word. We learned how to know God and how to become like him by beholding his glory in the Word of God (chapters 6 and 7). We also learned how to become wise by hearing and doing his words (chapters 8 and 9). Our cooperation with God in these responsibilities will prepare us to be servants who are more useful to our Master because we are more like our Master.

Where We Are Going

Part 3 will now take our growth in Christ one step further. In Ephesians 4:24, Paul exhorts us to "put on the new self." That means that our changed lives must reveal Christ to others. God uses the first two responsibilities of restraining the flesh and renewing our minds to establish Christlike character within us. God intends next to use what he has produced in our lives to have a Christlike influence on others. Christ made it clear that we are to be "salt of the earth" and are to shine as "the light of the world."

> You are the salt of the earth, but if salt has lost its taste, how shall its saltiness be restored? It is no longer good for anything except to be thrown out and trampled under people's feet.
>
> You are the light of the world. A city set on a hill cannot be hidden. Nor do people light a lamp and put it under a basket, but on a stand, and it gives light to all in the house. In the same way, let your light shine before others, so that they may see your good works and give glory to your Father who is in heaven. (Matt. 5:13–16)

These verses are a call to spiritual leadership. Please do not be distracted by the word *leadership*. The call to spiritual leadership does not mean that every believer must hold some official position in the church or must have a certain kind of personality. In a classic work, J. Oswald Sanders writes, "Leadership is influence, the ability of one person to influence others to follow his or her lead."[1] We sometimes call this spiritual influence *ministry, discipleship, shepherding, spiritual parenting,* or *mentoring*. Whatever name we use, the purpose is the same—challenging others to change and to grow into Christlikeness.

We learned in the last chapter that Christlikeness shows itself most notably in servanthood—being responsive to the needs of others and to the will of our masters. It is this kind of character—that of a servant—that provides the backdrop for our influence, or leadership, in the lives of others. We are called to make a difference spiritually in the lives of others as the servants of God, the one who has commanded us to serve others.

1. J. Oswald Sanders, *Spiritual Leadership: A Commitment to Excellence for Every Believer,* updated edition (Chicago: Moody Publishers, 2007), 29.

How to Make a Difference

The principle of influence—of making a difference in the lives of others—is easily stated and easily understood.

> You have to *be* different to *make* a difference.
> You cannot change anything by adding more of the same.

Suppose you have in front of you a glass of unsweetened iced tea, but you do not like unsweetened tea. You wish to add something to your glass of tea to change the taste. You cannot change the taste by pouring more unsweetened tea into the glass. You must add something different to the glass, such as sugar, lemon, or ginger ale.

To have an influence on other people, you cannot be just more of the same kind of people they are. You must be different to make a difference. This is the significance of our Lord's command that we be salt and light. A first-century housewife who wished to preserve a piece of meat without the benefits of refrigeration could not wrap the meat in another piece of meat to store it. She needed to preserve it with salt—something different from the meat itself. If a first-century man needed to walk to his neighbor's house at night in the darkness, he had to take a lamp of some kind to light his way. The darkness could be changed only by light—something different from the darkness.

Likewise, the greatest spiritual impact is made on people by someone who is different from them. Others must see someone like Christ in us—not someone like the rest of the world—if we are to have any godly influence on them. We can catch some of the flavor of this mandate by examining a very important passage in the Old Testament written to Israel's leaders—primarily its fathers. In it, we find the three specific functions of spiritual leadership that will be the subject of our study in this chapter and the two to follow. Notice Moses's words:

> You shall love the Lord your God with all your heart and with all your soul and with all your might. And these words that I command you today shall be on your heart. You shall teach them diligently to your children, and shall talk of them when you sit in your house, and when you walk by the way, and when you lie down, and when you rise . . . lest you forget the Lord. (Deut. 6:5–7, 12)

When Moses spoke these words, he was about to pass the torch of leadership to Joshua, his God-appointed successor. The people of Israel stood assembled on the east bank of the Jordan River. Moses delivered his farewell address and recapped the past forty years. He recounted the Lord's hand on the nation. While his memory surveyed the wilderness wanderings, his prophetic eye visualized the pitfalls that lay before the children of Israel in the yet-to-be-conquered land of Canaan. Canaanite influence and paganism could easily swallow up the people of God and render them useless in representing Israel's holy God before the nations.

The dangers to God's people have not changed in the few thousand years since that day on the Jordan bank—nor have God's strategies. If God's name is to be proclaimed to the unbelieving world and his ways passed on to the next generation of believing children, it will be done only by those who take seriously the charge given in Deuteronomy 6. Parents and leaders addressed by Moses in this passage could not be laid-back or cavalier about their spiritual responsibilities. Moses charged them to be (1) God-loving examples, (2) Word-filled teachers, and (3) ministry-minded overseers.

These three characteristics are the fruit of the kind of life we have been discussing in the previous chapters of this book. Those who have been exposing themselves to God cannot help but be filled with devotion to the lover of their souls. His Word will be their daily delight, and they will be obsessed with calling others to "taste and see that the LORD is good" (Ps. 34:8). Believers who are putting on the new self will be passionate about their God and passionate about making disciples of others.

Let's look more closely at what it means to be a God-loving example. In chapters 11 and 12, we will examine what it means to be a Word-filled teacher and a ministry-minded overseer.

Loving God with All Your Heart

Moses instructed the people that to have any lasting influence on their children, they must "love the LORD [their] God with all [their] heart and with all [their] soul and with all [their] might" (Deut. 6:5).

I sincerely hope that you have not come this far in your study of this book without having spent much time pursuing a personal relationship with God. I am afraid that, like most of Israel in Moses's day, we too have very little impact for God on others because we have very little passion for God. Like the rest of the world, we are too often passionate about matters of little consequence. By our actions and reactions, we betray that we have ascribed great value and worth to many things other than God. Dr. Bob Jones Sr. used to say, "What you love and what you hate reveal what you are." Our loves—our strong desires are exposed in a number of ways.

For example, we worry only about things that are of great importance to us. We never worry about things that do not matter to us. Determine what a person worries about, and you have discovered his treasures. Does he worry most about his appearance and dress before others, his acceptance by certain individuals, his financial security, his pecking order among his peers, or his performance in his work? His anxieties reveal his priorities.

Similarly, how a person chooses to spend her resources of time, money, and energy reveals her priorities. Are they spent primarily—if not in amount, at least in preoccupation—on her leisure and recreational activities, her work, or her family? While none of these is evil in itself, none is worthy of first place in any believer's life.

A person's anger is another indicator of his priorities. Find out what highly displeases him, and you have exposed what he values. No one is displeased if something he values little is taken away or is threatened. But begin to rob someone of his treasures, and you will have a fight on your hands. It may be his control, his reputation, his possessions, his position, or his health. Our anger reveals what areas of life are most precious to us. Our anger exposes what we have not yet surrendered fully to God to deal with as he wishes for his glory and for our good.

We hear much today about the apathy of the church. No one is ever apathetic! We are all passionate about something—be it our autonomy, our pleasures, our sports, our wardrobe, our solitude, our control, or any one of a countless number of idols. Those who have influence for God are passionate about God. They love him with heart, soul, mind, and body!

Please do not miss the thrust of the previous four chapters about renewing the mind. Those who are pursuing their God will find they are not ill rewarded. Biblical change leads to a passionate relationship with the God of heaven that makes every other love pale in comparison. When we do not pursue him in this way, we are, in the words of

C. S. Lewis, "half-hearted creatures, fooling around with drink and sex and ambition when infinite joy is offered us, like an ignorant child who wants to go on making mud pies in a slum because he cannot imagine what is meant by the offer of a holiday at the sea."[2] John Piper echoes the sentiment: "The irony of our human condition is that God has put us within sight of the Himalayas of His glory in Jesus Christ, but we have chosen to pull down the shades of our chalet and show slides of Buck Hill—even in church."[3]

Moses instructed the people of Israel that the next generation would "forget the Lord" (Deut. 6:12) unless they saw examples of those who loved God with all their heart, soul, and mind. The process for developing that kind of passion has been explained in chapters 6 and 7. The result is a God-exhilarated lover, and, like all true lovers, such a lover is extravagant. Think with me about some of the lovers of God in the Scriptures.

Mary's Extravagant Gift

Jesus enters the home of a leper in Bethany just days before he is to hang in public shame at Golgotha. He is soon to experience the desertion of his disciples, the mocking scorn of the Jewish establishment, and the wrath of God against our sin. In an extraordinary act of devotion, Mary of Bethany, the sister of Martha and Lazarus, breaks the seal on an alabaster jar of ointment and lavishes it on the feet and head of her blessed Lord Jesus. The perfumed oils slowly fill the room with fragrance as the disciples are quickly filled with anger. "What extravagance!" they cry. "This ointment is worth an entire year's wages; it could have been sold and the money given to the poor!" (see Matt. 26:6–13; Mark 14:3–9; John 12:1–8).

Jesus's rebuke to the disciples is penetrating: "Why do you trouble the woman? For she has done a beautiful thing to me" (Matt. 26:10). Such extravagance is the sign of a lover—not a lover in a sexual sense but any person who has an intense devotion toward and delight in another. The gifts of lovers to each other are often misunderstood by others; lovers often appear to overdo it.

2. C. S. Lewis, *The Weight of Glory and Other Addresses* (repr., New York: HarperCollins, 2009), 26.

3. John Piper, *Desiring God: Meditations of a Christian Hedonist*, rev. ed. (Colorado Springs: Multnomah Books, 2011), 102.

A similar incidence of devotion by another woman, this one a former harlot, is recorded in Luke 7:36–50. The Lord comes to her defense and praises her extravagant gift as a demonstration of her love. She had experienced extravagant forgiveness. No other gift but an extravagant one would be appropriate in return.

Do those following us see our devotion to our Lord in our extravagant gifts, or do they see us give to the Lord in a miserly and reluctant fashion? Perhaps that is why our joy is so small. Did not Paul teach us, "whoever sows sparingly will also reap sparingly" (2 Cor. 9:6)? What if those who follow us were to see us as cheerful givers instead of grudging givers?

I submit that the reason we do not love him passionately—as did these devoted worshipers who gave their extravagant gifts—is that we have not contemplated often the extent of his "inexpressible gift" to us (2 Cor. 9:15). Those who have reflected much on his forgiveness may even be accused of overdoing it in their giving, but that is to be expected—they are lovers!

Mary's Extravagant Attention

In Luke 10:38–42, we find Mary at Jesus's feet again. This time she is giving extravagant time to the Lord. Martha thinks she is overdoing it and should be doing something useful and practical. I say again, however, that lovers are extravagant! They cannot get enough of each other's time. Thoughts of the loved one return to their minds often throughout the day and even invade their dreams at night. They take time to mull over every action and word of the loved one, seeking to savor each one to the fullest.

Such was the experience of David, the lover of God. He found great delight in the testimonies, words, commandments, and statutes of God (see Pss. 1:2; 119:16, 24, 35, 47, 70, 77, 174). Ponder the extravagance in David's longing to spend time with God.

> O God, you are my God; earnestly I seek you;
>   my soul thirsts for you;
> my flesh faints for you,
>   as in a dry and weary land where there is no water.
> So I have looked upon you in the sanctuary,
>   beholding your power and glory.
> Because your steadfast love is better than life,

> my lips will praise you.
> So I will bless you as long as I live;
> in your name I will lift up my hands.
>
> My soul will be satisfied as with fat and rich food,
> and my mouth will praise you with joyful lips,
> when I remember you upon my bed,
> and meditate on you in the watches of the night. (Ps. 63:1–6)

God-loving examples to the next generation are people who cannot get enough time with God. They can miss the evening newscast, the day's sports scores, the stock-market report, the latest office gossip, and the night's feature television special, but they cannot miss their time with God! They will be found consistently in the Word and in the house of God. They may be accused of overdoing it, but that's to be expected—they are lovers!

David's Extravagant Praise

David, the sweet psalmist of Israel, had a lot of time to think. He spent most of his early life on hillsides watching sheep or in caves watching out for his enemies. He didn't waste the time, however. He thought much of God. And the more he thought, the more overwhelmed he was with Israel's God. The book of Psalms bursts with the extravagant praise of a man who had seen God. Note the exuberance of "a man after [God's] own heart" (1 Sam. 13:14) in the last of David's writings, Psalm 145. The next time you read that passage, notice how many times he uses the word *all* to make sure he doesn't leave anything out. Here is a God-intoxicated man who cannot find the words to express the greatness of the God whose "greatness is unsearchable" (v. 3).

His extravagant praise was misunderstood, however—even by his own wife! The occasion was the return of the ark of the covenant to Jerusalem. Its possession by the Philistines had brought great shame on Israel. David's earlier attempt to bring it back had ended in bitter tragedy because God's methods for carrying the ark had been ignored. The time finally came when David ventured to bring it back again. The Scriptures describe the event in 2 Samuel 6:13–15.

> And when [the priests] who bore the ark of the Lord had gone six steps, he sacrificed an ox and a fattened animal. And David danced before the Lord with all his might. And David was wearing a linen ephod. So David and all the house of Israel brought up the ark of the Lord with shouting and with the sound of the horn.

Then follows in verse 16 the sad commentary on the heart of his own wife. "As the ark of the Lord came into the city of David, Michal the daughter of Saul looked out of the window and saw King David leaping and dancing before the Lord, and she despised him in her heart."

How tragic! She misunderstood his praise because she did not share David's gratitude. His heart was full of thoughts of God's deliverance from his enemies and of God's selection of him as king. He was not performing for anyone's entertainment or just "letting himself go" in the name of worship. The one-time celebration of the return of Israel's ark warranted an extraordinary display of praise to Israel's God. He was accused of overdoing it, but that was to be expected—he was a lover!

Paul's Extravagant Service

It was the apostle Paul's last stop before his final trip to Jerusalem. There he would be arrested, accused, imprisoned, and eventually escorted to Rome, where he would die for his Lord. He addressed the elders of the church at Ephesus and fondly recounted his previous visits. The Holy Spirit had already told him that "imprisonment and afflictions" awaited him in Jerusalem (Acts 20:23). He remained resolute, however. "But I do not account my life of any value nor as precious to myself, if only I may finish my course and the ministry that I received from the Lord Jesus, to testify to the gospel of the grace of God" (v. 24).

Paul reminded them of "the words of the Lord Jesus, how he himself said, 'It is more blessed to give than to receive'" (v. 35). They prayed together, and "there was much weeping on the part of all; they embraced Paul and kissed him, being sorrowful most of all because of the word he had spoken, that they would not see his face again" (vv. 37–38).

Just before he reached Jerusalem, he stopped in the home of the evangelist Philip. While Paul was there, the prophet Agabus informed him that he would be arrested in Jerusalem and turned over to the Gentiles. As might be expected, his friends wept and begged him not to go to Jerusalem. Paul replied, "What are you doing, weeping and breaking my heart? For I am ready not only to be imprisoned but even to die in Jerusalem for the name of the Lord Jesus" (Acts 21:13).

Here is extravagant service! He was accused of overdoing it, but that's to be expected—he was a lover!

The Extravagance of Our God

No one's extravagance of any type can outdo the extravagance of our God! His love is extravagant; his sacrifice was extravagant; his promise to do "far more abundantly than all that we ask or think" (Eph. 3:20) is extravagant, and the reception of his saints "into the eternal kingdom" (2 Peter 1:11) will be an abundant, extravagant entrance. He is that kind of God! He may be accused of overdoing it, but that's to be expected—he is the lover of our souls!

How can we be anything but passionate toward God if we spend any time at all beholding his works and his glory? Jonathan Edwards writes, "We are nothing if we are not in earnest about our faith, and if our wills and inclinations are not intensely exercised. The religious life contains things too great for us to be lukewarm."[4] He further laments the condition of his day—how he would grieve if he knew the condition of ours.

> We find that people exercise the affections in everything else but religion! When it comes to their worldly interest, their outward delights, their honor and reputation, and their natural relations, they have warm affection and ardent zeal. In these things their hearts are tender and sensitive, easily moved, deeply impressed, much concerned, and much engrossed. They get deeply depressed at worldly losses, and highly excited at worldly successes. But how insensible and unmoved are most men about the great things of another world! How dull then are their affections! Here their love is cold, their desires languid, their zeal low, and their gratitude small. How can they sit and hear of the

4. Jonathan Edwards, *Religious Affections: A Christian's Character before God*, ed. James M. Houston (Minneapolis: Bethany House Publishers, 1996), 8.

> infinite height, depth, length, and breadth of the love of God in Christ Jesus, of His gift of His infinitely dear Son offered up as a sacrifice for the sins of men, and yet be so insensible and regardless! Can we suppose that the wise Creator implanted such a faculty of affections to be occupied in this way? How can any Christian who believes the truth of these things not realize this?[5]

Is it any wonder that so few believers of the next generation want what we purport to possess? Who would want to be like us? If we are not known to be God-loving believers by our obvious extravagance for the lover of our souls, why should those who follow us bother with him either?

Let us put away our obsessions with anything but Christ! Let us fill our souls with his life-giving Word, listen obediently to the promptings of his Spirit, and delight ourselves in extended times of fellowship with the one who has loved us with an everlasting love. Then, and only then, can we expect the next generation to be attracted to him rather than to the world. Oh believer, "love the Lord your God with all your heart and with all your soul and with all your might" (Deut. 6:5)!

To Know Him Is to Love Him

I have spoken much already about the necessity of reflection and meditation on the Word. If the fire that burns within us is from God, it will have both the heat of passion and the light of truth as revealed in God's Word. May God deliver us from academic studies that have not penetrated the heart. Light without heat warms no one. May we be spared, as well, from the heat of supposed movements of the Holy Spirit that are not based on the clear teaching of Scripture. Heat without light is a darkness that destroys. John Piper so astutely observes,

> "True worshipers will worship the Father in spirit and truth." True worship does not come from people whose feelings are like air ferns with no root in the solid ground of biblical doctrine. The only affections that honor God are those rooted in the rock of biblical truth.
>
> Else what meaning have the words of the apostle: "They have a zeal for God, but it is not according to knowledge" (Romans 10:2)? And

5. Edwards, 27.

> did not the Lord pray, "Sanctify them in the truth; your word is truth" (John 17:17)? And did he not say, "You will know the truth and the truth shall make you free" (John 8:32)? Holy freedom in worship is the fruit of truth. Religious feelings that do not come from a true apprehension of God are neither holy nor truly free, no matter how intense.[6]

There can be no true enjoyment of God except that which is based on his own revelation of himself. Mere poetic fantasies or imaginary dialogue with God will not suffice. Those who have great impact for God are those who have a great passion for him fueled by meditation on his Word. They are also those who "are strong" and "have overcome the evil one" because "the word of God abides in [them]" (1 John 2:14).

Take a few moments to ask yourself what your present experience of God and his Word is. What does your example reveal about your passion for God? No one can know him intimately and not love him passionately.

Are You Thirsty for God?

If the discussion in this chapter of the God-loving heart has stirred any desire within you to raise the shades of your chalet and view the Himalayas for yourself, then you have experienced the "hunger and thirst for righteousness" of which our Lord spoke in Matthew 5:6. It is the same longing for rest that Jesus spoke of in Matthew 11:28 when he said, "Come to me, all who labor and are heavy laden, and I will give you rest." It is a thirst he intends to quench and a rest he intends to give to those who come to him and who stop searching for relief in other sources.

It is this thirst that God will use to draw us to his Word. In it we will find the living water. We will find rest for our souls. In short, we will find God. When he is revealed to us as we behold his glory, we will be stunned by his mercy to us, humbled by his grace, and thirsty for knowledge of him.

Have You Been Tasting God?

Scriptural sermons, biblical Christian music, short readings of the Scripture, and books like this on the Christian walk will allow you to

6. Piper, *Desiring God*, 102.

"taste and see that the LORD is good" (Ps. 34:8). But even these aren't enough. These brief exposures to God and his ways are nothing more than the pizza or sausage samples offered at the end of the supermarket aisles. They offer only a small taste of the product; they are not the meal. You may have tasted the Lord in recent days, but you will not be full until you have feasted at his banquet hall and filled yourself with the knowledge of who he is.

Do You Know the Joy of Abiding in Christ?

After you have spent a day with God reflecting on what he has revealed about himself, confessing your sin, turning your heart toward him in praise, and offering yourself to him to use as he wills, you will begin to experience the joy of abiding in Christ (see John 15:11). Others will take notice that you have been with Jesus (see Acts 4:13). As the hymn writer said, "Thy friends in thy conduct, his likeness shall see."[7]

Such God-loving believers make a difference in the lives of others because they are filled with "all joy and peace in believing" (Rom. 15:13). Even Christian circles are filled with believers who are not filled with joy or peace. They are an unhappy lot and just as agitated and restless as the unbelievers around them who know not God. Who wants to follow their unhappy examples? The best advertisement is a satisfied customer. Think of the woman in John 4 who, after she had met the Lord at the well in Samaria, returned to call the entire city to drink of the same source that had quenched her thirst.

Masters at Meditation

You may protest, "I understand what you wrote about meditation in earlier chapters, but I am not good at that kind of thing. I could never learn how to reflect on God's Word that way." The truth is that *all* of us are masters at meditation. We all are very skilled at taking one thought and mulling it over and over in our mind. Earlier I used the example of worry, but we also do it every time we experience a temptation of any sort.

Consider the first temptation in the garden of Eden, recorded in Genesis 3:6. When Satan presented Eve the option of eating the forbidden fruit, the Bible says, "So when the woman saw that the tree was

7. William D. Longstaff, "Take Time to Be Holy," 1882.

good for food, and that it was a delight to the eyes, and that the tree was to be desired to make one wise, she took of its fruit and ate." Notice what happened here. Eve listened to the word of the serpent: "You will not surely die. For God knows that when you eat of it your eyes will be opened, and you will be like God, knowing good and evil" (vv. 4–5). Her next move was to reflect on that information and consider how the fruit would benefit her.

When we hear preaching on this passage in Genesis 3, our attention is often drawn to the appeals to the lust of the flesh ("the tree was good for food"), the lust of the eyes ("it was a delight to the eyes"), and the pride of life ("the tree was to be desired to make one wise"). Perhaps there is a parallelism here with the threefold appeal John presents in 1 John 2:16, but I feel that an emphasis on these draws attention away from the real dynamics of this situation.

Eve was drawn into this temptation because she began to consider that the fruit was good and delightful (pleasing) and desirable. The next logical action was for her to take it. Her passions were inflamed by meditating on the virtues and benefits of the fruit. She was then only a short step away from actually choosing to take it. She saw it eventually as something "desired to make one wise."

Notice, too, that the qualities Eve ascribed to the fruit were qualities that belonged to God himself. He only is truly good. He only is truly delightful. He only is "to be desired to make one wise." Proverbs 3 describes the dynamics at play here. Rather than trusting God and his words, Eve "lean[ed] to her own understanding" (v. 5). She was "wise in [her] own eyes" (v. 7). How could she make such a disastrous choice? She meditated on a lie. This is the essence of temptation.

Sin starts with a deception—often a twisted truth. We mull over and over in our minds the deception, considering the benefits of indulgence until we are so convinced of its virtues that we choose to embrace it. Only then do we find that a hook is imbedded in the lure.

Understand then that we *will* meditate. We will meditate on truth, inflaming our desires for God, or we will meditate on lies, inflaming our desires for things that please ourselves in opposition to him. Meditation is not an option. Our only option is the choice of fuel for our reflection.

This book is my effort to tempt you with God. I want you to see that he is good, he is delightful to the eyes, and he is "desired to make one wise." If you will spend enough time reflecting on him and considering his virtues, it will be but a small step for you to choose him as the satisfaction for your thirsty soul.

I think now you can see why people who are passionate for God spend much time listening to and reflecting on the words of their lover. They have refused the lies of the serpent and have filled themselves with the truths of the Creator.

Let us then put away our preoccupation with lesser things. The next generation must be tempted with God. They must see by our passionate, God-loving lives that he is good, that he is delightful, and that he is desirable to make one wise. I am afraid that those who observe our lives may be led to the delusion that other things—such as prestige, money, sports, recreation, control, or relationships with others—are the ultimate good, delightful, and desirable pursuits of life. We must tempt them with God!

Take Time to Reflect

For a thorough discovery of how others see you, use the study sheet "God's Love versus Self-Love" in the appendix C. Go through the entire sheet yourself, underlining the phrases on both sides of the chart that you know apply to you. Give your underlined paper to your spouse, child, friend, or coworker and tell him that you are sure there are items you have missed. Ask him to go through the sheet and underline in another color of ink or pencil the additional areas from both sides of the chart that he sees apply to you. If there are areas that you have already underlined that he wishes to underline in his own color to let you know he heartily agrees with your evaluation, encourage him to do so.

Assure him that no matter what he underlines, you will not be defensive or argumentative. In order for you to have honest feedback, he must feel that you will not retaliate or challenge him. You may ask him for a clarification of his choices so that you can know specifically how to improve, but he must not feel threatened by your follow-up questions. You must approach this assignment with him in genuine humility. Any self-protective and self-serving responses on your part will only confirm with him any previous suspicions on his part that you are out to please yourself instead of God and others.

You might also ask yourself the following questions:

- What extravagant gifts have I recently (or ever) offered to God?
- When was the last time I gave God any extravagant attention?
- When was the last time I gave God any extravagant praise?
- Am I known by those who follow me as one who gives God extravagant service?
- What extravagances of God regularly occupy my thoughts?

A Word to Disciple Makers

The Power of Example

In Mark 3:14, Jesus "appointed twelve . . . so that they might be with him." Through exposure to their Lord, the disciples gained his vision of the lost, learned the lessons of servanthood, and acquired a desire for personal godliness as they observed his life and character.

People have a difficult time doing or being something they have not seen modeled in some way. For example, it is much easier for a child to learn to water-ski if she has grown up watching her parents and older siblings doing it than it would be if she had never seen a water-skier and had to learn to water-ski by reading a book or watching a video. The information gained through a book or video may be extremely helpful and logical, but seeing it carried out again and again by an experienced skier and trying it out under the skillful eye of a veteran skier is by far the best way to learn.

Jesus gave many lectures (discourses) to his disciples, but he was always an example of what he was teaching. When he wanted to teach them about servanthood, he washed their feet. When he wanted to teach them to respect God-ordained authority, he paid his taxes. God wants each one of us who is maturing in his relationship with him to be close-up illustrations of godliness to those around us.

Of course this is frightening. Anyone in a position of being an example has a very vulnerable position. Not one of us comes equipped with a bulletproof life. We will be disappointed, hurt, and misunderstood by those we try to help. Because of this vulnerability, many avoid leadership positions and consequently never grow. God is grieved when he finds this attitude. He says, "Though by this time [taking into consideration how long you have been saved] you ought to be teachers, you need someone to teach you again the basic principles of the oracles of God. You need milk, not solid food" (Heb. 5:12).

Paul testifies that he learned to rejoice in vulnerability because it gave him an opportunity to see God work firsthand in his life. He says, "For the sake of Christ, then, I am content with weaknesses, insults, hardships, persecutions, and calamities. For when I am weak, then I am strong" (2 Cor. 12:10). Vulnerable situations in life compelled him to look more steadfastly at Christ, who strengthened him in the difficulties (see Phil. 4:13). Consequently, he grew.

Although vulnerability is scary for us, our Lord greatly values our ministry to others. He says that "whoever does [his commandments] and teaches them will be called great in the kingdom of heaven" (Matt. 5:19). He puts a high priority on living out what we know and being an instrument of influence on others.

A dad who drives recklessly in traffic says something to his children about himself: "Dad is not safe and cares only about his own thrill-seeking." He skews his children's view of their father. A dad who wears a police badge and drives recklessly when off duty says something to his children about the entire realm of law enforcement. He skews their view of everything he represents by his badge. Sometimes we wonder why the children of pastors or Christian workers "go bad." Perhaps by percentage there are no more failures than in the church congregation, but maybe there is a dynamic here that Christian leaders overlook. Their example to their children is important not just for their own integrity as parents but for the integrity of everything they represent as ambassadors of Christ.

The apostle Paul was very cautious not to cast a reflection on the gospel ministry by his own life. He said that he lived in such a way as to be "put no obstacle in anyone's way, *so that no fault may be found with our ministry,* but as servants of God we commend ourselves in every way" (2 Cor. 6:3–4). Paul wore a "badge" that said he was the minister of God. He knew that any personal actions would be either a credit or a discredit to the ministry.

All of us should be concerned about our example, but if you are a disciple maker with a badge (a father, deacon, pastor, teacher, or person with any position of spiritual leadership), you must be doubly aware of how your example affects others. You represent more than just yourself when you wear a badge.

11

BEING A WORD-FILLED TEACHER

And these words that I command you today shall be on your heart. You shall teach them diligently to your children. (Deut. 6:6–7)

In the last chapter we saw that "putting on the new self" means having a Christlike influence that makes a difference in the lives of those around us. We saw from Deuteronomy 6:5 that God's first concern for spiritual servant-leaders is that they become God-loving examples.

In the two verses that follow, Moses set forth the second function of Israel's leaders. They were to become Word-filled teachers. He commanded them to saturate their own hearts with the ways and the words of the living God. They were then to saturate the minds of their children with the same. Here are his instructions to that end, followed by the apostle Paul's parallel emphasis in the New Testament.

> And *these words* that I command you today *shall be on your heart.* You shall teach them diligently to your children. (Deut. 6:6–7)

> Let the *word* of Christ *dwell in you* richly, *teaching* and admonishing one another in all wisdom, singing psalms and hymns and spiritual songs, with thankfulness in your hearts to God. (Col. 3:16)

All of us are teaching all the time. We teach by our example, as we saw in the last chapter. We also teach whenever we open our mouths and give advice, comment, or instruction. God's concern is not just that we teach, for we will always be doing that, but that we be *Word-filled* teachers.

Get Ready for Dangerous Days

In 2 Timothy 3, Paul warns his disciple Timothy that "in the last days there will come times of difficulty" (v. 1) and that to survive these dangerous days Timothy must continue in the things he has been taught from "the sacred writings" by his godly mother and grandmother (v. 15). Paul warns Timothy that he will see an increase in false teachers, who will be "always learning [yet] never able to arrive at a knowledge of the truth" (v. 7). These "evil people and impostors will go on from bad to worse, deceiving and being deceived" (v. 13). Timothy will need to remain assured of the truth—his only protection against faulty thinking and error.

In order to bolster Timothy's confidence in the things he has learned, Paul reminds him that the Scriptures have a particular nature that sets them apart from other kinds of knowledge. Notice his words:

> All Scripture is breathed out by God and profitable for teaching, for reproof, for correction, and for training in righteousness, that the man of God may be complete, equipped for every good work. (vv. 16–17)

These verses teach four important functions of the Word. The Bible teaches us what is right for us ("teaching"), what is wrong with us ("reproof"), how to make it right ("correction"), and how to keep it right ("training in righteousness"). God uses the Word in these ways to equip believers for ministry to others ("equipped for every good work"). Word-filled teachers will skillfully use the Scriptures for these purposes in the lives of those they disciple. Let's look at each function in more detail.

The Scriptures Teach Us What Is Right

Some popular false teachers and leaders today tolerate anyone except those who claim that doctrine is important for biblical unity. Some today pronounce that the sole test of faith is whether one loves Jesus, but the real question to be asked is "Which Jesus?" Paul was fearful that the believers of his day would be deceived by teachers who were "false apostles, deceitful workmen, disguising themselves as apostles of Christ" (2 Cor. 11:13). He said,

> But I am afraid that as the serpent deceived Eve by his cunning, your thoughts will be led astray from a sincere and pure devotion to

> Christ. For if someone comes and proclaims *another Jesus* than the one we proclaimed, or if you receive a *different spirit* from the one you received, or if you accept a *different gospel* from the one you accepted, you put up with it readily enough. (2 Cor. 11:3–4)

> I am astonished that you are so quickly deserting him who called you in the grace of Christ and are turning to a *different gospel*—not that there is another one, but there are some who trouble you and want to distort the gospel of Christ. But even if we or an angel from heaven should preach to you a *gospel contrary* to the one we preached to you, let him be accursed. As we have said before, so now I say again: If anyone is preaching to you a *gospel contrary* to the one you received, let him be accursed. (Gal. 1:6–9)

The apostle John had the same concern when he wrote,

> Beloved, do not believe every spirit, but test the spirits to see whether they are from God, for many false prophets have gone out into the world. By this you know the Spirit of God: every spirit that confesses that Jesus Christ has come in the flesh is from God, and every spirit that does not confess Jesus is not from God. This is the spirit of the antichrist, which you heard was coming and now is in the world already. (1 John 4:1–3)

> Everyone who goes on ahead and does not abide in the teaching of Christ, does not have God. Whoever abides in the teaching has both the Father and the Son. If anyone comes to you and does not bring this *teaching*, do not receive him into your house or give him any greeting, for whoever greets him takes part in his wicked works. (2 John 1:9–11)

Teaching, or doctrine, was important to John and Paul, and it must be important to us if we are to be Word-filled teachers. What the Scriptures say is important because of what the Scriptures are.

The Scriptures Are Inspired

To survive the dangerous days ahead, we and our children, like Timothy, must understand that the Word of God is inspired by

God—literally, *God-breathed.* The Scripture writers were not setting forth their own ideas or parroting the mythology of their day. They were writing the exact words that God desired to have preserved for every generation to follow. Peter said that "no prophecy [revelation from God] was ever produced by the will of man, but men spoke from God as they were carried along by the Holy Spirit" (2 Peter 1:21).[1]

The Scriptures Are Infallible

Since the Scriptures are God-breathed, they take on the nature of the Author. He is omniscient—knowing all things—and, therefore, is not ignorant of anything. He hasn't left out anything important, nor has he revealed anything that can be contradicted by new information in the future. He has revealed completely and truthfully everything necessary for us to know. He cannot make a mistake.

Not only is he wise enough to be without error in all that he said, but he is also omnipotent—all powerful—and, therefore, competent enough to make sure his will is transmitted without error to his creatures. His infinite perfections ensure that all his purposes—including his purpose of transmitting his words to mankind without error—will be fulfilled.

The Scriptures Are Authoritative

Bob Jones Sr. affirmed the Bible's authority with the declaration "Whatever the Bible says is so!" Today, many in their rebellion to God's authority take the position "Whatever *I choose* to believe is so!" They set themselves up as the final authority—the final decision-maker—about what is true and what is not. Their arrogance is astounding! The Bible stands in judgment on our beliefs and behavior—not vice versa.

The Bible is the final authority about salvation. It is the exclusive source of information about how we can be redeemed from our lost condition. No church, religious group, government, or well-intentioned individual can add to or subtract from the Scripture's clear teaching without usurping God's authority. Heed the words of the apostle Peter: "*There is salvation in no one else,* for there is *no other name* under heaven given among men by which we must be saved" (Acts 4:12).

1. For a more thorough discussion of inspiration, see E. J. Young, *Thy Word Is Truth* (Grand Rapids: Eerdmans, 1957).

The Bible is also the final authority about how we are to live after we are saved. It is the final authority about sanctification. The apostle Peter speaks about this as well: "His divine power has granted to us *all things* that pertain to [eternal] life and godliness [the way we live in this life], through the knowledge of him who called us to his own glory and excellence" (2 Peter 1:3).

In this passage, Peter echoes what we have seen in Acts 4:12—namely that the Bible is the exclusive source of information about how to have eternal life. But he also declares that the Bible is the only source of information about how to live a godly life on this earth while we wait for heaven. Some might protest, "Why should I believe that the Bible is the final authority regarding the way I live when I don't believe it is the final authority on other topics—like history, chemistry, space exploration, nutrition, welding, or accounting?" That is a fair question and has a simple answer.

First, the Bible does not claim to say everything there is to know about history, although everything it says about historical events is entirely accurate. Therefore, we can go to other sources of information to learn other facts about history. The Bible does not claim to say everything there is to know about astronomy, although everything it says about the heavens is entirely accurate. Therefore, we can go to other sources of information to learn other facts about astronomy. The same is true about many other subjects mentioned in the Bible.

The Bible *does* claim, however, to say everything there is to know about how to live on this earth with a sense of well-being, contentment, peace, and joy. It covers "all things that pertain to life and godliness." Therefore, to go to sources that do not point you to the God of the Scriptures for help to solve the problems of living is to rely on a competing source of information for help. According to God, this is a great evil (see Jer. 2:13). Although science may discover some things that may be *helpful* to our well-being, nothing we can discover outside the Bible is *essential* to our well-being.

Second, if what we have discovered on our own is truly helpful, it can already be found in the Word of God in a much purer form. Our problem, however, is that when we attempt to help others, we are often at a loss to know what the Bible says about the issues that confront us from day to day. We are *not* Word-filled teachers.

Finally, please note that our counsel must be dipped from the mainstream of divine revelation. Too often an entire counseling or parenting strategy is built on isolated passages of Scripture. Those passages are indeed part of the river but were never intended by God to be used to provide a complete system of counseling or parenting. It is noteworthy that God says, "My word . . . shall not return to me empty, but it shall accomplish that which I purpose, and shall succeed *in the thing for which I sent it*" (Isa. 55:11). God promises to bless his Word—but only to accomplish the purposes he originally designed it for. Thus, the advice of this book, and of any other human instrument, must flow from the center of God's stream of truth about sanctification if it is to have God's blessing when dealing with the subject of change.

The Scriptures Teach Us What Is Wrong

Second Timothy 3:16–17 also informs us that the inspired Scriptures have a second function. They are used by God to teach us what is wrong with us and how that wrong is to be addressed. Word-filled teachers must know what the Bible says about how to reprove others who are not right.

Telling others they are wrong goes against the grain of these times in which individuals feel they alone are the determiners of what they should or should not do. The truth of the matter, however, is that we are prone to go our own way, even those of us who are believers. Therefore, we must

> reprove, rebuke, and exhort, with complete patience and teaching. For the time is coming when people will not endure sound teaching, but having itching ears they will accumulate for themselves teachers to suit their own passions [they will follow teachers who will tell them what they want to hear], and will turn away from listening to the truth and wander off into myths. (2 Tim. 4:2–4)

How to Respond to What Is Wrong

The Bible gives specific instructions on how to address someone who is wrong in doctrine or in practice. Perhaps the most important element in confronting is the necessity of prayerful self-examination before dealing with the sins of others. Notice this emphasis in the following passages:

> Why do you see the speck that is in your brother's eye, but do not notice the log that is in your own eye? Or how can you say to your brother, "Let me take the speck out of your eye," when there is the log in your own eye? You hypocrite, *first take the log out of your own eye,* and then you will see clearly to take the speck out of your brother's eye. (Matt. 7:3–5)

> If anyone is caught in any transgression, you who are spiritual should restore him in a spirit of gentleness. *Keep watch on yourself,* lest you too be tempted. (Gal. 6:1)

God does not give us permission to remove specks from the eyes of others—even our children—until we have done some spiritual lumberjacking and have removed the logs from our own eyes. We cannot be used by God to call anyone to obedience to us or to God if we are doing so from a position of our own disobedience. Again, this is why Moses commanded Israel's leaders to be sure that the words of God had saturated their own hearts before they attempted to teach them to their children.

Please note that Jesus himself considered this willingness to rebuke and chasten an expression of his love for his people. He loved them too much to allow them to continue in their sin. In Revelation 3:19, he said the following to the Laodicean church: "Those whom I love, I reprove and discipline, so be zealous and repent."

Rebuke must be accomplished in a way that reveals the loving heart of the one who is doing the rebuking. Believers who are allowing the Word of God to convict their own conscience about their relationship with God and with their neighbors are not mean-spirited as they deal with others. They know human sinfulness all too well as they have seen it exposed within their own hearts, and they desire to help others to be rescued from the storms of the flesh also. Many problems that arise from the manner in which believers confront one another are eliminated if teachers themselves are Word-filled. If they are not, their issues of concern are most likely wrong and so is the manner of confrontation.

How to Know What Is Wrong

We must let the Scriptures not only prescribe the manner in which we rebuke wrongdoing but also define for us the true nature of the problem we are addressing. As we have seen before, we must deal with both the surface sin and the heart issue. We can learn some important lessons about rebuke by examining God's rebukes of his people.

Notice God's rebuke of Moses for striking the rock in Numbers 20:1–13. There is no doubt that Moses is angry with the people. In fact, the Scriptures teach us much of the nature of anger in this passage. When God deals with Moses for mishandling this situation, however, God does not rebuke Moses for his anger, but rather for his unbelief (v. 12). God is the ultimate reality. Any evaluation of a situation that leaves him out of the picture is going to result in wrong conclusions because not all the facts are being considered.

Acts 17:28 reminds us that "in [God] we live and move and have our being." He is our environment. To ignore the nature and ways of the God who surrounds and sustains us is as dangerous as trying to swim while ignoring the nature and ways of water. Swimmers who do not consider the absence of oxygen underwater destroy themselves either by their ignorance or by their stubbornness in ignoring the nature of water.

Ignoring God is not just dangerous; it is offensive to God. Notice again Jeremiah 2:13, the passage we looked at in chapter 4. God says, "For my people have committed two evils: they have forsaken me, the fountain of living waters, and hewed out cisterns for themselves, broken cisterns that can hold no water." God says in effect, "You sin against me in two ways. First you forsake me as the essential component of life. Then you further insult me by looking elsewhere for a solution." The root of this abandonment of God for other solutions is unbelief. Thus most of God's rebukes to people in the Bible are leveled at their unbelief. Note just a couple examples:

> You rebelled against the commandment of the LORD your God and did not believe him or obey his voice. (Deut. 9:23)

> For they are a perverse generation,
> children in whom is no faithfulness. (Deut. 32:20)

God often reproved his people in the Old Testament for their unbelief, even though the more obvious problem seemed to be their complaining, covetousness, fear, or immorality. They indulged in sin because of their failure to see God in the picture. They were out of touch with reality. The writer of Hebrews puts his finger on their problem. He says, "The message they heard did not benefit them, because they were not united by faith with those who listened" (Heb. 4:2). Notice that they were refused entrance into the promised land "because of unbelief" (3:19). From a human standpoint, we might say they could not go in because they were afraid. God called it unbelief. The writer was concerned that his New Testament audience might also "fall by the same sort of disobedience" (4:11).

The same pattern unfolds in the New Testament when Jesus rebukes his disciples. Jesus saved Peter from sinking after Peter walked on the water, and then he rebuked him in Matthew 14:31: "O you of little faith, why did you doubt?" When the disciples panicked in the storm, he said, "Why are you so afraid? Have you still no faith?" (Mark 4:40). To the disciples who could not cast out the demon, he replied in Matthew 17:17, "O faithless and twisted generation, how long am I to be with you? How long am I to bear with you?" And to the two disciples he spoke with on the road to Emmaus, he stated, "O foolish ones, and slow of heart to believe all that the prophets have spoken" (Luke 24:25). These rebukes are only representative; there are many others.

Often parents of wayward teens will rebuke them for their ingratitude. In desperation, and perhaps in sorrow, they may say, "After all I've done for you, you don't appreciate it. How could you be so ungrateful?" But Jesus could have rebuked his disciples for their ingratitude, yet he did not. Instead he cut to the heart of the matter and asked, "After all the times you have seen me work, how could you still not believe?" Wise parents will ask the same question. They will not reprove their teens for ingratitude when their real problem is unbelief.

The apostles had the same concern. Paul summarized the believer's proper mindset when he restated the Old Testament truth "The righteous shall live by his faith" (Hab. 2:4; see also Rom. 1:17; Gal. 3:11). He set forth Abraham as the model of faith because "no unbelief made him waver concerning the promise of God, but he grew strong in his faith as he gave glory to God" (Rom. 4:20). The writer of Hebrews reminds us that "without faith it is impossible to please" God (11:6), and then he catalogs in the same chapter many examples of those who walked by faith. These were honored in this chapter, God's hall of faith, because they saw the promises afar off and saw "him who is invisible" (v. 27). They did not live as mere worldlings—unaware of the greater realities of God and his ways.

We too are exhorted to "hold fast the confession of our hope without wavering" (10:23). Scripture urges us,

> Take care, brothers, lest there be in any of you an evil, unbelieving heart, leading you to fall away from the living God. But exhort one another every day, as long as it is called "today," that none of you may be hardened by the deceitfulness of sin. (3:12–13)

This faith—this eye that sees the invisible—is at the heart of godliness. It should come as no surprise then that God's people are rebuked more for their unbelief—their failure to see God in their circumstances—than for anything else. In fact, as we have seen, unbelief rests at the core of anger, despair, covetousness, immorality, anxiety, and all other vices because believers have taken their eyes off their God as the source of all delight and provision and have looked elsewhere—and have always been disappointed in the long run.

The lesson here for disciple makers is obvious. Don't just rebuke others for their outward sin. Be aware of how that sin is a manifestation of hearts of unbelief. This is the pattern of the prophets, the apostles, and the Lord himself. The Scriptures truly tell us what is wrong.

The Scriptures Teach Us How to Make the Wrong Right

Paul told Timothy that the inspired Scriptures have a third function in the life of believers: correction. That is, they teach us how to make the wrong things in our lives right with God and others. The word *correction* comes from a Greek word that means to make something stand up again or to right something again.

Suppose that while backing out of a parking lot at your church on Sunday morning, you hit a car parked behind you, denting its fender. If you put your immediate plans for dinner on hold for a few minutes while you located the owner and made arrangements for the dented fender to be repaired to the owner's satisfaction, and if you then followed up later to be sure the fender indeed was restored to its original condition, you fulfilled the meaning of the word *correction.*

Much is wrong with man. We saw our desperate condition in part 1 of this book. We must be restored. The process involves more than saying, "I guess I need to be more careful in the future so that I don't sin in that area again." Proverbs 28:13 captures the two most crucial elements of this process—confession and forsaking. It says, "Whoever conceals his transgressions will not prosper, but he who confesses and forsakes them will obtain mercy."

The first part of making any offense right with God or others is confession. Confession involves agreeing with your accusers—God or any other person you have wronged—that you are indeed guilty of the charges that have been brought against you. The most direct manner for confessing your sin is to say to those you have wronged, "I was wrong when I [name or describe the offense so that your accusers know you see it the way they see it]. Will you forgive me?" By asking forgiveness in such a way, you assume full responsibility for the wrong and seek to be reconciled with the estranged party. Statements such as "I'm sorry" or "I apologize" never address the matter fully. We can be sorry that something happened yet not assume any responsibility for it. For example, I might be sorry that I hit Joe's car in the parking lot last Sunday, but I'm not willing to do anything about it. An apology, though it can include a full acceptance of responsibility, often does not.

Although God is willing to forgive anyone who comes to him in repentance, he does not extend forgiveness to us until we agree with his charges against us and take full responsibility for our sin (see Pss. 32:5; 38:18; 51:1–3; Luke 15:18; 1 John 1:7–10). This confession of sin makes reconciliation possible. Being reconciled to someone means that the former estranged relationship has been exchanged for one of peace and favor. Notice God's response to repentant sinners:

> I, I am he
> who blots out your transgressions for my own sake,
> and I will not remember your sins. (Isa. 43:25)

> Let the wicked forsake his way,
> and the unrighteous man his thoughts;

> let him return to the Lord, that he may have compassion on him,
> and to our God, for he will abundantly pardon. (Isa. 55:7)

There is much confusion today about confession, reconciliation, and forgiveness. I challenge you to make a thorough Bible study of these topics so that when you disciple others in these areas, you can give them Word-filled advice.

The second part of correction, according to Proverbs 28:13, is forsaking, which means the offender must be willing to make restitution, as did Zacchaeus (see Luke 19:8). It may mean accepting certain restrictions—some temporary, some permanent. For example, Adam and Eve never were allowed back into the garden of Eden after their sin. Moses never got to go into the promised land until Jesus himself called him to the Mount of Transfiguration for a conference about the exodus of Christ. The prodigal son of Luke 15 was restored to fellowship and honor with his father but never received another inheritance to spend. Luke 15:31 says that all the remaining estate of the father had been willed to the elder brother. There was nothing left to give the repentant prodigal.

The difference in the attitude of King David when he was confronted by Nathan about his adultery (see 2 Sam. 12:1–25, especially v. 13) and the attitude of King Saul when he was confronted by Samuel about his rebellion against God is instructive (see 1 Sam. 15:10–35, especially v. 30). David accepted every consequence without protest. Saul wanted to negotiate any negative outcomes, whereas David grieved over his estrangement from God and was willing to accept whatever measures God chose to counter the tendencies of his lustful heart. He wanted his fellowship and usefulness to God to be restored to their former condition.

Reconciliation is the heart of the gospel! God specializes in it. If we are to reflect him, we must also become masters at staying reconciled to God and others. Our heart should break when we see those around us unreconciled to God and others. We truly have been given a ministry of reconciliation (see 2 Cor. 5:18–21). Study this great doctrine. Become a Word-filled teacher on the subject of reconciliation.

The Scriptures Teach Us How to Keep It Right

Finally, Paul says that the inspired Word of God is useful for "training in righteousness" (2 Tim. 3:16).The word for *training* here is picturesque. It is the Greek word *paideia,* which means "upbringing, training, instruction, chiefly as it is attained by discipline, correction."[2] It "denotes the training of a child, including instruction; hence, discipline, correction. . . . [It is] the Christian discipline that regulates character."[3] From this Greek root we get the word *pedagogy*—the study of how to teach and instruct. It is the kind of instruction and structured oversight that should characterize any godly parenting effort. We could accurately translate it *child training.*

Children do not effectively rear themselves. Someone must provide the instruction and structured oversight that insist that the right principles and practices be learned and diligently applied. This is what a mother does when she sees to it that her grade-school child comes home from school and practices the piano for the required thirty minutes. The child may need some instruction about fingering, counting out the meter, or finding the correct notes. If the mother has any musical background, she can help with this part of the pedagogic process. In addition, her training in music will include generous doses of encouragement. Her training will also include warnings, rebukes, and chastening actions when the child is not cooperating or is disobeying. This process remains in force until the job is done—until the child is becoming skillful in playing the piano and is practicing without external prodding.

All of this is implied in the rich word *paideia.* Paul does not say here that it is "training in piano playing," however. His thrust is "training in righteousness." Disciple makers, like a creative mother who trains her child in piano, must bring to bear all the instruction, accountability, and discipline necessary to see that their disciples are growing in their skill of right living—righteousness. That requires specific training in the aspects of life that are particularly difficult at the moment, along with whatever encouragement, correction, and discipline are needed to spur learners on to continue their practice of right living on their own.

Much parenting and other forms of discipleship fail right here. For a mother to train her child to have the discipline necessary to practice the piano on his own, the mother herself must have a strong measure of

2. Walter Bauer, William Arndt, and Wilbur Gingrich, *A Greek-English Lexicon of the New Testament and Other Early Christian Literature* (Chicago: University of Chicago Press, 1979), 608.

3. W. E. Vine, *An Expository Dictionary of New Testament Words* (Old Tappen, NJ: Fleming H. Revell Company, 1940), 183.

discipline in her own life. If she gives in easily when the child complains or whines or if she responds to the child's complaints by yelling or by firing off a sharp lecture, she exposes her own lack of character. In the same way, pastors, teachers, or other disciple makers who respond with impatience and browbeating to their church members' or students' failures are not giving godly "training in righteousness." They are rather teaching that some matters are so grievous that people cannot help losing control.

The actual process of giving structured oversight will be discussed at length in the next chapter. The important concept to understand here is that Word-filled teachers are skillful in providing this kind of direction for their followers. Sometimes students in a Christian high school or university complain that rules or instructions are repeated too often. They may protest, "The principal or administration is treating us like children." That is true! They are being treated just as God treats his children. He uses whatever repetition, instruction, and methods of chastening are necessary to get the job of perfecting his children accomplished. If we are to reflect Christ to others, we can do no less.

Word-filled teachers, then, know what is right because they possess a thorough understanding of Bible doctrine. Second, they can recognize what is wrong and know how to humbly yet directly confront those who are "caught in any transgression" in order to "restore [them] in a spirit of gentleness" (Gal. 6:1). Third, Word-filled teachers know how to guide others in making the wrongs right. They can teach offending brothers and sisters how to confess their sin to God and others and how to forsake its practice. Last, they know how to provide the diligent instruction and oversight that will enable the ones they are leading to persevere in godly practices until their lives are characterized by righteousness—consistent right living.

I hope you are beginning to see the powerful impact that you can have on others for Christ if you are a God-loving example and a Word-filled teacher. There is yet one more characteristic of godly disciple makers—one I have alluded to. They must be ministry-minded overseers. That is the topic of our next chapter.

Take Time to Reflect

1. Are you seriously studying the Word and doctrinally sound books about the Word in order to become a Word-filled teacher? Chapters 8 and 9 in this book are extensive discussions about the importance of biblical meditation. Review them and put them into practice.
2. Does your advice echo the words of Scripture? Does the Word of God control your thinking so much that your advice flows out of your mouth in the actual words of Scripture, or does your advice sound more like whatever counsel is popular at the moment in evangelical Christianity or in the secular mainstream? Are you better known as a ______-filled teacher—fill in the blank with whatever author or speaker you follow most closely—or are you known as a *Word*-filled teacher?
3. Do you have regular, planned times of study, or is your study a more haphazard, catch-as-catch-can approach? Word-filled teachers become Word-filled on purpose.

A Word to Disciple Makers

How to Handle Hurt

IN CHAPTER 11, we saw that disciple makers must rely on the authoritative teaching of Scripture rather than trying to devise their own solutions. Let's look an issue where an other-solution approach is common: the matter of helping those who have great hurt in their past.

Our hearts are increasingly heavy in these "times of difficulty [dangerous days]" (2 Tim. 3:1) as we meet many who have been abused and hurt at the hands of others. The number of incidents of childhood sexual abuse continues to rise. The frequency of divorce and the resulting single-parent homes have wreaked untold emotional, economic, physical, educational, and spiritual disaster in the lives of today's children. The result is that more and more of us who minister to others are dealing with people who carry much emotional or spiritual baggage.

How are we to address their hurt and pain? Is God silent about it? Must we search through the rubble of secular psychology to discover something that we might use to help them? Should we look for drugs to alter their moods or calm their agitation? Need we turn to alternative Eastern religions to find some way to calm their troubled souls? Do we teach them to look deep within themselves for the solution? I hope by now in our study of biblical change that you can see the futility of all of these options. The Bible teaches us correct doctrine; it teaches us what is right.

God is the expert at addressing people in pain. Most of the Bible was written to hurting people. The Old Testament Scriptures were written about and to hurting people who were in the chains of slavery at the hands of Egyptians, Assyrians, and Philistines. The New Testament Gospels are records of our Lord's words to Jews living under the cruel rule of Roman gentiles. The Epistles were written to small, largely gentile churches whose congregations often contained many slaves, many of whom were owned by evil masters.

Think with me about the conditions in which the believers in the first church in Jerusalem lived. Early in the first century as the gospel began to make its impact in that capital city, the believers were increasingly targeted for persecution because of their newfound faith in Jesus Christ. Acts 7:54–60 describes Stephen's martyrdom at the hands of the Jewish religious leaders—one of whom was Saul of Tarsus. Acts 8:1–3 tells of Saul's continued terrorist actions against the church. The early believers were finally driven out of Jerusalem into Judea and Samaria and eventually into Asia Minor. They were rejected in their Jewish homeland because they were Christians. They were further persecuted in the gentile-ruled cities of Asia Minor because they were Jews. No matter where they went, they suffered greatly. They were denied jobs, land, and status. Their families were ridiculed and maligned. Often they were jailed or killed because they were believers.

James and Peter, copastors in Jerusalem who wished to encourage their scattered flock, wrote letters to these hurting people. Notice their God-inspired counsel:

> Count it all joy, my brothers, when you meet trials of various kinds, for you know that the testing of your faith produces steadfastness. And let steadfastness have its full effect, that you may be perfect and complete, lacking in nothing. (James 1:2–4)

> Blessed be the God and Father of our Lord Jesus Christ! According to his great mercy, he has caused us to be born again to a living hope through the resurrection of Jesus Christ from the dead. . . . In this [hope] you rejoice, though now for a little while, if necessary, you have been grieved by various trials, so that the tested genuineness of your faith—more precious than gold that perishes though it is tested by fire—may be found to result in praise and glory and honor at the revelation of Jesus Christ. (1 Peter 1:3, 6–7)

Don't miss the thrust of these apostles' writings. They are telling us to allow God to use times of great pain to refine our souls and to prepare us for the day when we will stand before our Lord.

Think with me for a moment about this advice. Is this the emphasis of most of today's Christian books on helping hurting people? Will they tell us to prepare our "minds for action," to be "sober-minded," and to "set [our] hope fully on the grace that will be brought to [us] at the revelation of Jesus Christ" (1 Peter 1:13)? You see, we are right back where we started in chapter 1: God's recovery program is sanctification.

How then do we deal with great pain? Peter tells us we are to increase our intake of the Word and be doubly careful that we are not "conformed to the passions of [our] former ignorance" (1 Peter 1:14). During times of increasing affliction, we are to "long for the pure spiritual milk, that by it [we] may *grow up* into salvation" (2:2). We are to *grow out* of our pain.

Notice how many times in his two epistles the apostle Peter uses the words *know, knowing, knowledge, known, remember, remembrance, mind,* and *grow.* This is the kind of counsel from divine inspiration that Peter and James gave their scattered flock. If we are to be Word-filled teachers, our counsel must echo theirs, or we must ask ourselves some important questions: Did God forget to tell us the things we need to know in these "times of difficulty"? Should we expect him to send us a supplement to our Bible to fill in the holes where he forgot to say what we need to know to handle today's kinds of problems?

The answer, of course, is obvious. He reminds us that his Word is entirely sufficient to equip every believer for *every* good work (see 2 Tim. 3:17). Our problem is that we do not know him and his Word well enough to know his ways. We must become Word-filled teachers. That means that when we are advising anyone about the problems of living, we must be saying exactly what God himself said. As we have seen in 2 Timothy 3:16–17, God's inspired Word will always tell us what is right. It is the *only* infallible source of truth. It accurately contains "*all things* that pertain to life and godliness" (2 Peter 1:3).

12

BEING A MINISTRY-MINDED OVERSEER

You shall teach them [the words of God] diligently to your children, and shall talk of them when you sit in your house, and when you walk by the way, and when you lie down, and when you rise. (Deut. 6:7)

In the last two chapters, we looked at Deuteronomy 6 and saw in verse 5 that Moses taught Israel's leaders to be God-loving examples. In verses 6 and 7 he called them to be Word-filled teachers. Moses continued his instruction with a third responsibility: for them to be ministry-minded overseers.

There are two thrusts in this third emphasis. First, Israel's leaders were to be *ministry-minded*—intentionally interacting with their followers to stimulate spiritual growth. Like our Lord, who illustrated truth with familiar wildlife and from every possible angle of daily life—fishing, farming, housecleaning, shepherding, building, and military strategic planning—they were to be alert to both the incidental and the intentional opportunities to have a spiritual influence on others. Second, they were to be ministry-minded *overseers*. It was their responsibility to structure the daily experiences and environment of their children so as to saturate them with the ways and the words of the living God so that they achieved spiritual goals.

Consider for a moment the conditions in your circle of Christian friends, your church, and your ministries. How many of the spiritual leaders are known for being God-loving examples, Word-filled teachers, and ministry-minded overseers? Tragically, there are often glaring holes in the consistency of the example, shallowness in the level of biblical teaching and application, and very little personal involvement of leaders in the spiritual direction and accountability of those under their authority. The unhappy result is that the people of God in general, and children of Christian families in particular, are not being discipled into useful servants for Christ. We need to see the urgency of our condition today, be broken by our failure, and earnestly endeavor to get our mission of discipleship back on track.

Before we go any further, please note that the emphases in chapters 10 through 12 of this book are sequential. You cannot effectively oversee others unless you are the right kind of example—one known for being God-loving—and are a teacher whose mind is saturated with the Word of God. If you are not making strong progress in these first two areas, you will not have a ministry mindset as you oversee others. Your interactions with them will not focus on stimulating their growth in Christlikeness because you are not experiencing that growth yourself. Your efforts to manage others will focus on lesser goals of achieving a certain level of production and attainment or controlling behavior and results.

What does God mean when he commands spiritual leaders to be overseers? All of us can think of leaders who have been tyrannical, cultic, or authoritarian, and we shudder at the damage that has been done in the lives of countless saints who have followed such leaders. Thankfully, that is not what God asks us to be. Ezekiel 34 contains his scathing rebuke of the spiritual leaders in Israel—the shepherds—who used their position of leadership for personal gain, and James 3:1 warns that "teachers" will "be judged with greater strictness." God does not take the misuse of spiritual leadership lightly.

God warns against having a self-serving mentality—the opposite of servant-leadership. He tells church leaders,

> Shepherd the flock of God that is among you, exercising oversight, not under compulsion [not because you have to], but willingly, as God would have you; not for shameful gain [not because of what you get out if it], but eagerly; not domineering [as those who overpower others] over those in your charge, but being examples to the flock. (1 Peter 5:2–3)

Similarly, Jesus warned his disciples about adopting the gentile mentality of seeking power over the lives of others.

> The kings of the Gentiles exercise lordship over them [overpower their followers], and those in authority over them are called benefactors [a title of honor]. *But not so with you.* Rather, let the greatest among you become as the youngest, and the leader as one who serves. (Luke 22:25–26)

Spiritual Parenting

God provides the perfect picture of oversight in spiritual matters: parenting. God deals with us as his children. He presents himself as our Father. When we parent others the way God parents us and when we are truly God-loving and Word-filled, we will stay away from the excesses of gentile, self-serving lordship. As Christlike servant-leaders, we can have a genuine spiritual influence on others.

The apostle Paul used the imagery of child-rearing often. He saw himself as a spiritual parent who took responsibility for the growth of others until they demonstrated Christ to others by their lives. Notice his passion in Galatians 4:19: "My little children, for whom I am again in the anguish of childbirth *until Christ is formed in you.*" He knew his job of oversight was not finished until his followers were "put[ting] on the new self, created after the likeness of God in true righteousness and holiness" (Eph. 4:24).

The theme of parental supervision for the spiritual development of others is a common thrust throughout the entire Bible. For example, the writer of Proverbs instructed and warned his "son" by his brief cause-and-effect reality bites of life. The apostle John acknowledged that his readers were at various stages of development. Some were "little children" in the faith (1 John 2:12), others were "young men" (vv. 13, 14) who were effectively engaged in spiritual battle, and still others, who were reproducing their lives in others, were called "fathers" (vv. 13, 14).

With the paradigm of spiritual parenting in mind, I want to propose a simple developmental model for discipling others. We can summarize its emphases as

1. learning self-denial through submission to authority
2. learning the application of self-denial
3. serving God and others.

These three emphases follow roughly the major outline of this book and are best illustrated through the actual parenting process within a Christian home.

First, in part 1, we learned about restraining the flesh. This is the first item of business in any discipling-parenting endeavor. In the home, children in their preschool years must be taught how to obey. In the same manner, the first major step in spiritual growth for all believers is learning the meaning of self-denial—we cannot have our own way. We must yield instead to God and to the authorities God has placed in our lives.

Second, as we saw in part 2, disciples must learn how to live wisely. That will require the development of a renewed mind—one that thinks as God thinks. We must be taught the proper applications of self-denial in the various arenas of our lives. We must also learn the biblical motivations for our self-denial—love for God and others. We must learn to turn our faces to God for help and thus exercise faith that trusts God for the power to say no to ourselves.

Parents of school-age children who are truly discipling their offspring are alert to the increased opportunities to train their children in the finer points of God-dependent self-denial during the grade school and junior high years. These lessons can be introduced even in the preschool years, but as children increasingly interact with those outside their homes during the school-age years, their opportunities to apply these lessons increase as well and become a primary discipleship emphasis.

Parental Discipleship Emphases by Maturity

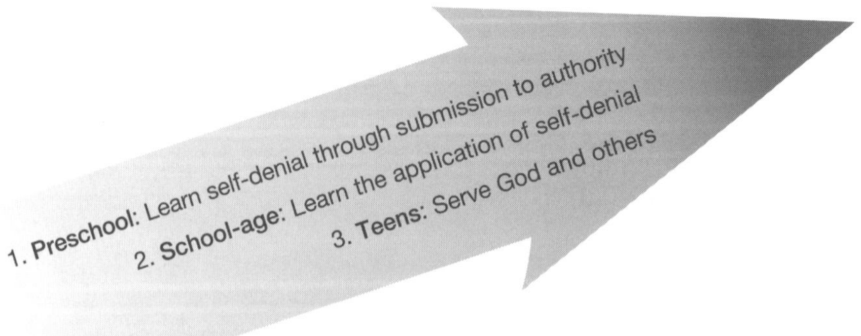

Third and finally, during the teen years the discipling-parenting focus should be able to move to coaching as parents see their teens consistently practicing God-dependent self-denial on their own. Teenagers are thus becoming useful servants for Christ. Teenagers—and any other disciples—who have moved effectively through the first two discipleship emphases bear fruit in the lives of others. This corresponds to part 3 of this book—reflecting Christ to the world around us.

These three emphases build on one another. Although each emphasis can be started in the very earliest times of a child's life, some concepts cannot be fully understood or practiced until the child has developed more fully mentally and physically. Each emphasis must be maintained throughout life.

Although submission is the first lesson to be learned in any discipling endeavor, it can never be put aside. It is the foundation for the training that is to follow. Likewise, the submissive heart introduced in the preschool years and the training in biblical motivations and practical applications of God-dependent self-denial learned in the school-age years must both be continued for effective service to be a reality in the teen years.

The Atomic Structure of Christianity

Before we look at these emphases in detail, we need to realize the importance of God-dependent self-denial in our Christian walk. Consider how a wrong view of the fundamental makeup of the world crippled science for centuries. We will continue to experience a similar "dark ages" in Christianity today if we do not grasp this basic component for godliness.

In the sixth century BC, Greek philosophers proposed that everything in the universe was composed of four basic substances: earth, air, fire, and water. As early as the fifth century BC, other philosophers became convinced that there must be something unseen that was even more basic than these four substances. Much later, in 1803, John Dalton wrote a series of postulates that became the foundation of our modem atomic theory. Continued scientific discovery supports the atomic theory and has led to a much better understanding of the most basic particles of matter. These discoveries propelled mankind into the present nuclear age. Not understanding the basic building blocks of matter greatly hindered scientific progress.

The Main Principle of Discipleship

Christianity has a similar basic component that lies at the heart of everything godly. That component is death. Jesus told his disciples,

> If anyone would come after me, let him deny himself and take up his cross daily and follow me. For whoever would save his life will lose it, but whoever loses his life for my sake will save it. (Luke 9:23–24)

> Truly, truly, I say to you, unless a grain of wheat falls into the earth and dies, it remains alone; but if it dies, it bears much fruit. Whoever loves his life loses it, and whoever hates his life in this world will keep it for eternal life. (John 12:24–25)

In the biblical worldview, life comes only from death. This theme of death was a common one for our Lord. He himself stated that he came to die. His death made eternal life a reality for all who trust in him. His death also made freedom from the power of sin a possibility, as we saw in chapter 5 when we discussed how believers are to mortify their flesh. Christ's work for us at Calvary demanded his death. Our work for Christ on this earth demands our death to self in return. We must then become skillful at dying—to self. That daily dying must be done in the right way and for the right reasons, however, if it is to produce the right result.

Ministry-minded overseers never forget the absolute necessity of this atomic-level component as they disciple others. Matter cannot be explained without atoms, and the Christian life cannot be understood, nor reproduced, without the ongoing death to self that Jesus called self-denial.

With this reality in mind, let's look at how we can effectively oversee the discipleship of others as they grow in Christ.

The Preschool Years: The Rebel Broken

As we have seen, our Lord said that disciples who are following him must deny themselves. In the first step of any discipleship effort, disciples must be taught the meaning of self-denial: you cannot have your own sway. Children in their preschool years should be taught the meaning of the word *no* by Christian parents who understand this essential discipleship element. They must learn that someone other than themselves is in charge and that they are not their own masters. Paul underscored this in the familiar verse, "Children, obey your parents in the Lord, for this is right" (Eph. 6:1). Parents who insist on obedience from their children have an opportunity to begin laying the foundation for teaching self-denial.

A Word of Caution

Parents who insist on obedience for the sheer benefit of the parent, however, are sabotaging any true discipleship efforts. For example, parents who yell at their children so that their television ballgame isn't interrupted by the children's noise are not teaching their children anything constructive. You cannot teach self-denial from a position of self-indulgence.

Similarly, children reared by cruel, strict, authoritarian parents who rule with an iron fist will initially comply to avoid their parents' wrath and rejection but are not being taught biblical self-denial for God and others. Subsequently, when rearing their own children, they will often resort to similar destructive parenting techniques. Others who react to the way they were raised may become permissive parents. Neither parenting approach honors God, nor do they promote godliness in their children. Both parenting approaches may provoke obedience from the child, but neither teaches godly self-denial.

Obedience or Self-Denial

Keep in mind that obedience and self-denial are not necessarily the same. Obedience may be just the outward compliance to the demand of an authority. Self-denial is the practice within the heart that says no to what the sinful heart wants for itself at that time. We are practicing self-denial when we treat self as if it were dead—no longer having any influence on us.

Of course, preschool-age children cannot understand the difference between obedience and self-denial, but it isn't necessary at this early age. They can—and must—learn, however, and as early as possible, that they are subordinates. They are not rulers but obeyers. They must also be taught as soon as possible to ask God for help to obey. The self-denial that must become a regular practice of life must eventually become a God-dependent self-denial. Parents can reinforce this as they pray with their preschoolers at structured teaching times and at times of correction. Parents can pray, "And dear Jesus, help Johnny to obey Mommy and Daddy. It will be too hard for him unless you help him to please you instead of himself." This teaches Johnny early on that God is the most important component in his obedience.

Later you can teach your children the principles covered in part 1 of this book that outline the more complete aspects of this God-dependent self-denial.

Kindergarten Christianity

Sometimes parents of youngsters who are not behaving in school tell school officials their children have "always had a hard time taking no for an answer." What that generally means is that their children were not consistently given no for an answer when they were at home or that their parents did not consistently make the no stick. These children did not learn God-dependent self-denial as a way of life. They did not learn to say no to themselves and yes to their "masters." Without a basic attitude of submission to authority, they cannot be delivered from their own flesh and ignorance, nor can they be trained to become useful to God or anyone else. Enabled by their parents, they are sabotaging their own future.

This lesson of self-denying submission to God and authorities is the primary lesson of "spiritual kindergarten." It is kindergarten Christianity. Children can make no real progress until this lesson is in place.

This is why Christian teen camps place so much emphasis on salvation and surrender. Until these issues are settled, nothing else of spiritual consequence can be accomplished in the campers' lives. The same is true in Christian education. Unless the chapel messages, classroom instruction, and interactions with the faculty are used by God to bring the students to a point of submission to God and other authorities, no real discipleship for Christ can be accomplished. Without students whose hearts are gladly submissive to God, the training and education by the Christian school produces only more highly skilled rebels. Students will be better educated in their fields of interest but will use their education to serve only themselves. All Christian counseling must start here as well. If couples struggling with problems in their marriages or individuals overwhelmed with some difficulty are not submissive to God and his ways, no significant progress is possible. This lesson of God-dependent self-denial isn't optional. It is foundational!

These early lessons in self-denial can be effectively taught, however, only by "masters" who have the self-denial to persevere in their supervision until the lesson is learned. Preschool children can be trained to obey immediately and sweetly. A one-year-old can be trained to stop arching his back in protest while he sits in his highchair or to come to his mother when she calls his name or to stop reaching out for a forbidden object when his father says, "No, Johnny." A three-year-old can be taught to sit attentively in her parent's lap for a few minutes while her parent reads to her out of a colorful book of Bible stories. A four-year-old can learn to pick up his toys and put them in the toy box when it is time for him to go to bed.

Be Not Weary in Well Doing

These lessons—and dozens like them—will require that a parent consistently and calmly both repeat the command and carry through with the appropriate consequences if the command isn't obeyed. Children must learn they cannot have their own way. Parents must be aware of this basic ministry thrust of discipleship at this developmental level and must consistently and competently oversee that discipling relationship in the preschool years until their children know they cannot have their own way.

A young mother can grow very weary of telling her toddler the same thing over and over again. It is very frustrating for her to have to interrupt whatever she is doing to stop him from getting into trouble or to insist that he obey her in some matter or to administer correction when he disobeys her. Consider this, however. If she were in a factory assembly line where her job was to place a part on an automobile body, she would not grow frustrated if more cars kept coming down the line for her to assemble. Even though she had already put plenty of parts on car bodies, she would expect to continue to do the same task as long as it was her job.

Training toddlers—or children at any age—is the same. Parents should expect to give the same instructions, the same reminders, and the same corrective measures over and over and over again. That is a parent's job. It is *paideia*—child training—and the repetition of these matters is a primary teaching tool.

After Paul introduces the principle of sowing and reaping in Galatians 6:7–8, he encourages us to persevere with the exhortation of verse 9: "Let us not grow weary of doing good, for in due season we will reap, if we do not give up."

So you see, parenting—or any other discipling relationship—is not primarily about controlling behavior and teaching good Christian habits. It is the process by which God-loving, Word-filled leaders structure and supervise the experiences and environment of those they lead so that they come face to face with God and his ways and his Word. It is about ministering—intentionally interacting (through conversation, instruction, and even correction and chastening) with those they lead for the purpose of stimulating spiritual growth.

In the early years of childhood—and in the early days of any spiritual discipleship effort with others—spiritual growth will come in the form of learning to take no for an answer from God and other authorities and learning to give immediate and cheerful obedience. That is the foundation for everything else in the Christian life.

In the next level, disciples or children can learn the reasons behind each limitation and can learn a higher motive for obedience, but in their early years they must be trained to submit to the will of those who are discipling them. There is no life without death in God's worldview. It is your job as an overseer to make sure this component of God-dependent self-denial is given its appropriate place in the daily experiences of those you lead. It is the foundational principle for spiritual growth.

If self-denial still does not seem a paramount issue to you, again let me encourage you to master the truths of part 1 of this book. You can build nothing godly in your own life or in the lives of others unless you and they are practicing God-dependent self-denial.

A Word of Comfort

If you were not reared and discipled with the kind of godly parenting described above, please do not despair. Every time your heart is tempted to be bitter or to imitate the wrong child-rearing style of your parents, you have an opportunity now to practice the self-denial for God and others that your parents did not teach you earlier. Of course, you will not be learning self-denial by putting away your toys or obeying a parental command. But you will be learning godly self-denial by submitting to God's way of handling the hurts and hardships from your past and responding in faith towards God as you let God parent you.[1]

The School-Age Years: The Disciple Trained

The flesh, when manifesting itself, will produce chaos. The apostle James said that the result of listening to fleshly *wisdom* is "*disorder* and every vile practice" (James 3:16). Paul said that "God is not a God of *confusion* but of peace" (1 Cor. 14:33). In both of these passages, the Greek word for *disorder* or *confusion* means "a state of disorder, disturbance, confusion, tumult, . . . commotions."[2] The Bible teaches that when the flesh is not restrained by structure and authority, it can produce only chaos and "every vile practice."

In the preschool years, children can be trained to cheerfully *take orders*. In this second time of life, they are taught to *value order*. They cannot become *productive* citizens of their households, churches, and communities unless they are abandoning the chaotic lifestyle of selfish living.

We will look at the motivations for this orderliness later in this chapter and will learn in the next chapter how to keep this orderliness in life from becoming a legalistic straitjacket. For now, I want you to see the importance of orderliness if the disciples you are training are ever to be productive for God or for anyone else.

Learning Law and Order

Children who are given responsibilities to clean their rooms, rake the leaves, pick up their toys, clear the table, vacuum the floor, take out the trash, and wash the car are being trained to bring order out of chaos. To participate in these chores, they must learn to cheerfully *take* orders, which is the first major thrust of discipleship, and they must learn to *value and practice orderliness*. They are learning law and order—foundational principles of civilized and productive people. They are learning to be constructive instead of destructive.

1. Steve Viars's book *Putting Your Past in Its Place: Moving Forward in Freedom and Forgiveness* (Eugene, OR: Harvest House, 2011) provides wonderful, godly counsel for sorting out the issues of the past so that they do not sabotage your present ministry to others.

2. W. E. Vine, *An Expository Dictionary of New Testament Words* (Old Tappen, NJ: Fleming H. Revell Company, 1940), 227.

Please understand that we are not to live for order. We are to live for Christ and value order. Order in our lives does not make us godly; rather, it makes us useful to God. People whose lives have order are constructive in their deeds and words instead of destructive. They determine their activities by priorities, not by what pressures them most at the moment. They know how to schedule their time and work toward worthy goals. They know as well that anything worthwhile in life comes through processes of sowing and reaping and cause and effect. That means they are willing to put continued effort—repetition—into something and are willing to wait for the outcome. Ordered people understand and live out the principles embodied in such old sayings as "A place for everything, and everything in its place" and "Failing to plan is planning to fail."

By contrast, the lives of chaotic people are characterized by haphazard efforts to accomplish the things that press them most and by the spontaneity of doing whatever they feel like doing at the moment. They live for whatever pleases them the most at that moment and hope for the best in the future.

Unfortunately, many parents live such chaotic lives themselves that they never teach these lessons at home. Nobody lives by any set schedule in such homes. Mealtimes when family members sit around the table and fellowship with each other are nonexistent. Family members eat whatever they want whenever they are hungry. Families do not make decisions based on any order of priorities—spiritual, financial, or otherwise. Bedtimes vary from night to night, and the lives of family members are filled with crisis and calamity.

Tragically, in such homes parents approach their child-training responsibility with the same mentality as they would approach a pile of dirty dishes on the kitchen counter. Instead of attending to their responsibilities on a regular, systematic basis, they ignore them until they are out of control. Then both the dishes and the children are handled with grudging disgust. The lack of structured, principled, and godly problem-solving habits in homes like these leads to all sorts of emotional upheaval in the family members. The rule of life in homes like these is "every man for himself." Children growing up in such homes do not learn from their parents to be productive citizens, and more tragically, they do not learn from their parents to become useful disciples of Jesus

Christ because no one with a ministry mindset is overseeing their training and development.

The grade-school years (approximately ages six through twelve) provide wonderful opportunities for parents to build on the lessons of the preschool years. Children who have learned the meaning of self-denial ("you cannot have your own way") in their preschool years can now be taught the applications of God-dependent self-denial in the expanded experiences of life, particularly as they become more active in their interaction with others outside their own homes. These are the years when they will become a part of many other social settings and experiences outside of home and school—church groups, youth organizations such as 4-H, Bible clubs, little league sports, summer camps, children's choirs, and overnight stays with trusted relatives. They are no longer under the continual, watchful eye of their parents as they were when they were preschoolers. Other adults now supervise increasingly greater portions of their lives.

Parents must carefully oversee the selection of new authorities in their children's lives so that a biblical thrust of self-denial is reinforced and maintained in these extended settings. Children are not helped if they spend large amounts of time in the homes of friends whose parents allow the children to fight and pick on each other, to be rude and disrespectful to adults and other family members, to watch movies and television programs that are sensual or teach worldly values, or to play without adequate supervision.

Sending children to school classrooms, summer camps, vacation Bible school, or soccer practices that are loosely run and poorly supervised undermines what they need to be taught at this age as well. If children return from these activities more out of control, more disrespectful, and more self-serving than is usual for them at this time in their lives, wise parents will discreetly probe to find out what went on and counter the effects of it with instruction and, if necessary, reproof and correction. If the negative influence continues to have its chaotic effect, parents may need to curtail and perhaps eliminate certain activities from their children's lives.

Children who play games in which they have to wait their turn and play by the rules benefit from the reinforcement to practice self-restraint and experience the need for and the benefits of orderliness. In elementary schools, orderliness is taught and reinforced when children walk with other class members to the bathroom and to the drinking fountain in single file without talking, raise their hand to ask a question, stack their books neatly in their desks at the end of the day, abide by a dress code, address teachers and other adults respectfully, and say "excuse me" when they bump into someone. All these practices help teach children to take orders and to value orderliness.

These examples of chaotic versus orderly living are not techniques that in themselves guarantee godly and orderly children and disciples. They are merely examples of the kinds of structures and strategies that God-loving, Word-filled, ministry-minded disciple makers will use as they *oversee* the restraint of the fleshly impulses of those they lead. Disciples can thus be trained in the day-to-day *applications* of God-dependent self-denial. Remember, the goal by the teen years is to have children who are useful to the Lord in productive service. That means they should have had much practice in self-restraint.

Empowerment for godly living, as we have seen in parts 1 and 2, comes from walking in the Spirit. You will have many opportunities to teach your child-disciple to look past both discouraging and exhilarating events to the all-seeing God, who enables believers to do right and judges the heart. He records not the temporal score or the placement in the contest but rather notices the humility of heart that accepts the outcome as coming from God. Teach those you are discipling to look to God for strength to think and do right in both their losses and their victories. They must learn *God-dependent* self-denial.

The *motivation* for denying self is found in the first and second great commands—demonstrating love for God and our neighbor. Even young children can be taught to examine their motivation for their actions. For example, if eight-year-old Johnny and his six-year-old sister Susan are fighting, most parents simply separate them into different rooms, make them take some time out, or punish them in some other fashion without ever addressing the real issues of their children's hearts. How much better it would be if the parent dealing with the situation would stop the fight and then address the heart. "Johnny, let me ask you a question. When you were treating your sister the way you were just now, were you pleasing God or pleasing yourself? And Susan, when you hit Johnny when he teased you, were you pleasing God or pleasing yourself?" If Johnny and

Susan live in a home where their parents are God-loving and Word-filled, even an eight-year-old like Johnny and six-year-old like Susan will already have a sense of awe and respect for God and will recognize that they are pleasing themselves and not God when they mistreat each other.

The next step in this parenting scenario is to use the situation to teach the process of biblical reconciliation. Sinning children—and that's what they and you need to see them as—need to be reconciled to God *and* their siblings. Johnny, in the situation above, can learn to say to his sister, "I was wrong when I teased you. Will you forgive me?" His sister, even at six, can learn to say, "I forgive you, and I was wrong when I hit you. Will you forgive me?" They can then both pray and ask God to forgive them for pleasing themselves instead of him. This approach takes longer than sending them to their room—and they may still need to be separated for a period of time—but it addresses the real problem: the heart. This kind of parenting is done by ministry-minded overseers. They are not just overseeing the behavior of their children but are sensitive to every opportunity to have a spiritual ministry with their children.

Not for Kids Only

Often when we are discipling adults who are just beginning to put their lives back together after their recent conversion or after repenting of going their own way for a period of time, we need to help them to bring a measure of order back into their lives. Their lives reflect the chaos of fleshly living—usually in several areas.

For example, we may have to help them to establish some rules in their financial lives—perhaps destroying credit cards or setting up a budget or contacting all their creditors and arranging for payments on overdue debts. We may have to help them to set up some principles of communication that will help them to solve problems with other family members without blowing up or clamming up. They may need to establish some consistent penalties for their children's misbehavior instead of doing whatever they feel like doing at the moment. They may need to establish some regular routines of exercise and rest or work out a diet that will help them lose the weight that is endangering their health. They may need to switch jobs, eliminate corruptive friends, forsake sensual music, or address ungodly habits. Most important, they may need similar structure in their devotional time with the Lord and in their personal

Bible study. Without regular and generous exposure to the glory of God, they cannot be changed into the image of Jesus Christ.

I think you get the picture. People whose lives are not useful to the Lord at the moment have a great need for some structure and order so that their lives do not continue to spiral into greater chaos. Again, bringing these areas into subordination to scriptural principles alone does not make people godly. Only the Spirit of God working through the Word of God can make someone godly. These attempts to eliminate the chaotic effects of fleshly living in the past only keep them from further corruption and make them more useful in service for Christ when they do begin walking in the Spirit again.

How Well Do You Smell Smoke?

Before moving on to the third emphasis in disciple making, I want to make one last comment about your interaction with your children or your disciples. You cannot establish rules that will cover every possible manifestation of fleshly living. In fact, the fewer rules you can have while getting the job done, the better. The real culprit that hinders your children's or your disciples' usefulness to God is any manifestation of the flesh in their lives. You have to be a "flesh-sniffer." You will not be sensitive to the rule of the flesh in their lives, however, if you are living a fleshly life yourself.

Most people who smoke do not realize how keenly nonsmokers can smell cigarette smoke. No matter how furtive a smoker may be, every nonsmoker in the area can tell within minutes that someone has lit a cigarette. The smoker doesn't smell smoke as keenly as the nonsmoker.

When we who lead are indulging in the flesh, not only do we hurt our influence by our poor example, but we also do not "smell" the fleshly indulgence of our children or those whom we disciple. We will not pick up on the attitudes, words, and choices that reveal a self-centered heart. Fleshly living will become only further entrenched, making any change in the future that much harder to make.

God-loving, Word-filled, ministry-minded leaders do not need all kinds of techniques to get their discipleship of others on track. They already know *what* God has dealt with them about and know *how* God has delivered them from their own self-centered ways. They have plenty of wisdom (they know the next right move) because God has already parented them in those areas. We are to rear our children the way God rears us. Our problem is often that we do not know what to do with our children or disciple because we have not been listening to God as he has tried to disciple us by his Spirit into lives of spiritual usefulness for him.

The Teen Years: The Servant Deployed

The Bible does not present maturity as a result of reaching a certain age but of becoming fruitful for Christ (see John 15:1–6). By now I think you can see that the purpose for training in God-dependent self-denial and for renewing of the mind toward Christlikeness is that the ones you are discipling will become effective servants for Christ. You want them during their teen years to be God-loving, Word-filled, ministry-minded believers themselves—servant-leaders.

Ideally, Christian teenagers (ages thirteen through nineteen) who have been biblically discipled by God-loving, Word-filled, ministry-minded parents should be consistently living the applications of God-dependent self-denial by this time in their lives. They will be away from home much of the time at school or work and should evidence their commitment to pursuing loving actions toward God and others at their own expense. If teenagers have learned well the lessons in the previous years, their parents can function more as coaches who provide wisdom for new situations and problems and as cheerleaders who give generous doses of encouragement for their teenagers to persevere in God-dependent self-denial. They should be increasingly active in service at school and church, influencing others for Christ.

Short-term missions trips and community projects can be wonderful tools for teaching teenagers the satisfaction and joy that can come from denying self for God and others. Many teens return from these activities excited about seeing how God used them when they stopped thinking about themselves and started giving themselves in service for Christ.

The tragedy of short-term missions trips and service projects is that they are often the first time teenagers have really had to deny themselves for God and others. They could be many more miles down the road toward genuine usefulness to Christ had their hearts' selfishness been exposed earlier through other service opportunities arranged by the spiritual leaders in their lives. Teens can be greatly used by the Lord in nursing home and rescue mission services and in ministries of assistance to others in the congregation. During the summer months they can serve as support staff at Christian camps—working in the dining hall, helping on the grounds crew, or serving as counselors.

Often, however, teenagers are kept out of church and youth activities because holding a steady job makes participation at camps and mission trips impossible. Teenagers may truly need a job to save for college or help support their families, but many teens are working simply to have more spending money. Parents who encourage this are taking the risk of producing savvy consumers and not God-dependent, self-denying servants.

Ministry-minded parents who feel their teenagers must work will carefully oversee where they work, how much they work, with whom they work, and why they work. They will be sure that their teenagers' work outside the home reinforces the discipleship thrusts they are attempting to make. The wrong jobs worked for the wrong reasons can unravel years of Christian parenting in teenagers' lives and stifle their parents' and church leaders' attempts to teach them Christian service.

Once when my wife and I were holding a family conference at a church, an eighth-grade girl came to us just before Sunday school and gave us a container of cookies she had baked for us. I visited with her for a few moments and expressed our gratitude for her thoughtfulness. I learned later from the youth pastor that she was part of a small group of the teens who called themselves the Doulos Group: Servants for Christ. He told me that they prepared treats like those for visiting preachers and missionaries and did service activities for needy families in the church. The parents who encouraged this kind of activity and the youth pastor who helped to coordinate their efforts were teaching those teens the joy of service. The young people were becoming useful to Christ. They were learning to demonstrate their love for God and others in concrete ways. They were being equipped "for the work of ministry" (Eph. 4:12). They were becoming servant-leaders.

On a broader scale this is the kind of opportunity that needs to be available to anyone in the church. It is not my goal in this chapter to give you an encyclopedia of ideas for working with teenagers. I am rather trying to demonstrate that the kind of spiritual leaders God uses are overseers who provide structure and accountability with a ministry mindset—they desire to see their disciples change and grow in Christlikeness.

Getting Them Ready for the Biggest Day of Their Lives

Why should we go to such effort to teach our children and disciples the principles, applications, and motivations of God-dependent self-denial? One day as I was thinking about my responsibilities to disciple my wife and daughters, I realized that "the biggest day" of my daughters' lives was not the day they would get married or the day that one of them had our first grandchild. And though my wife and I consider the day we were married a stellar day, it was not "the biggest day" of our lives. That day is yet to come. It will be the day when we all stand before Jesus Christ to give an account of our usefulness to him during this earthly pilgrimage. The significance of that day is defined by the significance of the one before whom we will appear.

All our work on earth—every thought and action—will be tried by the fires of his omniscience, and the degree to which we lived to please ourselves or lived to please our Lord will be exposed. Everything we have done will be evaluated for its effect on his purposes on the earth and will be consequently discounted and disqualified or rewarded and celebrated. It will be a momentous, awe-inspiring day for us! It will eclipse every other day any of us have ever had up to that time.

My greatest joy in that day will be in seeing *his* joy, if my wife and children can give a good account to him. The apostle John urged his "little children" (see 1 John 2:1, 12–13, 18, 28; 3:7, 18; 4:4; 5:21) to continue in what he had taught them so that "when [Christ] appears, [they could] have confidence and not shrink from him in shame at his coming" (2:28). Paul was driven by the same forward look. He said in 1 Thessalonians 2:19, "What is our hope or joy or crown of boasting before our Lord Jesus at his coming? Is it not you?" (see also 1 Cor. 1:8; 2 Cor. 1:14; 5:10; Phil. 1:9–11; 2:16).

May we too be driven by a passion to delight our God by preparing for him another generation of God-loving, Word-filled, and ministry-minded disciple makers who can stand before him and hear, "Well done, good and faithful servant. . . . Enter into the joy of your master" (Matt. 25:21). This is our mission—getting them ready for the biggest day of their lives!

Take Time to Reflect

Second Corinthians is Paul's autobiography of the ministry. To gain a biblical perspective of his ministry mindset, read through the entire book and note the verses in which he speaks of his concern for the spiritual growth of others. Either underline or highlight them in your Bible or write them out in a notebook. Notice the following examples from 2 Corinthians 1:

> . . . that we may be able to comfort *those who are in any affliction.* (v. 4)
>
> If we are afflicted, it is for *your comfort and salvation.* (v. 6)
>
> Our hope for *you is unshaken.* (v. 7)
>
> . . . and supremely so toward *you.* (v. 12)
>
> . . . that *you might have a second experience of grace.* (v. 15)
>
> Not that we lord it over your faith, but we work with you for *your joy.* (v. 24)

This epistle is filled with references such as these that show Paul's continual burden for the spiritual growth and development of others. Our lives should reflect the same concern.

A Word to Disciple Makers

Ministering in the Milieu

The mandate of Deuteronomy 6:7 to "talk of [the words of God] when you sit in your house, and when you walk by the way, and when you lie down, and when you rise" underscores the necessity for spiritual leaders to take advantage of informal times to teach the ways and words of God. The mundane activities of normal living are also the cauldron in which many problems of living with others come to the boiling point. Ministry-minded leaders are alert to their followers' failures, conflicts, weaknesses, habits, strengths, and temperaments. Those are uncovered in the milieu—in the midst of the normal events of life—as leaders watch the ones they are discipling relate to the daily ups and downs of living on a fallen planet with fallen people.

We all learn best when a need or weakness in our lives has been exposed in some way. It is at that point of need that we are most teachable. Wise disciple makers personalize their discipleship "curriculum" as they see needs arise. Lessons are more potent, and in most cases disciples are more open to receiving help when they have just been exposed.

This ministry in the milieu is why family living is such a wonderful workshop for discipleship. Wise, alert, ministry-minded parents do not lack opportunities to bring God and his ways into everyday events. This same up-close contact is why experiences at a summer camp and the dormitory life at a conservative Christian college can be such powerful aids to spiritual growth if spiritual leaders or counselors have a ministry mindset. They also do not lack opportunities to address new challenges.

Nothing exposes our own spiritual deficiencies—and sometimes outright spiritual poverty—more than parenting and disciple making. Resist the urge to just "get away from it all" as a solution to the pressure, unless by that you mean to remove yourself from the milieu temporarily for a few hours to "argue yourself back to reality" by meditating on Scripture and spending time in prayer with God himself.

Don't think that just a change of scenery or pace will solve the problem. There is no doubt that these can be temporarily restorative—that is part of the reason for the day of rest Sabbath commanded by God in Exodus 20:8–11. The greater benefit for the cessation of normal activities, however, is so we can devote ourselves to the contemplation of God. That, as you have seen from chapters 6 and 7, is the greatest refreshment available to any person.

Often parents who use their work, media, sports, hobby, or other escapes as ways to get away from the pressures of family living will be heartbroken when their teenagers use similar get-away-from-it-all strategies to avoid home once they have the mobility to do so. We must not teach them that escape is a valid way of handling problems. They must learn by our example and by our coaching to run to God when they are under pressure.

13

LABORING TOGETHER WITH GOD

I planted, Apollos watered, but God gave the growth . . . and each will receive his wages according to his labor. For we are God's fellow workers. (1 Cor. 3:6, 8–9)

WHAT A PRIVILEGE that God has called us and equipped us to be God-loving, Word-filled, ministry-minded disciple makers—"fellow workers" with him! We are humbled by the responsibility and cry out with Paul, "Who is sufficient for these things?" (2 Cor. 2:16). How can we "serve God acceptably" (Heb. 12:28 KJV)? How can we give him the "reasonable service" (Rom. 12:1 KJV) of which he is worthy?

Before we close our study, we must ask ourselves some penetrating questions about ministry. What is God's part in the work, and what is our part? What will keep us from the excesses that have plagued the church through the centuries? We dare not teach on the one hand simply a passive approach to "let go and let God," nor can we merely impose a rigid system of discipline on others and expect biblical change to take place in their lives. As always, God gives us clear teaching—sound doctrine—that when "rightly handl[ed]" will allow each of us to stand before him at the judgment seat as "a worker who has no need to be ashamed" (2 Tim. 2:15).

Lessons from the Farm

Let's consider how we are laborers together with God. God chose to reveal his written Word and send his Son, the incarnate Word, to a nation called Israel—largely an agricultural nation of farmers and shepherds.

Even the New Testament epistles—although written to metropolitan populations like those in Corinth, Ephesus, Philippi, and Colossae—contain much agricultural imagery because of their readers' familiarity with vineyards, shepherds, and farms. The Bible's imagery of planting, watering, fertilizing, pruning, and harvesting was not chosen, however, merely because of the nature of the people (they were an agricultural community) but because of the nature of the truth that God was communicating to them. Since God created all growth processes—physical and spiritual—we should expect them to bear a remarkable resemblance to each other. The physical laws of God reflect the spiritual lawsof God.

Paul teaches us in 1 Corinthians 3:5–9 that if we can understand the divine role and the human role in the activities and responsibilities of a "plant grower" (a farmer), we can understand the divine role and the human role in the activities and responsibilities of a "people grower" (a disciple maker).

We are to be faithful farmers, planting and watering as God's laws of nature dictate and as God's grace enables us—practicing God-dependent self-denial. *God* is the sovereign Lord of the harvest, giving the increase as he sees fit.

It should not surprise us that we again encounter the paradox of divine sovereignty and human responsibility. In 1 Corinthians 3:6, Paul says, "I planted" (Paul did his part), but he readily admits that "neither he who plants nor he who waters is anything" (v. 7). In 1 Corinthians 15:10, Paul testifies that *he* labored, yet he said it was "the grace of *God*" that made him what he was. God frequently attributes some work to himself that he also commands us to do. Jonathan Edwards expressed the paradox this way:

> We are not merely passive, nor yet does God do some, and we do the rest. But God does all, and we do all.
>
> God produces all, and we act all. For that is what he produces, viz. our own acts. God is the only proper author and fountain; we only are the proper actors. We are, in different respects, wholly passive and wholly active.
>
> In the Scriptures the same things are represented as from God and from us. God is said to convert, and men are said to convert and turn. God makes a new heart, and we are commanded to make us a new

heart. God circumcises the heart, and we are commanded to circumcise our own hearts. . . . These things are agreeable to that text, "God worketh in you both to will and do."[1]

We can expect, therefore, to learn that even in our disciple-making oversight of others we are to do something and can expect God to do something. Paul teaches that "we are God's fellow workers" (1 Cor. 3:9).

Three Kinds of Farmers

As I have already mentioned, the Bible frequently illustrates truth by way of farming imagery. For example, the Word is presented as seed and the human heart is represented by soil in Luke 8. The Word is also presented in Isaiah 55:10 as rain and snow that "come down from heaven, and do not return there but water the earth, making it bring forth and sprout, giving seed to the sower and bread to the eater." The blessing of God is represented in verse 13 by the appearance of the fir and myrtle trees rather than the desert briars and thorn bushes. In the passage before us—1 Corinthians 3:5–9—Paul presents himself and Apollos as farmers and his audience, the Corinthian church, as the field.

In order for you to understand more accurately your role as a God-loving, Word-filled, ministry-minded disciple maker, I want us to consider in this chapter three kinds of farmers. They each represent a distinct approach to life and ministry. Two of them represent the wrong extremes. Only one of them honors God. Study the following chart to get an overview of where we are heading.

Undisciplined Farmers	**Disciplined Farmers**	
Gambling Farmers (Slothful)	Controlling Farmers (Legalistic)	Trusting Farmers (Faithful)
Please Self		Please God

In the last chapter we discussed the diligent oversight that ministry-minded disciple makers must have. The question before us now is

1. Jonathan Edwards, *The Works of Jonathan Edwards*, ed. Sereno Edwards Dwight (Edinburgh: Banner of Truth, 1974), 2:557.

"How can we provide biblical oversight for others by imposing structure and accountability on them without putting them into a legalistic strait-jacket, which dishonors God?"

Often in this day, people who impose any discipline on the lives of others are called legalists. Certainly legalism is a danger we must avoid, but I propose to you that the danger in legalism is not the discipline itself. People who are pleasing self by imposing discipline on themselves and others are just as destructive as people who are pleasing themselves by ignoring the discipline of themselves and others. The first leads to the fleshly self-discipline of a legalist, and the other produces the fleshly self-indulgence of a sluggard. Neither pleases God.

With that brief overview, let us move on to look more closely at each of the three kinds of farmers. We will specifically note how they respond to God's laws of nature. They represent the various responses believers can have to God's laws of any sort—natural or revealed.

Gambling Farmers

The first farmers we want to study we will call the gambling farmers. These farmers ignore the laws of nature and gamble on the outcome. God has created his world with certain built-in laws. God's laws are statements of reality—the way things are in his world. His laws in the natural world are often self-evident, and we cannot ignore them without paying certain consequences. For example, neither the law of gravity nor the laws of thermodynamics can be ignored without penalty. The same is true for the law of sowing and reaping—in both the natural and the spiritual realms.

Farmers cannot forget to sow their seed in the spring and then suppose that in midsummer they can plant "real hard" and still have a crop when the harvest season starts in early fall. They cannot ignore the built-in timetable of the seed. Neither can they ignore the seed's requirement for moisture by giving their fields one good watering at planting time and then ignoring their need for water throughout the rest of the growing season. Their seed will germinate and quickly perish from drought. Farmers who ignore these laws and still expect to have crops can only gamble that they will have a satisfactory outcome. God's laws cannot be ignored.

Gambling Farmers Are Lazy Farmers

The book of Proverbs presents such a man—the sluggard—and even likens him to a lazy farmer. Notice the picture Solomon portrays of him in Proverbs 24:30–34. Solomon is perhaps out for an afternoon drive in his chariot, inspecting the fields of his sharecropping tenants. He pauses by a field that is in utter disarray. Solomon steps out of his chariot, walks over to the deteriorating stone wall, and ponders what he sees. He later reports:

> I passed by the field of a sluggard,
> by the vineyard of a man lacking sense,
> and behold, it was all overgrown with thorns;
> the ground was covered with nettles,
> and its stone wall was broken down.
> Then I saw and considered it; [Solomon isn't critical; he is reflective.]
> I looked and received instruction. [He tries to reap a lesson from this field for himself as he ponders the sluggard's excuses.]
> A little sleep, a little slumber,
> a little folding of the hands to rest, [Then he reflects on the eventual outcome of the man's laziness.]
> and poverty will come upon you like a robber,
> and want like an armed man. [Though the consequences would come slowly as a man traveling by foot, his end would nonetheless be as if he had been robbed of everything valuable to him.]

Solomon realizes that the end of this man's laziness will be total ruin. The man has good intentions, for "the soul of the sluggard craves"—he *wants* a good crop—but he "gets nothing"; by contrast, "the soul of the diligent is richly supplied" (Prov. 13:4). The sluggard in Proverbs 26 makes little excuses—soft choices—for himself: the job is too big and dangerous (v. 13); he doesn't "do" mornings (v. 14); and he doesn't like to be pushed—he will get to it when everyone backs off and quits hounding him (v. 15). If you try to hold him accountable, he can give you reason after reason to justify his inactivity (v. 16).

Sluggards and Second Chances

A primary characteristic of this lazy farmer is that he begs for a second chance when he begins to experience some of the fallout of his slothfulness. Solomon puts it this way: "The sluggard does not plow in the autumn [another one of his excuses]; he will seek at harvest and have nothing" (Prov. 20:4). Such people have indulged themselves, ignoring the laws of life, and now, when the reaping time comes, they don't like the crop—or lack thereof—and beg for someone to bail them out.

This is the teenager who isn't allowed to play sports because he has failed his academics and then begs his school for another chance to prove himself if he can just be allowed to play this season. This is the college student who has had her fun and games in school, accumulating a long list of disciplinary offenses, and then begs for another chance when she is placed on probation or denied further enrollment. This is the thirty-five-year-old husband and father who has ignored his family while he absorbed himself in his work or recreation and then begs his wife not to leave him when she threatens divorce. This is the family who has never really settled down in a local church. They have never joined and have attended only sporadically. They have always had some excuse for not attending regularly and for not joining. Now they are having marital problems or problems with one of the children, and they beg the pastor to help out. This is the employee who has frequently displayed an unruly temper, and though challenged by her superiors about it, has sought no biblical help. When she is finally fired, she begs for another chance.

All these individuals are ignoring the laws of God's world. They are not plowing, sowing, and tending their fields when the time is right. They always have some reason to explain why they can't get out into the fields. Now they look for some miraculous intervention by God and others to bail them out. They have a "lottery mentality" that ignores God's normal ways of provision through sowing and reaping, and then, like gamblers, they hope for a windfall from a "lucky number."

In New Testament passages such as 2 Thessalonians 3:11 (see also 1 Timothy 5:13), these people are described as lazy loafers who walk "in idleness" (a military term meaning to be out of order; insubordinate; not attending to one's own post) and are "busybodies" (wanderers who are not attending to their own business but are involved in the business of others). But most observations about sluggards are found in Proverbs:

The desire of the sluggard kills him, [His lusts are his ruin.]
for his hands refuse to labor. [He has his own ideas about how he will make life work through pursuing his own pleasures. God's way is labor.] (Prov. 21:25)

Whoever is slothful will not roast his game, [He doesn't even value what he has.]
but the diligent man will get precious wealth. (Prov. 12:27)

The way of a sluggard is like a hedge of thorns, [He is always running into difficulty.]
but the path of the upright is a level highway. (Prov. 15:19)

Whoever is slack in his work
is a brother to him who destroys. [And then he wonders why he got fired.] (Prov. 18:9)

Like vinegar to the teeth and smoke to the eyes,
so is the sluggard to those who send him. [You cannot depend on him to come through in his responsibilities.] (Prov. 10:26)

Sluggards' fleshly self-indulgence destroys every field of responsibility. This is why it is just no good to keep giving them another chance and another field, no matter how hard they beg and plead, after they have been ignoring reproofs and instruction. They will waste every chance until they have a different kind of heart. They need biblical change, which involves turning their hearts toward God in repentance and dependence. They need to develop a growing personal relationship with God by applying doctrine, reproof, correction, and instruction in righteousness. Until they have plowed, planted, and cultivated their souls according to God's laws of growth and change, no second chance will help them.

We need to see clearly as we leave our consideration of gambling, lazy farmers—Proverbs' sluggards—that their main problem is that they are pleasing self rather than pleasing God. That condition is always destructive, and from that they need to be rescued by the reproofs of life (see Prov. 12:24; 15:19; 19:15; 20:4; 24:34), by the appeals of concerned brothers and sisters, and by the corrective interventions of his superiors.

Controlling Farmers

The second kind of farmer we want to examine are controlling farmers. These farmers don't ignore the laws of nature as the gambling farmers do. Instead, they keep the laws of nature—religiously. They plant on time and study everything they can find on seeds, soil, and weather. They diligently keep the laws of nature to ensure the outcome they desire. They can usually turn out a pretty good crop and can often become self-confident. They aren't totally irreligious in their self-confidence, however. They may even ask God for help to understand how to farm well and might pray that God would send the right weather conditions. Most of the time it works. They have great crops!

Controlling farmers might even do so well that others seek them out for advice, and they quickly gravitate to those who have the same air of seriousness about farming. They may look at slothful farmers, however, with an air of smug contempt. When observing a sluggard's fields, they might say such things to themselves as "I couldn't live with myself if I let my fields degenerate like that" or "I don't understand what's wrong with that man! All he has to do is get out and get his hands dirty. Anybody ought to be able to figure that out!"

People who fall into the category of controlling farmers work from sunup to sundown just to make sure that they have done everything they can. In fact, they are so diligent that they can become quite driven and controlling—even perfectionistic—about their labor. They may become so intense about doing right that they make themselves—and everyone close to them—miserable by continually questioning their own motives, doubting whether they have really done their best, or wondering whether they have had enough faith to please God. They may become filled with self-doubt and consequently may redouble their efforts in order to make sure that everything is just right.

If these farmers are in leadership positions, they can become overly critical of the work or spiritual condition of others. They can quickly demoralize their followers with their fear-driven obsession to be sure they are doing right. Please note that the problem here is not their diligence in making their underlings accountable. That may be precisely what they should be doing in their leadership role. The problem is their confidence in themselves to get the job done and their flesh-driven fear of failure and of loss of control that motivates their diligence. They cannot often tolerate being vulnerable, and they don't like surprises. They want to know what is going on and want to be able to do something about it.

What Drives Controlling Farmers?

Actually, the dynamic behind the controlling farmer is the flesh, which desires to promote and protect itself. The biblical picture of an *unbelieving* "controlling farmer" is the New Testament Pharisee. But any time *believers* serve their employers with "eye-service, as people-pleasers" (Eph. 6:6), they are fleshly, controlling farmers. Any time *believers* use "wrath and anger and clamor and slander" (Eph. 4:31) to silence opponents or ridicule others into compliance, whether online or in person, they are fleshly, controlling farmers. When leaders like King Saul throw spears and temper tantrums to get what they want, they are fleshly, controlling farmers.

For a review of the insidious driving force of unrestrained flesh, return to chapter 2 of this book, "Recognizing the Evil Within," and chapter 3, "Identifying Your Own Way." Craig's father, in "A Case in Point" in chapter 3, is a good example of a fleshly, self-serving, controlling farmer.

Early Warning Signs

Wise, "flesh-sniffing" parents can see the beginnings of controlling-farmer tendencies in their children at an early age. We briefly touched on this approach to life in chapter 3 when we discussed various kinds of rebels. A budding controlling farmer may be the really good student who wins the scholastic and citizenship awards in elementary school or who receives the valedictorian, Christian leadership, or sportsmanship awards in high school.

For some children and teens, the good testimony and achievement may indeed be the result of a Spirit-filled, God-dependent walk with Christ. A child or teen may have already learned how to be the trusting farmer we will discuss next. For others, however, the fleshly, self-pleasing motive for being good and doing well can be seen in the great depression or anger that they exhibit when they have done their best but not achieved their goals. Or it can be seen in the snobbish, exclusive, haughty, or proud spirit they display when they win again. They may receive many "perishable" crowns, but their flesh-driven achievement will earn no "imperishable" crowns from the Judge who tries the heart (1 Cor. 9:25).

As they grow in their lust for control, we could characterize their lives by one word—*intense*! That intensity can make them difficult to live with. They may even find living with themselves to be a great burden at times. They may not wear well in relationships and may have a hard time getting close to people because relationships contain too many variables for them to be at ease. They are seldom risk free.

They may even begin to experience various physical problems. Their bodies cannot sustain the intensity with which they push themselves. They may suffer from any number of gastrointestinal disorders, stress-related illnesses, tension headaches, chronic pain or numbness, and insomnia. Because their minds are never at rest, their bodies are in a constant state of emergency as well. Physicians may tell them to eliminate some pressures in their lives, but they have difficulty understanding how they are to try harder not to try so hard.

Unfortunately, over time the physical effects can become chronic and the damage permanent. After all, it takes an enormous amount of physical and mental energy to be in total control! It will crush even the strongest of mortals. As you can see, the physical and relational price of being self-insured is high.

Don't Miss the Subtle Shift

Please realize here that the condition of controlling farmers is often unwittingly the stopover point for many who have left the ways of the gambling farmers and are moving toward the position of the trusting farmers. At some point these individuals saw that their lack of discipline was dishonoring to God. They realized their self-indulgent, chaotic, unproductive lives were evidence that they were living to please themselves rather than God. Bowing in humility before God, they repented of their slothfulness and determined to abandon their self-serving ways. They knew they must bring some order back into their lives so God would use them. They sincerely wanted to please God.

When they began applying some discipline to their lives, they began to see some very pleasing results. They liked the results so much, however, that they began to focus excessively on their disciplined living to produce more of the desired results and to ensure that the results they had achieved would continue. Their initial focus of wanting to please God has subtly shifted to an intense desire to please themselves by achieving and maintaining the results they have grown to admire.

They are not only somewhat contemptuous of others who don't share their concerns but also increasingly intolerant of anyone—especially family members and work associates—who would stand in the way of the results they are pursuing. Like those who worked with Frank in "A Case in Point" on pages 56–59, others might think controlling farmers are unnecessarily opinionated, but since they are usually right in the end, they generally follow their suggestions. After all, such farmers usually end up with better crops than their neighbors who do things a different way. It isn't wrong that they are usually right. It is wrong that in their minds they always have to be right. They are impatient with other opinions because they cannot see how they will get the results they want if they follow another way.

The Heart of the Matter

Herein is the reason we call these people controlling farmers and legalists. They do what is right—at least what is right in their own eyes—in order to ensure and control the outcome that they have decided they must have. They are at heart legalists—those who do the right things for self-advancing, self-preserving reasons.

Pleasing self is at the heart of legalism just as it is at the heart of slothfulness. Many today do not understand the issues of the flesh, and when they see the hard, joyless lives of Christian legalists who discipline themselves and others their own way, they abandon disciplined living altogether, supposing that the problem is their intense discipline. As a reaction to the fleshly rigidity of the legalists, they go to an opposite extreme of tolerant self-indulgence, often in the name of Christian liberty.

Since the flesh can produce only destruction (see Rom. 8:13), sluggards and legalists are both headed for ruin—the former through their neglectful orientation, the latter through their driven intensity. Sluggards do whatever they want to get what they want—leisure and fun. Legalists do right to get what they want—bumper crops. None of them, however, experience much peace or true rest in the soul because they are all flesh driven.

In addition, neither sluggards nor legalists will be able to give a good account at the judgment seat of Christ. On the foundation of salvation in Christ they have built only with the wood, hay, and stubble of fleshly self-indulgence or fleshly self-reliance. Their works will not stand the test of God's fire, and gambling and controlling farmers will suffer great loss in that day (see 1 Cor. 3:10–15).

Trusting Farmers

There is a better way—a way that truly reflects Christ. It is the way of trusting farmers.

Trusting farmers, like controlling farmers, keep the laws of nature—but for an entirely different and higher motive. They keep them not to ensure the results they want but because the Father they love has given them. They wish to honor their Father by obeying his rules. Although they would like to see certain results, they realize that the determination of those results is entirely up to their Father, the Lord of the harvest. They are more concerned that the fruit of the Spirit be manifest in their labors—no matter what results the Father gives—than that a certain amount of fruit come out of their fields as the result of their efforts. They are driven by a desire to please the Father in all things. They have taken seriously the apostle Paul's admonition in 1 Corinthians 10:31: "So, whether you eat or drink, or whatever you do, do all to the gloryof God."

Trusting farmers are diligent; they are disciplined; they labor to exhaustion—but not to *gain* God's favor. They throw their lives into their farms because they *have* God's favor. Every day of labor is just another page of a thank-you card to God for the riches of his grace to them in making them children of God. They trust God to help them to do right: not to get what they want but to faithfully give God what he deserves—unqualified trust and devotion—because he is a worthy Father. They want to hear the law of their Father so that they can do it, and they delight in the law of their Father because they love the Father and therefore love his will (see Rom. 7:22). God-loving people have no trouble loving God's law since his laws are reflections of his nature.

Trusting farmers get their greatest delight not in the bumper crop they reap while keeping the laws of God but in the pleasure they bring to their Father for having done his will. When the Father chooses not to allow a bumper crop for their efforts, trusting farmers are still at peace because they know they have pleased the Father in their part of the enterprise—they have been faithful (see 1 Cor. 4:2).

The Danger of Being Good without God

The danger for trusting farmers, of course, is that when doing right becomes the normal way of life for them, they may gradually become somewhat dependent on their own disciplined habits to keep up their image of godliness. They may drift into the ways of controlling, legalistic—self-dependent and self-glorifying—farmers. For a period of time, they may appear to be good without God. Their loving Father, however, will mercifully convict them or mercifully bring trials of some sort to once again expose their self-dependent ways. They may then bow with the humility of repentance and once again please God with their dependent, trusting hearts.

The Hallmark of Trusting Farmers

The most outstanding characteristic of trusting farmers is not the bumper crop of their fields but the fruit of God's Spirit that is so evident in their lives—no matter what the yield of their fields. If they do have crops that yield "a hundredfold," they will not be cocky and arrogant. They will be humbly grateful that their Father has allowed them to produce this much for his glory.

If the Father destroys the standing grain with a hailstorm, trusting farmers are humbly submissive to their Father's decision in that outcome as well. Since they delight to delight the Father, they are not shaken by the calamity the Father gives. They know they can always delight the Father by maintaining trusting hearts. They trust the God who promises that he is always present and always faithful to provide whatever is truly needed. They understand that the "righteous one shall live by faith" (Heb. 10:38). They know they cannot please the Father in any way without faith (see Heb. 11:6). They wish to be like Abraham, the father of the faithful, because

> no unbelief made him waver concerning the promise of God, but he grew strong in his faith as he gave glory to God, fully convinced that God was able to do what he had promised. (Rom. 4:20–21)

They have spiritual eyes that see God in everything.

Trust in the Father does not make them lazy. They do not think that since their Father ultimately controls the outcome, they do not need to labor so hard. They know that attitude would not delight the Father. They show as much discipline and orderliness as controlling farmers, but their motive is different. They work faithfully and diligently to delight the Father and trust the Father to control the outcome. That delight and trust in their Father is the secret of their peace, their contentment, and their joy. Their hearts bear much fruit, though their earthly fields through the providence of God may have been laid waste by their enemies or by the weather.

Trusting farmers heartily embrace the words of their Master, who said,

> Truly, truly, I say to you, unless a grain of wheat [his own ambitions] falls into the earth and dies, it remains alone; but if it dies, it bears much fruit. Whoever loves his life loses it, and whoever hates his life in this world will keep it for eternal life. If anyone serves me, he must follow me; and where I am, there will my servant be also. If anyone serves me, the Father will honor him. (John 12:24–26)

His greatest delight is in pleasing the Father by being faithful as a laborer "together with God" (1 Cor. 3:9 KJV). May God help all of us to be faithful, trusting farmers whom the Father can honor!

Take Time to Reflect

1. When your spiritual leaders "drive by your field," what do they see?
    - Evidence of a slothful farmer (chaos)?
    - Evidence of a legalistic farmer (control, intensity)?
    - Evidence of a faithful farmer (peace, joy, rest)?
2. Are you making small allowances and excuses for not getting the job done? What should you be doing instead?

3. Are you tolerating weeds and allowing the fences or boundaries to erode? What maintenance do you need to do in your life right now?
4. What is your tolerance for chaos in someone else's life? In your life?
5. Do you see your neighbors' chaos as a threat to their *usefulness* or as a threat to *your love for order*? What truths could you hold in mind to improve your perspective?
6. Do you panic (legalistic farmer) or trust (faithful farmer) when life goes out of control? Give examples to support your answer.

A Word to Disciple Makers

What about Mercy?

Some people believe that no one should suffer—ever! Their main concern is that people be happy and have a sense of well-being. Consequently, when courts, parents, employers, or school officials impose some sort of penalty for unacceptable behavior, they are accused of being unmerciful. We need to think biblically about God's mercy and compassion.

God's mercy contains two elements. The first is an inward concern for the miserable plight of someone, and the second is an outward action aimed at relieving that desperate condition even at great expense to the one relieving the suffering.

We especially see this kind of compassion in our Lord in his response to the various plights of people in the gospels. He was moved with compassion when he saw a leper who needed to be healed (see Mark 1:40–42); a widow whose son had just died, leaving her in a destitute condition (see Luke 7:11–15); a crowd who had been with him three days without food (see Matt. 15:32–38); and two blind men who needed their sight restored (see Matt. 20:30–34). His compassion always extended beyond their physical condition, however, to the greatest misery of all—a soul captivated by sin. His compassion led him to challenge the disciples to pray for laborers to go into the ripe fields of the world to spread the good news of God's mercy to sinners (see Matt. 9:36–38).

To represent Christ well to the world means that we too must be moved with compassion when we see the dire state of the condemned lost. We must be willing to relieve their misery at great personal cost to bring them to Christ for his mercy and forgiveness. On another level we are also to be concerned about the physical dilemma of those around us, "especially to those who are of the household of faith" (Gal. 6:10).

But what is the biblical response to someone who is suffering the consequences of his own sin as the lazy farmer of Proverbs did? Should we bail him out of the consequences of his actions? To answer that question we will need to look more closely at exactly what God is working to accomplish when he shows mercy.

We have already seen that God's mercy moves him to rescue us from our pitiful plight. Before salvation, our most urgent need was to be rescued from the penalty of our sin. After salvation, our most urgent need is to be rescued from the power of sin in our lives. One of the merciful ways God extracts us from the power of sin in our lives is to allow us to experience its consequences. Notice how the writer of Hebrews records God's loving intervention in the lives of his sinning children: "The Lord disciplines the one he loves. . . . All discipline seems painful rather than pleasant, but later it yields the peaceful fruit of righteousness to those who have been trained by it" (Heb. 12:6, 11). The most merciful thing God can do is to chasten us—though it is painful at the time—in order to deliver us from the miserable end of our self-indulgent living. He does this to produce the fruit of righteousness in us.

God-loving, Word-filled, ministry-minded disciple makers are more concerned that their disciples be extracted from the bent of their sinful hearts than from the immediate unpleasantness of their chastening. Chastening produces a test of their faith: Will they begin to view life from God's perspective now that God has their attention, or will they continue to go their own way? Can they see God in the picture now? And most important, will they submit to God now?

In every trial—and that includes the trial of chastening—James exhorts us to let it have its perfecting work in us so that we may be "perfect and complete, lacking in nothing" (James 1:4). Without the consequences, both natural and imposed, the human heart will continue to gamble on the outcome—as we have seen in the case of the sluggard. Sluggards do not need to be removed from the unpleasantness of their condition. They need to experience the unpleasantness to help them to change. The writer of Hebrews agrees that it is not a "pleasant" experience. Rather it is "painful," but it will produce the righteous fruit of godliness in believers who are "trained by it" (Heb. 12:11).

To cut short a trial by removing sin's grievous consequences is to short-circuit the merciful efforts of God to deliver us from our self-centered living—the most dangerous and miserable condition possible for believers. The unpleasantness is part of the rebuke, correction, and instruction in righteousness that equip "the man of God" for usefulness in the future (2 Tim. 3:17).

Of course, that correction and penalty must be administered by overseers with hearts that are truly concerned about the desperate spiritual condition that has been exposed by the wrong choices. If you as a disciple maker want your disciples to see the hand of God in their lives through the correction you administer, you must deliver the consequences in a manner that can be readily seen as the hand of God. You cannot have a mean-spirited, you're-going-to-pay-for-that attitude. That will only erect an enormous stumbling block in the path of your disciples' restoration to usefulness for God. You would be fulfilling your responsibility as an overseer, but you would certainly not be exhibiting ministry-mindedness in your actions. Thus we have the continual reminders of Scripture to examine our own lives before we deal with the faults of others (see Matt. 7:3–5; Gal. 6:1; 1 Tim. 4:15–16).

EPILOGUE

It is better to go to the house of mourning [for a funeral] than to go to the house of feasting [for a party], for this [death] is the end of all mankind, and the living will lay it to heart. Sorrow is better than laughter, for by sadness of face the heart is made glad. The heart of the wise is in the house of mourning, but the heart of fools is in the house of mirth. (Eccl. 7:2–4)

As I pondered what would be a fitting end to this book, God sent a momentous event into my life. On February 24, 1998, my father stepped into the presence of his Creator and Redeemer. Ten years earlier he had been hospitalized for quadruple bypass surgery. Five years after that he suffered a stroke that forced him into an early retirement at age sixty-three. A heart attack on February 20 put him into the hospital with pneumonia and serious damage to his heart. During his brief four-day stay in the coronary care unit, the condition of his heart continued to degenerate as the pulmonary specialists labored to clear up his lungs. He was conscious for brief moments but could not talk because of ventilator tubes. He could nod his head in answer to my questions and knew that he would not be coming out of this one. He assured me that although he was physically uncomfortable in the present, he was not fearful about the future. He knew he would soon be with his Lord. I prayed often with Dad in those brief four days. Sometimes he was awake while I prayed—often, he wasn't.

During that time, I frequently thought about the words of Solomon at the start of this epilogue. Funerals are more instructive than parties, according to the wisest king, for funerals cause us to consider our own end. In Dad's presence, I was compelled to consider the end of all mankind, and my heart was "made glad." Eternity was even more real to me, and I saw illustrated in his death what has been the theme of this book.

For believers, every death—whether a death to self or, as in Dad's case, death to life itself—though it bring momentary sorrow as they pass through a brief veil of tears, is but the means of entrance into a fuller possession of Christ. Dad had to die to possess his heavenly inheritance in Christ. In the same way, I must die to self to possess more of Christ here on earth. Death is at the heart of the gospel message. The death of God's dear Son paid the fearsome penalty for my sin, provided the power for godly living now, and guaranteed that I shall dwell with him forever in the future. I was saved by his death and have been called to a paradox: a life of death.

Although I can only imagine the fullness of joy Dad experiences now in the presence of God, I can experience "a foretaste of glory divine"[1] as I repudiate any earthly source of joy and seek it only as a by-product of fellowship with Christ. The thought of heaven is sweeter not primarily because Dad is there but because its reality was impressed more deeply on my heart as I watched him step from time to eternity. I sensed as I stood by his bed that the thin veil that separates earthly life from heaven is as temporary and as frail as the curtain that separated Dad's small room from the main floor of the coronary care unit.

I want to get better at dying. I want to struggle less when the challenge to die to something here on earth confronts me. At Dad's bedside, I thought much of how exhilarating it must be to stand in the presence of God—entirely complete by the work of his own hands. Oh, how my heart yearned for that presence! I felt again the impact of the words of Paul, who also longed for his own complete redemption.

> I consider that the sufferings of this present time are not worth comparing with the glory that is to be revealed to us. For the creation waits with eager longing for the revealing of the sons of God. . . . For we know that the whole creation has been groaning together in the pains of childbirth until now. And not only the creation, but we ourselves, who have the firstfruits of the Spirit, groan inwardly as we wait eagerly for adoption as sons, the redemption of our bodies. (Rom. 8:18–19, 22–23)

1. Fanny Crosby, "Blessed Assurance," 1873.

The thought of becoming entirely whole in body and fully restored in spirit to the likeness of Christ makes the thought of dying seem almost trivial. Since Dad's death, I have pondered eternal things more often and more deeply, and the thought of dying to anything of earth has indeed come much easier. Truly,

> this light momentary affliction is preparing for us an eternal weight of glory beyond all comparison, as we look not to the things that are seen but to the things that are unseen [a life of faith—*beholding* the invisible]. For the things that are seen are transient, but the things that are unseen are eternal. (2 Cor. 4:17–18)

Though this book has been about how to die well, it has also been about how to behold well. We have all heard people say that the departed are "in a better place." Heaven isn't a better place because it is a place of mansions and streets of gold. It is a better place because in it we have a better view—a view of God and of the Lamb, a view unobstructed by the soul's depravity and the body's mortality. My prayer is that God has used this book to stir within you a desire to see the unseen. Biblical change, as you have read from these pages, is the product of *beholding* the glory of God. One day that change will be complete because we will behold him, unhindered by the limitations of this earthly existence.

John the apostle spoke of that change when he wrote, "Beloved, we are God's children now, and what we will be has not yet appeared; but we know that when he appears *we shall be like him, because we shall see him as he is*" (1 John 3:2). Paul testified of that change:

> Behold! I tell you a mystery. We shall not all sleep, but we shall all be changed, in a moment, in the twinkling of an eye, at the last trumpet. For the trumpet will sound, and the dead will be raised imperishable, and we shall be *changed*. (1 Cor. 15:51–52)

Our eyes shall behold the Bridegroom in all his splendor. As his bride we shall sit down at the marriage feast of the Lamb, who has loved us and bought us with his blood, and as his bride we shall "dwell in the house of the Lord forever" (Ps. 23:6). What a blessed hope!

John the Beloved closes the final chapter of his revelation with the heart cry of the redeemed: "The Spirit and the Bride say, 'Come.' And let the one who hears say, 'Come.' And let the one who is thirsty come; let the one who desires take the water of life without price" (Rev. 22:17). The Bridegroom replies, "Surely I am coming soon," and all the redeemed join with the apostle in exclaiming, "Amen. Come, Lord Jesus!" (v. 20). And we too, who have been beholding him "in a mirror dimly" (1 Cor. 13:12), cry out with the hymn writer, "And Lord, haste the day when the faith shall be sight,"[2] when we shall be completely *changed into his image*!

2. Horatio G. Spafford, "It Is Well with My Soul," 1873.

Appendix A

THE MAP METHOD OF MEDITATION

FIND A PORTION of Scripture relevant to your problem or find one that deals with a Bible truth you wish to master. Use the MAP method (Memorize, Analyze, and Personalize) to meditate on it. Always meditate on Scripture that God's Spirit particularly draws to your attention as you are reading his Word.

Memorize the Passage

During temptation you must know *exactly* what God has said, *word for word*. Merely having a general idea about what is right is not enough when dealing with the deceptive nature of your own heart. Those who cannot remember God's exact words are in danger of leaning on their "own understanding" (Prov. 3:5).

Memorizing often occurs automatically if the passage is studied intensely enough in the analysis step. Another way to memorize verses is by writing out the first letter of each word in a verse. (Include the punctuation just as it appears in the text.) For example, Psalm 119:105 says, "Your word is a lamp to my feet and a light to my path." The first letters are: *Y w i a l t m f a a l t m p*. The first letter of each word gives enough of a prompt so that you can recall the word, but since the whole word is not present, you do not find yourself merely reading the words mindlessly.

Analyze the Passage

Study the passage, asking the Holy Spirit to give you a thorough understanding of its message. You can do an intensive study of the passage by listing the major words of the verses and then using an English dictionary to find out the meaning for each word. If possible, look up each word in a Greek or Hebrew dictionary or check the meaning of each word in *Strong's Exhaustive Concordance* or an online resource like www.e-sword.net or www.blueletterBible.com. Once you are sure of each word's meaning, put the passage in your own words (i.e., paraphrase it). A more extensive study involves using a commentary or a good study Bible to help you to understand more about who wrote the passage, to whom it was written, and why it was written. Most important, pray that God will illuminate your understanding. Ask him to teach you what he wants you to know from the Scriptures.

Personalize the Passage

Plan concrete changes in your life that are consistent with your understanding of the passage. Such plans include schedules, steps, and details. Ask yourself, "When have I failed to obey this truth in the past? When am I likely to meet a temptation again? What should be my godly response the next time I am tempted?" Think through this game plan thoroughly and *in advance* of the next temptation. Use the passage in a personal prayer to God. For example, a person meditating on James 4:1–11 may begin a prayer this way: "Lord, you tell me here in James 4:1 that the conflict I am having with John is the result of my own desires to have something my way. I know that isn't pleasing to you. Instead of responding in anger to John, I need your help and grace, which you promise in James 4:6, where you say that you oppose the proud but give 'grace to the humble.' Help me to humble myself and not to insist on my own way. I want to allow you to lift me up in your time."

Appendix B

FOOLS BY DEFAULT

We need to be reminded that becoming wise is not an automatic matter. All of us are born fools (see Prov. 22:15) and will continue to become "better" fools unless we submit ourselves to the disciplines of wisdom. The fact that we are *fools by default* should not surprise us if we understand human depravity. Neither should it surprise us that unless we take specific measures to counteract that default status, we will progress only to become increasingly useless as servants of God.

Proverbs, the parental training manual for wisdom, goes to great lengths to acquaint us with the ways of the fool so that we can avoid his path and his end. Solomon describes for us three grades of fools in Proverbs 1:22. He says, "How long, O *simple ones,* will you love being simple? How long will *scoffers* delight in their scoffing and *fools* hate knowledge?"

Simple Ones

Simple ones are budding fools. The word *simple* means "easily led, gullible . . . willful and irresponsible."[1] Simple ones are open-minded and therefore vulnerable to all kinds of enticement. They have not developed a discriminating judgment about what is right or wrong (see Prov. 1:22; 9:13, 16–18; 14:15). They are thoughtless and naive—not about sin but about sin's effects *on them*. Because they are undiscerning, they easily drift into moral corruption. They are aimless, but their tempters and temptresses are not (see 1:10–14; 7:6–27; 22:3). Apart from godly tutelage, simple ones are on the road to death (see 1:32; 7:7, 27; 22:3). If they refuse to learn, they will graduate to fools (see 14:18). In the end, along with the other types of fools, they will be judged because they have rejected God's wisdom and discipline (see 1:22–25, 32).

1. Derek Kidner, *The Proverbs: An Introduction and Commentary* (Downers Grove, IL: IVP, 1964), 39.

Fools

Fools are the common, ordinary, generic, garden-variety fools. The word *fool* means "dull and obstinate."[2] They are slow—but not in mental capacity. They are slow in their willingness to obey and have an inclination to make wrong decisions because of their stubbornness.

Proverbs describes fools as self-confident (see 12:15; 14:3, 16; 18:2; 26:12; 28:26), unreliable (see 26:6), and a grief to their parents (see 15:20; 17:21). They are restless (see 17:24; 20:3), deceptive (see 10:18; 14:8; 17:7), resentful of correction (see 15:5; 17:10), and unteachable (see 1:7, 22; 13:19; 17:10; 18:2; 23:9; 26:11; 27:22). They do not prepare their hearts for wisdom (see 17:16), often appear illogical (see 26:7, 9), and delight to speak of evil (see 12:23; 15:2, 14; 19:1). In addition, they make light of sin (see 14:9), slander others (see 10:18), are known as mischief makers (see 10:23; 26:18–19), have an anger problem (see 12:16; 14:16; 27:3; 29:11), and will eventually fall (see 1:32; 3:35; 10:8, 10; 11:29).

Young people who are weak in discernment exhibit characteristics of simple ones. They are easily swayed by peers and seem to end up in trouble unintentionally. These characteristics should raise concerns on the part of their parents and leaders. There is much that can be done to counter their simple-mindedness, as the following chart points out. The concern should escalate greatly, however, if their lives are moving from this state of impressionableness to a state of stubbornness. If they now defend their actions and deceive others to cover their actions, they are fast becoming common fools. If those actions and attitudes become their lifestyle, parents should have serious doubts about whether they know Christ as their Savior.

There is yet another level of fool, however.

Scoffers

Scoffers are deliberate, mean-spirited troublemakers. They are not content to be evil themselves but are bent on corrupting others. They reject rebuke (Prov. 13:1), hate those who correct them (see 15:12), mock justice (see 19:28), and enjoy despising good (see 1:22). They are

2. Kidner, 40.

hotheaded and arrogant (see 21:24) and are therefore odious to society (see 24:9; 29:8).

Satan himself is the master scoffer—the ultimate fool. He was characterized by Jesus as "a murderer" and "a liar" (John 8:44). Those two characteristics are dominant elements in the lives of these fools. They are becoming conformed more and more to the image of their master, Satan.

The progression of evil in these classes of fool and Proverbs' instruction about how to deal with each one can be summarized in the following chart.

	Simple Ones (Budding Fools)	Fools (Common Fools)	Scoffers (Full-Blown Fools)
Characteristics	Unguarded Defenseless Weak Impressionable	Unrestrained Disobedient Stubborn Involved in evil	Uncontrollable Devilish Mean Incorrigible

Remember, the measure of how foolish people remain is determined by their *response* to instruction and correction (wisdom's teaching methods). Those who have no heart for them will remain fools (see 1:7; 12:15; 13:1; 14:16; 15:5; 17:10; 23:9; 28:26). We are fools by default and can be wise only on purpose.

Appendix C

GOD'S LOVE VERSUS SELF-LOVE

"Just two choices on the shelf—loving God or loving self."

God's Love Described in 1 Corinthians 13[1]	**Self-Love**
1. **patient** (v. 4)—sacrifices self to wait for God's way and timing; has the divine power to wait; is long fused; doesn't retaliate even when it has the power; gives to others not what they deserve but what God gave us	1. **impatient**—desires own way and own timing; suffers if can't have its way *now*; is impatient; resents any departure from its own schedule; won't wait for God to work; snaps at people
2. **kind** (v. 4)—sacrifices self to meet others' needs; has passion to be active and useful in the lives of others; is kind in words and deeds; does the unexpected, undeserved, and unrewarded	2. **unkind**—nasty and hurtful in words and deeds; acts in favor of "me" instead of others; always puts conditions on others' love
3. **does not envy** (v. 4)—sacrifices self to cheer for or weep with others; does not boil, seethe, or stew; is content with God's control; doesn't compare for the purpose of looking "down on" or "up to"	3. **envious**—boils, seethes; laughs when others weep; weeps when others laugh; resents and wants what others have; wants to be what others are; is displeased by prosperity of others; judges others' worthiness by comparing it with its own

1. This chart is adapted from Ken Collier, "Two-Choices Chart," unpublished. Used by permission.

4. **does not boast and is not arrogant** (v. 4)—sacrifices self to remain small; doesn't "parade to gain applause"; is not proud; points to God, not self; doesn't brag or boast; doesn't inflate self	4. **proud**—is a "windbag"; praises self; will become anything so others will notice; brags; attempts to impress others; tries to appear to be what it is not; never admits it is wrong; is mad when others are too selfish to notice; points to what it's accomplished
5. **is not rude** (v. 5)—sacrifices self by being a lady or a gentleman; doesn't present the love of God in an ugly, misshapen way; is proper and courteous; does the right thing at the right time	5. **rude, crude, boorish**—draws attention to self by being loud, silly, moody, or harsh or by having poor manners, inappropriate actions, words, or timing; gives too much attention to fashion (fads) or appearance
6. **does not insist on its own way** (v. 5)—sacrifices self by not demanding rights; is not selfish; is a servant; gives; is not grasping for "my rights, my time, my money, my comfort, my thing" (see Rom. 12:10; Phil. 2:3)	6. **selfish**—rejects God's way for own way; seeks to please self
7. **is not irritable** (v. 5)—sacrifices self to be calm; is not soon angry for its own causes; is not oversensitive and touchy (see Heb. 10:24)	7. **explodes**—is an earthquake in the spirit; reacts in anger instead of acting in kindness; retaliates; is given to sudden outbursts; is angry for selfish reasons
8. **is not resentful** (v. 5)—sacrifices self by not keeping score; is not jealous; does not take permanent account of something for the purpose of bringing it back up; believes the best about a person; gives the benefit of doubt; forgives	8. **won't forgive**—uses "indelible ink"; builds a case for evil; enters wrongs into a ledger so that they can't be forgotten; is jealous; thinks evil
9. **does not rejoice at wrongdoing, but rejoices with the truth** (v. 6)—sacrifices self to love what God loves and hate what God hates; is excited to do the biblical thing; doesn't take iniquity by the hand and escort it into some other area of life	9. **rejoices in iniquity**—entertains sin; escorts sin right into its life; gets a thrill out of sin—its own or someone else's
10. **bears all things** (v. 7)—sacrifices self to cover others' weaknesses; covers, supports, protects; covers anything it can righteously cover; bears, not bares	10. **uncovers and exposes someone's sin to others unnecessarily**—bares, doesn't bear sin

11. **believes all things** (v. 7)—sacrifices self to believe the best about God and others; puts the best interpretation on events; believes in the best outcome; doesn't look to condemn; looks to save, not to judge	11. **wants to judge**—condemns; plays up doubts; believes the worst; is cynical, suspicious
12. **hopes all things** (v. 7)—sacrifices self by not giving up; anticipates a good outcome when God's truth wins out; hopes in every situation, against all evidence; confronts people with the truth in the hope that they will obey and change; knows that failure is never final as long as God's grace operates	12. **hopeless**—acts hopeless; talks hopeless; feels hopeless; gives up; quits praying; doesn't trust God or follow his way
13. **endures all things** (v. 7)—sacrifices self by staying put when it feels like quitting; bears all things at all costs; digs a trench and stays put; stays when it feels like running	13. **quits**—does not make the sacrifices necessary to remain faithful to God-given or agreed on responsibilities
14. **never ends** (v. 8)—always accomplishes God's work on earth and in heaven; is supernatural in its origin and its results	14. **always fails!**—"the one who sows to his own flesh will from the flesh reap corruption" (Gal. 6:8)

BIBLIOGRAPHY

Adams, Jay E. *How to Help People Change*. Grand Rapids: Zondervan, 1986.

———. *A Theology of Christian Counseling*. Grand Rapids: Zondervan, 1979.

———. *A Thirst for Wholeness: How to Gain Wisdom from the Book of James*. Woodruff, SC: Timeless Texts, 1998.

Arndt, William, and F. Wilbur Gingrich. *A Greek-English Lexicon of the New Testament and Other Early Christian Literature*. Chicago: University of Chicago Press, 1979.

Augustine. *The Confessions of Saint Augustine*. Translated by John K. Ryan. New York: Doubleday, 1960.

Bauer, Walter, William Arndt, and Wilbur Gingrich. *A Greek-English Lexicon of the New Testament and Other Early Christian Literature*. Chicago: University of Chicago Press, 1979.

Bounds, E. M. *The Weapon of Prayer*. Reprint. Radford, VA: Wilder Publications, 2008.

Bridges, Jerry. *The Pursuit of Holiness*. Colorado Springs: NavPress, 1978.

———. *Trusting God*. Colorado Springs: NavPress,

Bruce, A. B. *The Training of the Twelve*. Grand Rapids: Kregel Publications, 1971.

Chafer, Lewis Sperry. *He That Is Spiritual*. 1918. Reprint. Grand Rapids: Zondervan, 1967.

DeHaan, Dan. *The God You Can Know*. Chicago: Moody Press, 1982.

Edwards, Jonathan. *Religious Affections: A Christian's Character before God*. Edited by James M. Houston. Minneapolis: Bethany House Publishers, 1996.

———. *The Works of Jonathan Edwards*. Vol. 2. Edited by Sereno Edwards Dwight. Edinburgh: Banner of Truth, 1974.

Fugate, J. Richard. *What the Bible Says about Child Training*. Apache Junction, AZ: Foundation for Biblical Research, 1996.

Horton, Ronald A., ed. *Handbook of Christian Education*. Greenville, SC: BJU Press, 2017.

Hull, Bill. *Jesus Christ, Disciplemaker*. Grand Rapids: Fleming H. Revell, 1984.

Kidner, Derek. *The Proverbs: An Introduction and Commentary*. Downers Grove, IL: IVP, 1964.

Lewis, C. S. *Mere Christianity*. Reprint. New York: HarperCollins, 2001.

———. *The Weight of Glory and Other Addresses*. Reprint. New York: HarperCollins, 2009.

Lutzer, Erwin W. *How in This World Can I Be Holy?* Chicago: Moody Press, 1974.

———. *How to Say No to a Stubborn Habit*. Wheaton: Victor Books, 1979.

McCallum, Dennis, ed. *The Death of Truth*. Minneapolis: Bethany House Publishers, 1996.

Murray, Andrew. *Humility*. Reprint. Grand Rapids: Bethany House Publishers, 2001.

Orr, James, ed. *The International Standard Bible Encyclopedia*. Vol. 3. Grand Rapids: Wm. B. Eerdmans, 1956.

Owen, John. *Sin and Temptation*. Edited by James M. Houston. Minneapolis: Bethany House Publishers, 1996.

Packer, J. I. *Knowing God*. Downers Grove, IL: InterVarsity Press, 1973.

Petersen, J. Allan. *Your Reactions Are Showing*. Lincoln: Back to the Bible, 1967.

Petersen, Jim. *Lifestyle Discipleship*. Colorado Springs: NavPress, 1993.

Piper, John. *Desiring God: Meditations of a Christian Hedonist*. Revised edition. Portland: Multnomah Books, 2011.

Ray, Bruce A. *Withhold Not Correction*. Phillipsburg, NJ: Presbyterian and Reformed, 1978.

Ryle, J. C. *Holiness*. 1879. Reprint. Darlington, England: Evangelical Press, 1997.

Ryrie, Charles C. *Balancing the Christian Life*. Chicago: Moody Press, 1969.

Sanders, J. Oswald. *Spiritual Leadership: A Commitment to Excellence for Every Believer*. Updated edition. Chicago: Moody Publishers, 2007.

Sorenson, David. *Training Your Child to Turn Out Right*. Independence, MO: American Association of Christian Schools, 1995.

Sproul, R.C. *The Soul's Quest for God*. Wheaton: Tyndale House Publishers, Inc., 1992.

Spurgeon, Charles Haddon. *Morning and Evening*. Peabody, MA: Hendrickson Publishers, 1991.

———. *The New Park Street Pulpit*. Vol. 1, 1856. Reprint. Grand Rapids: Zondervan, 1963.

Stormer, John A. *Growing Up God's Way*. Florissant, MO: Liberty Bell Press, 1984.

Tozer, A. W. *The Attributes of God*. Camp Hill, PA: Christian Publications, 1997.

———. *Evenings with Tozer: Daily Devotional Readings*. Chicago: Moody Publishers, 1981.

———. *The Knowledge of the Holy*. New York: Harper & Row, 1961.

———. *The Pursuit of God*. Camp Hill, PA: Christian Publications, 1993.

Trench, Richard C. *Synonyms of the New Testament*. Grand Rapids: Wm. B. Eerdmans Publishing Co., 1880.

Tripp, Paul David. *Age of Opportunity: A Biblical Guide to Parenting Teens: Revised and Expanded*. Phillipsburg, NJ: Presbyterian and Reformed, 2022.

Tripp, Tedd. *Shepherding a Child's Heart*. Wapwallopen, PA: Shepherd Press, 1995.

Veith, Gene Edward, Jr. *Postmodern Times*. Wheaton: Crossway Books, 1994.

Viars, Steve. *Putting Your Past in Its Place: Moving Forward in Freedom and Forgiveness*. Eugene, OR: Harvest House, 2011.

Vine, W. E. *An Expository Dictionary of New Testament Words*. Old Tappan, NJ: Fleming H. Revell Company, 1940.

Warfield, B. B. "Imitating the Incarnation." Appendix D in *The Person and Work of Christ*. Edited by John J. Hughes. Phillipsburg, NJ: P&R Publishing, 2023.

Williams, Charles. "Paul's Testimony to the Doctrine of Sin." Chapter 2 in *The Fundamentals: A Testimony to the Truth*, vol. 3, edited by R. A. Torry and A. C. Dixon. Los Angeles: The Bible Institute of Los Angeles, 1917.

Young, Edward J. *Thy Word Is Truth*. Grand Rapids: Eerdmans, 1957.

INDEX OF SCRIPTURE

Proverbs

Mark

Luke

John

Acts

Romans

1 Corinthians

2 Corinthians

INDEX OF SUBJECTS AND NAMES

Also from P&R Publishing on Sanctification

Do you know who you are? In this Scripture-saturated devotional, pastor and biblical counselor Paul Tautges provides 90 meditations on your complete identity before God in Christ as saint, sinner, and sufferer. Day by day, center your thoughts and affections on the Savior and stay on God's good path as you live in a broken world.

"Paul explains how understanding our position in Christ . . . gives meaning and power to our struggle against sin and perseverance through suffering. This excellent volume is must-reading for anyone who feels they need help in becoming the person Jesus wants them to be."

—**Joni Eareckson Tada**, Founder, Joni and Friends International Disability Center

"[A] lovely series of meditations. . . . You will learn who you are in Jesus Christ, you will learn how he provides all that you truly need, and you will learn why it is fitting that you submit to his good and perfect will. . . . This is a book that blessed me and one I am certain will bless you as well."

—**Tim Challies**, Blogger, www.challies.com

Was this book helpful to you?
Consider writing a review online.
The author appreciates your feedback!

Or write to P&R at editorial@prpbooks.com
with your comments. We'd love to hear from you.